D1161502

Political and Social Life in the Great Age of Athens

Political and Social Life in the Great Age of Athens

A Source Book edited by
JOHN FERGUSON and KITTY CHISHOLM
at the Open University

Ward Lock Educational
in association with
The Open University Press

ISBN 0 7062 3628 9 paperback
0 7062 3641 6 hardback

First published 1978

Set in 11 on 12 point Imprint at
The Pitman Press, Bath, and printed and bound at
The Whitefriars Press Ltd, London and Tonbridge
for Ward Lock Educational
116 Baker Street, London W1M 2BB
A member of the Pentos Group
Made in Great Britain

CONTENTS

ACKNOWLEDGMENTS

The Open University and publishers would like to thank the following for permission to reproduce copyright material. All possible care has been taken to trace ownership of the selections included and to make full acknowledgment for their use.

B. T. Batsford for extracts from *Economic and Social History of Ancient Greece* by M. M. Austin and P. Vidal-Naquet (1977); Basil Blackwell for extract from *Ancilla to the Pre-Socratic Philosophers* by K. Freeman (1948); A. M. Hakkert for extracts from *Greek Historical Documents, the Fifth Century BC* by N. Lewis (1971); L.A.C.T. Publications (19B Roxborough Park, Harrow, Middlesex HA1 3BA) for extracts from *LACTOR 1: The Athenian Empire* edited by Professor J. K. Davies and R. W. J. Clayton, and *LACTOR 2: The Old Oligarch* edited by K. R. Hughes and M. A. Thorpe; The Loeb Classical Library (Harvard University Press: William Heinemann) for extracts from the following: Isocrates *Antidosis, The Team of Horses, To Demonicus, Trapeziticus* translated by G. Norlin; Lysias, translated by W. R. Lamb; Vitruvius, translated by F. Granger; Pliny *Natural History* translated by H. Rackham; Pliny *Natural History* translated by D. E. Eichholz; Macmillan Publishing Co., Inc. for extracts from *Aristotle's Constitution of Athens and Related Texts* translated by Ernst Kapp and Kurt von Fritz © 1950 by Hafner Publishing Company, Inc; Oxford University Press for extracts from *The Dialogues of Plato* translated by Benjamin Jowett (4th edition 1953); Penguin Books Ltd. for extracts from the following: *Demosthenes and Aeschines* translated by A. N. W. Saunders (Penguin Classics, 1975) pp. 273–4 © A. N. W. Saunders, 1974; Herodotus *The Histories* translated by Aubrey de Sélincourt, revised by A. R. Burn (Penguin Classics, revised edition 1972) pp. 238–40 © the Estate of Aubrey de Sélincourt, 1954 © A. R. Burn, 1972; Plato *The Symposium* translated by Walter Hamilton (Penguin Classics, 1951) pp. 100–111 © Walter Hamilton, 1951; *Crito* from Plato *The Last Days of Socrates* translated by Hugh Tredennick (Penguin Classics, second revised edition 1969) pp. 89–94 © Hugh Tredennick, 1954, 1959, 1969; Plutarch *The Rise and Fall of Athens: Nine Greek Lives* translated by Ian Scott-Kilvert (Penguin Classics, 1960) pp. 153, 170, 178–81, 184–5, 197–8, 236–7, 253–4, 301 © Ian Scott-Kilvert, 1960; Thucydides *History of the Peloponnesian War* translated by Rex Warner (Penguin Classics, revised edition 1972) pp. 87, 103, 335–6, 358–60, 404–5 © Rex Warner, 1954; Xenophon *A History of My Time (Hellenica)* translated by Rex Warner (Penguin Classics, 1966) pp. 62, 67–70 © Rex Warner, 1966; Xenophon *The Persian Expedition* translated by Rex Warner (Penguin Classics, 1949) pp. 97, 98–9, 105, 106, 164–5 © Rex Warner, 1949. Reprinted by permission of Penguin Books Ltd; Schocken Books, Inc. for extract from *Goddesses, Whores, Wives and Slaves* by Sarah B. Pomeroy (1975).

Illustrations: Alinari, Rome for no. 4; Ashmolean Museum, Oxford for nos. 5, 6 and 12; British Museum for nos. 2, 8, 10, 13 and 15; Mansell Collection for nos. 1, 3, 7, 9, 14, 16 and 17; National Archaeological Museum, Athens for no. 11.

LIST OF ILLUSTRATIONS

FOREWORD

A long preface is not needed, but one or two points must be clarified.

First, this is an anthology designed for an express purpose: to serve the needs of the Open University course A 292 *Greece 478–336 BC*. Its prime function is as a source book for that course: the basic material has been chosen by the members of the course team for their teaching purposes. But it seemed to us that it filled a gap, particularly with the heartening growth of courses on classical civilization available in schools and universities. We have tried to bear in mind these last needs.

Secondly, we have avoided narrative history, though we have included material that bears on it. Thucydides, Xenophon and Plutarch are still essential beyond the few passages cited here, as is the support of Bury-Meiggs or some other secondary history.

Thirdly, we have deliberately concentrated on Athens. Without this the anthology would either have been superficial or intolerably long.

We have gratefully drawn on the selective work of others, for example M. N. Tod *A Selection of Greek Historical Inscriptions* (2 vols); R. Meiggs and D. Lewis *Greek Historical Inscriptions*; N. Lewis *Greek Historical Documents: The Fifth Century BC;* J. Wickersham and G. Verbrugghe *Greek Historical Documents: The Fourth Century BC;* G. Dittenberger *Sylloge Inscriptionum Graecarum*; J. M. Edmonds *The Fragments of Attic Comedy*; and others. We are particularly appreciative of the work of the LACT (London Association of Classical Teachers) Ancient History group and their publications, attractively called Lactors.

Translations are drawn from a variety of sources. To limit the costs of copyright we have sometimes used out-of-copyright versions even though more contemporary renderings are available. I have in addition translated a large number of the passages specially for this volume. Unattributed translations are my own.

This variety means that there is a variety of transliterations. Most students of classical civilization are aware that the familiar forms of Greek names come to us through the Latin: the Greek name of which the Latin is Aeschylus is, strictly transliterated, Aiskhulos, but there is no present agreement among English writers, and various inbetween versions are also found. The principles are explained in the A 292 Course Guide. This anthology provides a healthy variety. Similarly, there are differences in the handling of inscriptional evidence. Many inscriptions have come to us in a broken state. In epigraphical publications it is normal to use [] to indicate words which are missing, but which can be supplied with reasonable confidence. As this is not a technical epigraphical study I have dispensed with these in my own versions, but they properly remain in some other versions we use.

A number of expressions of thanks must be voiced. During my absence in the USA Lorna Hardwick as Acting Course Team Chairman, Jennifer Potter as Consultant, and (especially) Kitty Chisholm as Research Assistant took on the task of tidying up the first draft and seeing it into a stage ready for the printers. Passages or comments were received from other consultants and members of the course team too: Robert Cook and Anne Ward, Colin Cunningham, Ian Howarth, Alec Kassman. The typing or assemblage of individual passages, an exacting job, was due to Susan Darling, Pat Dixon and Karen Smith. Roger Lubbock and the Open University Publishing Division have as always been friendly and helpful as have the publishers themselves. Thanks to all of these.

John Ferguson

INTRODUCTION

The Funeral Speech

Thucydides cites a speech delivered by Pericles at the funeral of the Athenian dead in the first year of the war with Sparta (431–0). Some scholars regard it as Thucydides's own epitaph for Athens, written at the end of the century; others look on it as an authentic record, though not of course a verbatim report. It is a speech which has in the past been much idealized, and more recently pilloried. However that may be, it is how an Athenian saw his country and wanted others to see her.

For a full discussion see A. W. Gomme A Historical Commentary on Thucydides *(Oxford, Clarendon Press 1945).*

(35) Most of those who have stood in this place before me have commended the institution of this closing address. It is good, they have felt, that solemn words should be spoken over our fallen soldiers. I do not share this feeling. Acts deserve acts, not words, in their honour, and to me a burial at the State's charges, such as you see before you, would have appeared sufficient. Our sense of the deserts of a number of our fellow-citizens should not depend upon the felicity of one man's speech. Moreover, it is very hard for a speaker to be appropriate when many of his hearers will scarce believe that he is truthful. For those who have known and loved the dead may think his words scant justice to the memories they would hear honoured: while those who do not know will occasionally, from jealousy, suspect me of overstatement when they hear of any feat beyond their own powers. For it is only human for men not to bear praise of others beyond the point at which they still feel that they can rival their exploits. Transgress that boundary and they are jealous and distrustful. But since the wisdom of our ancestors enacted this law I too must submit and try to suit as best I can the wishes and feelings of every member of this gathering.

(36) My first words shall be for our ancestors; for it is both just to them and seemly that on an occasion such as this our tribute of memory should be paid them. For, dwelling always in this country, generation after generation in unchanging and unbroken succession, they have handed it down to us free by their exertions. So they are worthy of our praises; and still more so are our fathers. For they enlarged the ancestral patrimony by the Empire which we hold today and delivered it, not without labour, into the hands of our own generation; while it is we ourselves, those of us who are now in middle life, who consolidated our power

throughout the greater part of the Empire and secured the city's complete independence both in war and peace. Of the battles which we and our fathers fought, whether in the winning of our power abroad or in bravely withstanding the warfare of barbarian or Greek at home, I do not wish to say more: they are too familiar to you all. I wish rather to set forth the spirit in which we faced them, and the constitution and manners with which we rose to greatness, and to pass from them to the dead; for I think it not unfitting that these things should be called to mind at today's solemnity, and expedient too that the whole gathering of citizens and strangers should listen to them.

(37) For our government is not copied from those of our neighbours: we are an example to them rather than they to us. Our constitution is named a democracy, because it is in the hands not of the few but of the many. But our laws secure equal justice for all in their private disputes, and our public opinion welcomes and honours talent in every branch of achievement, not for any sectional reason but on grounds of excellence alone. And as we give free play to all in our public life, so we carry the same spirit into our daily relations with one another. We have no black looks or angry words for our neighbour if he enjoys himself in his own way, and we abstain from the little acts of churlishness which, though they leave no mark, yet cause annoyance to whoso notes them. Open and friendly in our private intercourse, in our public acts we keep strictly within the control of law. We acknowledge the restraint of reverence; we are obedient to whomsoever is set in authority, and to the laws, more especially to those which offer protection to the oppressed and those unwritten ordinances whose transgression brings admitted shame. (38) Yet ours is no work-a-day city only. No other provides so many recreations for the spirit – contests and sacrifices all the year round, and beauty in our public buildings to cheer the heart and delight the eye day by day. Moreover, the city is so large and powerful that all the wealth of all the world flows in to her, so that our own Attic products seem no more homelike to us than the fruits of the labours of other nations.

(39) Our military training too is different from our opponents'. The gates of our city are flung open to the world. We practise no periodical deportations, nor do we prevent our visitors from observing or discovering what an enemy might usefully apply to his own purposes. For our trust is not in the devices of material equipment, but in our own good spirits for battle.

So too with education. They toil from early boyhood in a laborious pursuit after courage, while we, free to live and wander as we please, march out none the less to face the self-same dangers. Here is the proof of my words. When the Spartans advance into our country, they do not come alone but with all their allies; but when we invade our neighbours we have little difficulty as a rule, even on foreign soil, in defeating men who are fighting for their own homes. Moreover, no enemy has ever met us in full strength, for we have our navy to attend to, and our soldiers are sent on service to many scattered possessions; but if they chance to encounter some portion of our forces and defeat a few of us, they boast that they have driven back our whole army, or, if they are defeated, that the victors were in full strength.

Indeed, if we choose to face danger with an easy mind rather than after a rigorous training, and to trust rather in native manliness than in state-made courage, the advantage lies with us; for we are spared all the weariness of practising for future hardships, and when we find ourselves amongst them we are as brave as our plodding rivals. Here as elsewhere, then, the city sets an example which is deserving of admiration. (40) We are lovers of beauty without extravagance, and lovers of wisdom without unmanliness. Wealth to us is not mere material for vainglory but an opportunity for achievement; and poverty we think it no disgrace to acknowledge but a real degradation to make no effort to overcome. Our citizens attend both to public and private duties, and do not allow absorption in their own various affairs to interfere with their knowledge of the city's. We differ from other states in regarding the man who holds aloof from public life not as 'quiet' but as useless; we decide or debate, carefully and in person, all matters of policy, holding, not that words and deeds go ill together, but that acts are foredoomed to failure when undertaken undiscussed. For we are noted for being at once most adventurous in action and most reflective beforehand. Other men are bold in ignorance, while reflection will stop their onset. But the bravest are surely those who have the clearest vision of what is before them, glory and danger alike, and yet notwithstanding go out to meet it. In doing good, too, we are the exact opposite of the rest of mankind. We secure our friends not by accepting favours but by doing them. And so we are naturally more firm in our attachments: for we are anxious, as creditors, to cement by kind offices our relation towards our friends. If they do not respond with the same warmness it is because they feel that their services will not be given spontaneously but only as the repayment of a debt. We are alone among mankind in doing men benefits, not on calculations of self-interest, but in the fearless confidence of freedom. (41) In a word I claim that our city as a whole is an education to Greece, and that her members yield to none, man by man, for independence of spirit, many-sidedness of attainment, and complete self-reliance in limbs and brain.

That this is no vainglorious phrase but actual fact the supremacy which our manners have won us itself bears testimony. No other city of the present day goes out to her ordeal greater than ever men dreamed; no other is so powerful that the invader feels no bitterness when he suffers at her hands, and her subjects no shame at the indignity of their dependence. Great indeed are the symbols and witnesses of our supremacy, at which posterity, as all mankind today, will be astonished. We need no Homer or other man of words to praise us; for such give pleasure for a moment, but the truth will put to shame their imaginings of our deeds. For our pioneers have forced a way into every sea and every land, establishing among all mankind, in punishment or beneficence, eternal memorials of their settlement.

Such then is the city for whom, lest they should lose her, the men whom we celebrate died a soldier's death: and it is but natural that all of us, who survive them, should wish to spend ourselves in her service. (42) That, indeed, is why I have spent many words upon the city. I wished to show that we have more at stake than men who have no such inheritance, and to support my praise of the dead by making clear to you what they have done. For if I have chanted the glories of the city it was these men and their like who set hand to array her. With them, as with few among Greeks, words cannot magnify the deeds that they have done. Such an end as we have here seems indeed to show us what a good life is, from its first signs of power to its final consummation. For even where life's previous record showed faults and failures it is just to weigh the last brave hour of devotion against them all. There they wiped out evil with good and did the city more service as soldiers than they did her harm in private life. There no hearts grew faint because they loved riches more than honour; none shirked the issue in the poor man's dreams of wealth. All these they put aside to strike a blow for the city. Counting the quest to avenge her honour as the most glorious of all ventures, and leaving Hope, the uncertain goddess, to send them what she would, they faced the foe as they drew near him in the strength of their own manhood; and when the shock of battle came, they chose rather to suffer the uttermost than to win life by weakness. So their memory has escaped the reproaches of men's lips, but they bore instead on their bodies the marks of men's hands, and in a moment of time, at the climax of their lives, were rapt away from a world filled, for their dying eyes, not with terror but with glory.

(43) Such were the men who lie here and such the city that inspired them. We survivors may pray to be spared their bitter hour, but must disdain to meet the foe with a spirit less triumphant. Let us draw strength, not merely from twice-told arguments – how fair and noble a thing it is to show courage in battle – but from the busy spectacle of our great city's life as we have it before us day by day, falling in love with her as we see her, and remembering that all this greatness she owes to men with the fighter's daring, the wise man's understanding of his duty, and the good man's self-discipline in its performance – to men who, if they failed in any ordeal, disdained to deprive the city of their services, but sacrificed their lives as the best offerings on her behalf. So they gave their bodies to the commonwealth and received, each for his own memory, praise that will never die, and with it the grandest of all sepulchres, not that in which their mortal bones are laid, but a home in the minds of men, where their glory remains fresh to stir to speech or action as the occasion comes by. For the whole earth is the sepulchre of famous men; and their story is not graven only on stone over their native earth, but lives on far away, without visible symbol, woven into the stuff of other men's lives. For you now it remains to rival what they have done and, knowing the secret of happiness to be freedom and the secret of freedom a brave heart, not idly to stand aside from the enemy's onset. For it is not the poor and luckless, as having no hope of prosperity, who have most cause to reckon death as little loss, but those for whom fortune may yet keep reversal in store and who would feel the change most if trouble befell them. Moreover, weakly to decline the trial is more painful to a man of spirit than death coming sudden and unperceived in the hour of strength and enthusiasm.

(44) Therefore I do not mourn with the parents of the dead who are here with us. I will rather comfort them. For they know that they have been born into a world of manifold chances and that he is to be accounted happy to whom the best

lot falls – the best sorrow, such as is yours today, or the best death, such as fell to these, for whom life and happiness were cut to the self-same measure. I know it is not easy to give you comfort, I know how often in the joy of others you will have reminders of what was once your own, and how men feel sorrow, not for the loss of what they have never tasted, but when something that has grown dear to them has been snatched away. But you must keep a brave heart in the hope of other children, those who are still of age to bear them. For the newcomers will help you to forget the gap in your own circle, and will help the city to fill up the ranks of its workers and its soldiers. For no man is fitted to give fair and honest advice in council if he has not, like his fellows, a family at stake in the hour of the city's danger. To you who are past the age of vigour I would say: count the long years of happiness so much gain to set off against the brief space that yet remains, and let your burden be lightened by the glory of the dead. For the love of honour alone is not staled by age, and it is by honour, not, as some say, by gold, that the helpless end of life is cheered.

(45) I turn to those amongst you who are children or brothers of the fallen, for whom I foresee a mighty contest with the memory of the dead. Their praise is in all men's mouths, and hardly, even for supremest heroism, you will be adjudged to have achieved, not the same but a little less than they. For the living have the jealousy of rivals to contend with, but the dead are honoured with unchallenged admiration.

If I must also speak a word to those who are now in widowhood on the powers and duties of women, I will cast all my advice into one brief sentence. Great will be your glory if you do not lower the nature that is within you – hers greatest of all whose praise or blame is least bruited on the lips of men.

(46) I have spoken such words as I had to say according as the law prescribes, and the graveside offerings to the dead have been duly made. Henceforward the city will take charge of their children till manhood: such is the crown and benefit she holds out to the dead and to their kin for the trials they have undergone for her. For where the prize is highest, there, too, are the best citizens to contend for it.

And now, when you have finished your lamentation, let each of you depart.

Thucydides 2, 35–46
tr. Sir Alfred Zimmern *The Greek Commonwealth* (Oxford 1911)

A POLITICS AND GOVERNMENT

Athens was a direct democracy. No Athenian would have recognized any modern state – Britain, USA, USSR or China – as a democracy; he would have regarded Parliamentary Democracy as being in reality 'Elective Oligarchy', for the Athenian system was 'direct' or 'participatory democracy'. Power lay with the Ekklesia (Assembly) which all citizens (i.e. free-born adult males with both parents of Athenian citizenship) were free to attend, to speak in the debates (though few did) and to vote. The business of the Ekklesia was in the hands of the Boule (Council) of 500, chosen by lot from those citizens who indicated their willingness to serve. The Boule was divided into ten Prytanies, each of which served as an 'Agenda Sub-Committee' for the Boule and Ekklesia for one month of thirty-six days or so. The President of the Boule and Ekklesia was chosen by lot from among the fifty citizens in the Prytany on duty. Most public offices, including the most senior, the archonship (of which there were nine), were filled by lot and rotated annually, though some were restricted to the wealthier classes. The Strategoi (literally 'generals') who came to exercise political as well as military leadership, were elected annually; even the poorest citizens were legally eligible for election (though few ever were elected) and there was no restriction on continuous re-elections. At the end of his year of office any official was subject to scrutiny of his tenure (euthynai) and prosecution before the Heliaia (law courts with mass juries of citizens over thirty years of age, numbering between 101 and 1,001 depending on the importance of the case). In order to ensure that so far as possible no citizen was prevented by his lack of 'private means' from participating in the process of government if he wished, payment was introduced in the fifth century for serving in the Boule and Heliaia, and in the fourth century even for attending the Ekklesia.

The best work on the details of the Athenian Constitution is C. Hignett *History of the Athenian Constitution* (Oxford University Press 1952). For an appreciation of its working and a discussion on the oligarchic nature of the sources see A.H.M. Jones *Athenian Democracy* (Blackwell 1957). A full account of the origins of Athenian democracy can be found in W. G. Forrest *The Emergence of Greek Democracy* (Weidenfeld – World University Library 1966) which also contains an appraisal of the achievements and failures of Athenian democracy, and a discussion of ancient criticisms of democracy. The inscriptions are an important record of actual decisions taken by the various parts of the democratic administration.

A1 Development of Democracy

Aristotle (384–322) was a philosopher/scientist who wrote extensively on politics and ethics as well as on the natural sciences. In the Politics *he discusses different forms of government.*

(a)

The first governments were kingships, probably for this reason, because of old, when cities were small, men of eminent virtue were few. Further, they were made kings because they were benefactors, and benefits can only be bestowed by good men. But when many persons equal in merit arose, no longer enduring the pre-eminence of one, they desired to have a commonwealth, and set up a constitution. The ruling class soon deteriorated and enriched themselves out of the public treasury; riches became the path to honour, and so oligarchies naturally grew up. These passed into tyrannies and tyrannies into democracies; for love of gain in the ruling classes was always tending to diminish their number, and so to strengthen the masses, who in the end set upon their masters and established democracies. Since cities have increased in size, no other form of government appears to be any longer even easy to establish.

Aristotle *Politics* 3, 1286b8–22
tr. B. Jowett (Oxford 1921)

(b)

I have shown already what forms of democracy are suited to particular cities, and what of oligarchy to particular peoples, and to whom each of the other forms of government is suited. Further, we must not only show which of these governments is the best for each state, but also briefly proceed to consider how these and other forms of government are to be established.

First of all let us speak of democracy, which will also bring to light the opposite form of government commonly called oligarchy. For the purposes of this inquiry we need to ascertain all the elements and characteristics of democracy, since from the combinations of these the varieties of democratic government arise. There are several of these differing from each other, and the difference is due to two causes. One (1) has been already mentioned, – differences of population; for the popular element may consist of husbandmen, or of mechanics, or of labourers, and if the first of these be added to the second, or the third to the two others, not only does the democracy become better or worse, but its very nature is changed. A second cause (2) remains to be mentioned: the various properties and characteristics of democracy, when variously combined, make a difference. For one democracy will have less and another will have more, and another will have all of these characteristics. There is an advantage in knowing them all, whether a man wishes to establish some new form of democracy, or only to remodel an existing one.

Founders of states try to bring together all the elements which accord with the ideas of the several constitutions; but this is a mistake of theirs, as I have already remarked when speaking of the destruction and preservation of states. We will now set forth the principles, characteristics, and aims of such states.

The basis of a democratic state is liberty; which, according to the common opinion of men, can only be enjoyed in such a state; – this they affirm to be the great end of every democracy. One principle of liberty is for all to rule and be ruled in turn, and indeed democratic justice is the application of numerical not proportionate equality; whence it follows that the majority must be supreme, and that whatever the majority approve must be the end and the just. Every citizen, it is said, must have equality, and therefore in a democracy the poor have more power than the rich, because there are more of them, and the will of the majority is supreme. This, then, is one note of liberty which all democrats affirm to be the principle of their state. Another is that a man should live as he likes. This, they say, is the privilege of a freeman, since, on the other hand, not to live as a man likes is the mark of a slave. This is the second characteristic of democracy, whence has arisen the claim of men to be ruled by none, if possible, or, if this is impossible, to rule and be ruled in turns; and so it contributes to the freedom based upon equality.

Such being our foundation and such the principle from which we start, the characteristics of democracy are as follows: – the election of officers by all out of all; and that all should rule over each, and each in his turn over all; that the appointment to all offices, or to all but those which require experience and skill, should be made by lot; that no property qualification should be required for offices, or only a very low one; that a man should not hold the same office twice, or not often, or in the case of few except military offices: that the tenure of all offices, or of as many as possible, should be brief; that all men should sit in judgment, or that judges selected out of all should judge, in all matters, or in most and in the greatest and most important, – such as the scrutiny of accounts, the constitution, and private contracts; that the assembly should be supreme over all causes, or at any rate over the most important, and the magistrates over none or only over a very few. Of all magistracies, a council is the most democratic when there is not the means of paying all the citizens, but when they are paid even this is robbed of its power; for the people then draw all cases to themselves, as I said in the previous discussion. The next characteristic of democracy is payment for services; assembly, law courts, magistrates, everybody receives pay, when it is to be had; or when it is not to be had for all, then it is given to the law courts and to the stated assemblies, to the council and to the magistrates, or at least to any of them who are compelled to have their meals together. And whereas oligarchy is characterized by birth, wealth, and education, the notes of democracy appear to be the opposite of these, – low birth, poverty, mean employment. Another note is that no magistracy is perpetual, but if any such have survived some ancient change in the constitution it should be stripped of its power, and the holders should be elected by lot and no longer by vote. These are the points common to all democracies; but democracy and demos in their truest form are based upon the recognized principle of democratic justice, that all should count equally; for equality implies that the poor should have no more share in the government than the rich, and should not be the only rulers, but that all should rule equally according to their numbers. And in this way men think that they will secure equality and freedom in their state.

Aristotle *Politics* 6, 1317a10–1318a10
tr. B. Jowett (Oxford 1921)

A2 The Constitution of Athens

As a scientist Aristotle worked from facts. For the political researches of the Lyceum he set his research workers to collect the histories of the constitutions of the Greek city-states – 158 in all. In 1890 the British Museum acquired four papyrus rolls containing an account of the Constitution of Athens. It is generally agreed that this is one of the collection. It is harder to say whether it is Aristotle's own work, but on the whole it seems likely: it can be safely dated to the last six years of his life. The work is loosely organized, and some of its historical statements are open to criticism, but it remains a major primary source for the history of the Athenian constitution. There is a valuable commentary in K. v. Fritz and E. Kapp Aristotle's Constitution of Athens and Related Texts *(Hafner, New York 1950), from which this translation is taken. See also J. M. Moore* Aristotle and Xenophon on Democracy and Oligarchy *(Chatto 1975).*

(23) By this time, then, the state had made great progress, having become gradually consolidated with the advance of democracy. After the Persian wars the Council of the Areopagus again acquired strength and was again in control of the public life. They acquired this leadership, not by any formal decree, but in consequence of the fact that it had been responsible for the battle of Salamis. For when the generals did not know how to deal with the emergency and made a public proclamation saying that everybody should care for his own safety, the Council provided sufficient money to distribute eight drachmae to each man and so prevailed upon them to man the ships. For this reason the people held it in high repute, and during this period the public order in Athens was in an excellent state. For in this period the Athenians were not only well trained for war, but also had a good reputation throughout Greece and obtained the leadership at sea against the will of the Lacedaemonians.

At this time Aristeides, the son of Lysimachus, and Themistocles, the son of Neocles, were the leaders of the people. The latter had the greatest renown for military skill, while the former was famous as a statesman and as the most upright man of his time. For this reason they used the one as a general, the other as a counsellor. Though they were political rivals, they collaborated in the reconstruction of the walls of the city. But it was Aristeides who instigated the defection of the Ionians from the alliance with Sparta, having availed himself of the opportunity offered by the fact that the Laconians had fallen into bad repute through Pausanias. For this reason it was also Aristeides who first assessed the contributions to be paid by the allied cities in the third year after the battle of Salamis, in the archonship of Timosthenes. He also administered to the Ionians the oath by which they swore to have the same enemies and the same friends as the Athenians. It was in confirmation of this oath that they cast the heavy pieces of iron into the sea.

(24) After this, when the Athenian state was growing in self-confidence and in the accumulation of much wealth, he [that is, Aristeides] advised the Athenians to seize the leadership and to give up their residence in the countryside to come to live in the city. For they would all have their livelihood there, some by participating in military expeditions, some by doing garrison service, and still others by participating in public affairs; and in this way they would keep hold of the 'leadership'. They followed this advice and placed themselves in control of the empire; and from then on they got into the habit of treating their allies, with the exception of Chios, Lesbos and Samos, as if they were their masters. These three they used as guards of the Athenian empire and, therefore, left their constitutions untouched and allowed them to rule over whatever subjects they happend to have.

They also made it possible for the masses to live comfortably, as Aristeides had proposed. For out of the income derived from the contributions made by the allies and from internal levies more than two thousand persons were maintained. For there were six thousand judges, one thousand six hundred bowmen, one thousand two hundred cavalry men, five hundred Councilmen, five hundred guards of the dockyards plus fifty guards on the Acropolis, about seven hundred state officials at home and about seven hundred abroad. In addition, when later they went to war, there were two thousand five hundred heavy-armed soldiers, twenty guard-ships, and other ships carrying the guardians, that is, two thousand men chosen by lot. Finally, there were the Prytaneum, the orphans, and the jail-keepers. All these persons received their livelihood from the state.

(25) This, then, was the way in which the people obtained their livelihoods. For seventeen years following the Persian Wars, the political order remained essentially the same under the supervision of the Areopagus, although it was slowly degenerating. But as the common people grew in strength, Ephialtes, the son of Sophonides, who had a reputation for incorruptibility and loyalty to the constitution, became leader of the people and made an attack upon that Council [that is, the Areopagus]. First he eliminated many of its members by bringing suits against them on the ground of administrative misconduct. Then, in the archonship of Conon, he deprived the Council of all those prerogatives which it recently had acquired and which had made it the guardian of the state, and gave some of them to the Council of Five Hundred, some to the [Assembly of the] people, and some to the law courts. He did this with the assistance of Themistocles, who was himself a

member of the Areopagus and was about to be tried for treasonable collaboration with Persia. For this reason Themistocles wished the Areopagus to be broken up, and therefore he told Ephialtes that the Council [that is, the Areopagus] was about to have him arrested, while at the same time he told the members of the Areopagus that he was going to reveal to them certain persons who were conspiring to overthrow the constitution. Then he led the deputies of the Areopagus to a place where Ephialtes could be found, as if he were going to reveal to them the conspirators who had assembled there, and talked to them with a great show of seriousness. When Ephialtes saw this, he was stricken with fear and took refuge at an altar wearing only his undergarment. Of course, everybody was surprised at these happenings; and at the next meeting of the Council of Five Hundred, and later, before the Assembly of the People, Ephialtes and Themistocles denounced the Areopagitae again and again until they succeeded in depriving the Areopagus of its power. . . . and not much later Ephialtes also was done away with, being assassinated by Aristodicus of Tanagra.

(26) In this way, then, the superintendence of the life of the community was taken away from the Council of the Areopagus. Following these events, the public order was further weakened by the efforts of popular leaders to stir up the common people. For it so happened that at this time the better people had no real chief, since their leader Cimon, the son of Miltiades, was rather young and had only recently begun to take an active part in politics, and since a great many of them had perished in war. For since in those times the expeditionary forces were made up from the roll of citizens, and since they were led by inexperienced generals who had been selected on the basis of the reputations of their families, the result was always that two or three thousand of those who had participated in the expeditions perished. In this way the ranks of the better men, of both the wealthy and poorer classes, were depleted.

In all other respects, they changed the administration, not paying the same attention to the laws as before; but the election of the nine Archons was left untouched except insofar as it was decreed, in the sixth year after Ephialtes' death, that the Zeugitae should be included in the preliminary choice of candidates from among whom the Archons were selected by lot. The first of that class to hold the archonship was Mnesitheides. Before that time all the Archons had been chosen from the Knights and the Pentacosiomedimni, while the Zeugitae held only the lower magistracies, except that occasionally the constitutional regulation may have been neglected.

In the fifth year after these events, in the archonship of Lysicrates, the thirty so-called 'local justices' were re-established. Two years later, in the archonship of Antidotus, in consequence of the increasing number of citizens, it was decreed, on a motion of Pericles, that a person should not have the rights of citizenship unless both of his parents had been citizens.

(27) After this, when Pericles started on his career as a popular leader and first earned renown, though still a rather young man, by prosecuting Cimon on his audits as a general, the constitution became even more democratic. He took away

some of the powers of the Areopagus, and, what is most important, he turned Athens' aspirations definitely toward its sea power. As a result of these changes, the masses gained still greater self-confidence and took more of the control of the state into their own hands.

In the forty-ninth year after the battle of Salamis, in the archonship of Pythodorus, the Peloponnesian War broke out. During this war the population was shut up in the city and became accustomed to being paid from public funds while on their military campaigns; and so, partly of their own will, partly without even noticing it, the common people chose to administer the state themselves.

Pericles was also the first to introduce payment for service on the law courts, a measure by which he tried to win popular favour to counteract the influence of Cimon's wealth. For Cimon, who possessed a truly regal fortune, performed the regular public services in a magnificent manner, and, in addition, supported a good many of his fellow demesmen. For anyone of the deme of Laciadae who wished to do so could go to him every day and received a reasonable maintenance; and his whole estate was unfenced so that anyone who liked could help himself to the fruit.

Pericles' resources were quite unequal to such lavish liberality. So he followed the advice of Damonides of Oea, who was generally believed to have been the instigator of most of Pericles' measures, and was later ostracized for that reason. This man had advised Pericles to 'offer the people what was their own', since he was handicapped as far as his own private means were concerned; and, in consequence of this, Pericles instituted pay for the judges. Some people blame him on this account and say that the law courts deteriorated, since after that it was always the common men rather than the better men who were eager to participate in drawing the lot for duty in the law courts. Also, after this corruption ensued; and Anytus was the first to set an example, after his command at Pylos, for he bribed the judges and was acquitted when he was prosecuted by some because he had lost Pylos.

(28) As long as Pericles was the leader of the people, the state was still in a fairly good condition, but after his death everything became much worse. For then the people first chose a leader who was not in good repute with the better people, while, in the earlier period, the political leadership had always been in the hands of the latter. For the first leader of the people, in the very beginning, was Solon, the second one was Pisistratus, both of whom belonged to the aristocracy of birth. After the overthrow of the tyranny, it was Cleisthenes from the noble family of the Alcmeonidae; and he had no political rival after Isagoras and his adherents had been exiled. After this Xanthippus was the leader of the people, and Miltiades the leader of the aristocracy. Then Aristeides and Themistocles [were the popular leaders]. After these, Ephialtes was the leader of the people, and Cimon, the son of Miltiades, of the wealthy class. Then Pericles was the leader of the common people, and Thucydides, a relative of Cimon, head of the other party.

After the death of Pericles, Nicias, who later died in Sicily, became the leader of the aristocratic party, and Cleon, the son of Cleaenetus, the leader of the people.

This man, more than anybody else, appears to have corrupted the people by his violent methods. He was the first who shouted on the public platform, who used abusive language and who spoke with his cloak girt up about him, while all the others used to speak in proper dress and manner. After this, Theramenes, the son of Hagnon, was the leader of the other party, and Cleophon, the owner of a lyre factory, the leader of the people. The latter was also the first to introduce the distribution of two obols. This distribution continued for some time. Then Callicrates of the deme Paeania abolished it, being the first to promise that he would add another obol to the two. Later, however, both of these leaders were condemned to death. For the people, even if they allow themselves to be deceived for some time, later begin to hate those who have induced them to do something improper.

After Cleophon there was an unbroken succession of popular leaders who distinguished themselves above all by their brazenness and by their eagerness to cater to the wishes of the masses, having nothing in mind but their most immediate interests.

The best Athenian statesmen, after those of the early period, seem to have been Nicias, Thucydides and Theramenes. In regard to Nicias and Thucydides, there seems to be almost universal agreement that they were not only true gentlemen but also statesmen, and that their attitude toward the city as a whole was the attitude of a father. But in regard to Theramenes, opinion is divided, because he happened to live in a time when public affairs were in a turmoil. But, if one tries not to judge lightly, it seems clear that he did not, as his detractors say, overthrow all constitutions, but that, on the contrary, he worked for the good of any established government as long as it did not transgress the [fundamental] laws, and that, in this way, he showed that he was able to serve the state under any kind of political set-up, which is what a good citizen should do, but would rather incur enmity and hatred than yield to lawlessness.

(29) Now as long as the fortune in the war was equally balanced, they retained the democracy. But when, after the disaster in Sicily, the Lacedaemonian side became stronger through the alliance with the Persian king, they were compelled to abolish the democracy and to establish the constitution of the Four Hundred. The speech initiating his resolution was made by Melobius, and the resolution itself was drafted by Pythodorus of the deme Anaphlystus. What chiefly won over the masses to support the resolution was the belief that the king of Persia would be more likely to take part in the war on their side if they had an oligarchical constitution.

The text of the resolution of Pythodorus was as follows: that the people should elect, in addition to the already existing emergency committee of ten, twenty others from those over forty years of age, and that these men together, after having sworn an oath to draft such measures as they considered best for the state, should then put down in writing proposals for the salvation of the country. Furthermore, they resolved that whoever wished to do so should be free to submit proposals of his own so that then they could choose what was best of all the proposals. Cleitophon supported the motion of Pythodorus in all respects, but added the proposal that the elected committee should also investigate the ancient laws which Cleisthenes had enacted when he established the democracy, so that, after having acquainted themselves with those measures, they might then deliberate as to what the best course would be. The implication was that the constitution of Cleisthenes was not really democratic but similar to that of Solon.

The committee, when elected, first proposed that it should be obligatory for the chairman of the Council to put to a vote all proposals made for the preservation of the state. Furthermore, they abolished the indictments for unconstitutional proposals, and all impeachments and citations, so that all Athenians who wished could freely give their advice in regard to the intended changes. They also ordered that if anyone should impose punishment on another man or should summon him, or bring him to court for this reason, such a person was at once to be indicted and to be brought before the generals, and that the latter were to hand him over to the Eleven for capital punishment.

After this, they established the following principles for the new political order; that the public revenue was to be used only for the war; that the public officials, with the exception of the nine Archons and the Prytanes in office, should serve without pay for the duration of the war; that these officials should each receive three obols a day; that, for the rest of the administration, the whole state should be entrusted, until the end of the war, to those of the Athenians who were most capable of serving the state with their persons and their property, to the number of not less than five thousand. These men should also be empowered to conclude treaties with whomever they wished. To effect this the people should elect from each tribe ten men over forty years of age who would have the task of drawing up the list of the five thousand, after having sworn a solemn oath over a full and perfect sacrifice.

(30) These were the proposals drafted by the selected committee. When these proposals had been ratified, the five thousand elected from their own number one hundred men who were entrusted with the task of drawing up the constitution. The commissioners so selected drew up and made public the following plan: Those [that is, of the five thousand] over thirty years of age were to be members of the Council, on an annual basis, without payment. To this Council were to belong the generals, the nine Archons, the Hieromnemon, the Taxiarchs, the Hipparchs, the Phylarchs, the commanders of the garrisons, the ten Treasurers of the Sacred Funds of the goddess Athena and the other gods, the Hellenotamiae, the Treasurers in charge of all other secular funds, twenty in all, the ten Commissioners of the sacrifices, and ten overseers. The Council was to appoint these men from a larger number of candidates selected by it in a preliminary election and chosen from among its own members of the current year. All the other officials were to be selected by lot and not from the members of the Council. The Hellenotamiae, who actually managed the finances, were not to take part in the sessions of the Council.

There were to be, in the future, four Councils, to be formed from the men of the age indicated; and that section of them which would obtain a place on the Council by lot was to serve as Councillors; but the others, too, were to be assigned to each term respectively. The hundred men were to divide themselves and the others as equally as possible into four sections and were to determine by lot who were to belong to each section; and for one year. . . . (?) The Councillors were to make resolutions that seemed best to them in regard to a safe and sound administration of the revenue and expenditures, and in regard to all other affairs, to the best of their ability; and, if they wished to confer about some matter with a greater number, each member was to be entitled to bring with him as an associate member whomever he wished from the same age group. The Council was to have a sitting every fifth day, unless there was need for more frequent meetings. The lot for the Council was to be cast by the nine Archons. The votes on divisions in the Council were to be counted by five men chosen by lot from the members of the Council; and from their number one was to be chosen every day by lot and entrusted with the task of putting the proposals to the vote. The five men selected were also to cast the lot among those who wished to appear before the Council, first concerning matters of religion, second for the heralds, third for the embassies, fourth for other matters; but, as to matters of war, the generals were to be free to bring them up for discussion whenever necessary without having to cast the lot for precedence. Furthermore, a Councillor who would not come to the Council house at the time previously announced was to pay a drachma for each day, unless he obtained leave of absence from the Council.

(31) This constitution they drafted for the future. But for the immediate present, they drafted the following political order: Four hundred men should form the Council according to the ancestral order, forty from each of the tribes, elected from bodies of candidates over thirty years old previously selected by their tribesmen. These men were to appoint the magistrates, to lay down the rules concerning the oath which they were required to take, and to take such measures in regard to laws and to the audit of public accounts as seemed best to them. The laws in regard to the political constitution which would be laid down were to be observed and it was not to be permitted to change them or to enact others. For the present, the generals were to be elected from the whole number of the five thousand, but the Council, after it had been constituted, was to hold a military inspection in full armour and to select ten men plus a secretary for them; and the men thus chosen were to hold office with full powers during the coming year and to consult with the Council if the need arose. Furthermore, they were to elect one Commander of the Cavalry and ten Phylarchs. But, in the future, the Council was to elect these magistrates according to the regulations drafted. Regarding all offices except the office of the Councillors and that of the generals, it was not to be permitted either to these officials or to anybody else to hold the same office more than once. And, for the time after the immediate present, in order to make provision that the Four Hundred be distributed over the four terms, namely, when the ordinary citizens will be admitted to serve in the Council together with the others, the hundred men are to divide them [that is, the Four Hundred] into sections.

(32) This, then, was the political order drafted by the hundred men who were elected by the five thousand. When these proposals had been ratified by the people under the chairmanship of Aristomachus, the Council for the year of the archonship of Callias was dissolved on the fourteenth of the month Thargelion before it had completed its term of office, and the Four Hundred entered on their office on the twenty-first of the same month. The regular new Council selected by the lot was to have entered into office on the fourteenth of Scirophorion.

In this way the oligarchy was established under the archonship of Callias, about one hundred years after the expulsion of the tyrants. The chief promotors of this constitutional change were Pisander, Antiphon and Theramenes, all of them men of good family and renowned for their outstanding political insight and well-balanced judgment. When this political order came into being, the five thousand were only nominally chosen. But the Four Hundred, together with the ten who had been entrusted with full powers, entered the Council house and ruled the city. They also sent an embassy to the Lacedaemonians and proposed to make an end of the war on the basis of the *status quo*. But when the latter were not willing to listen except on the condition that the Athenians abandon their maritime supremacy, they [that is, the new rulers] gave up the attempt.

(33) The constitution of the Four Hundred lasted for about four months. As one of their number, Mnesilochus held the office of Archon for two months in the year of the Archon Theopompus, who held the office for the remaining ten months. When they were defeated in the naval battle off Eretria and when the whole of Euboea with the exception of Oreos revolted, the Athenians were more embittered by the revolt than by anything that had happened before, for they drew more support from Euboea than from Attica itself. And, in consequence, they abolished the rule of the Four Hundred, entrusted the government to the five thousand capable of doing military service with full equipment, and decreed at the same time that there was to be no pay for any public office.

The chief promotors of the dissolution of the new rule were Aristocrates and Theramenes, who disapproved of the attitude of the Four Hundred. For the latter had decided everything by themselves and had never referred anything to the five thousand. It would appear that in this period Athens had a good form of government, when in a time of war, the government was in the hands of those able to serve with full equipment.

(34) These men, then, were quickly deprived of their political power by the people of Athens. In the sixth year after the overthrow of the Four Hundred in the archonship of Callias of the deme of Angele, after the naval battle of the Arginusae, it happened that the ten generals who had won the victory in the battle were all condemned by a single division [in the Assembly of the People], though some of them had not even taken part in the battle and others had been picked up from the sea by other vessels. This vote was the work of agitators who deceived the people by stirring up public anger. Moreover, when the Lacedaemonians offered to evacuate Decelea and to make peace on the basis of the *status quo,* some were very anxious to accept, but the majority would not listen to the proposal,

since they were misled by Cleophon, who came into the Assembly drunk and wearing his breastplate, and spoke against the conclusion of peace, declaring that he would never agree to it unless the Lacedaemonians surrendered all the cities. This was a great blunder; and it did not take long before they realized their mistakes. For in the following year, in the archonship of Alexias, they met with disaster in the naval battle at Aegospotami, as a result of which Lysander became master of the city and established the rule of the Thirty.

This happened in the following way. The peace had been concluded on the condition that they would return to 'the ancestral constitution'. On this basis the popular party tried to preserve the democracy; those of the nobles who belonged to the political clubs and the exiles who came back after the conclusion of the peace aimed at an oligarchy, while those who did not belong to the clubs but otherwise were considered as belonging to the best classes really wanted the ancestral constitution. To this last class belonged Archinus, Anytus, Cleitophon, Phormisius and many others. Their leader was Theramenes. When, however, Lysander sided with the oligarchs, the people were intimidated and felt compelled to vote for the oligarchy. The motion was drafted by Dracontides of Aphidna.

(35) In this way the rule of the Thirty was established, in the archonship of Pythodorus. When they had become masters of the city, they paid no attention to the other regulations concerning the constitution which had been passed. They did appoint five hundred Councilmen and also made appointments for the other magistracies from among persons previously selected from the Thousand. They associated with themselves ten governors of the Piraeus and eleven superintendents of the prison, and, furthermore, appointed three hundred lash bearers as their attendants. In this way they kept the city under their control. At first they showed moderation in dealing with their fellow citizens and pretended to be aiming at the ancestral constitution. They took down from the Areopagus the laws of Ephialtes and Archestratus about the Areopagitae. They abolished those of the Solonian laws which were controversial and also abolished the arbitrary power of the judges [to interpret the laws]. In doing this, they claimed to correct the constitution by removing ambiguities. For instance, the right of giving [by will] one's property to whomever one wished was made absolute; and the troublesome clauses by which it was limited (unless he be insane or not in full possession of his mental powers because of age or under the influence of a woman) were removed so that there might be no opening for sycophants. They applied the same principle to other matters.

This is what they did in the beginning. They made away with the professional denunciators ['sycophants'] and those mischievous and low politicians who curried favour with the people for the sake of their own evil aims. The citizens were delighted with these measures and believed that they did all these things out of the best intentions. But when they had acquired a firm hold on the state, they did not keep their hands off any kind of citizens but put to death persons who were distinguished by wealth or birth or reputation. For they intended to remove anyone whose influence they might have reason to fear, and, at the same time, wished to get hold of their possessions. In fact, after a short time, they had done away with more than one thousand five hundred persons.

(36) Theramenes, however, became indignant over the way in which the city was slowly going to pieces and exhorted the Thirty to cease such wanton conduct and to give the better classes their share in the government. At first, they merely opposed his suggestions; but when his counsel became known among the people, and the masses took the side of Theramenes, they were afraid that he might become the leader of the people and overthrow their despotic rule. So they started to make a list of three thousand people on the pretence that they would give them a share in the government. But Theramenes attacked them again on the ground of this measure, first, because, having promised to let the 'better people' participate, they admitted only three thousand, as if all merit were confined within that number; secondly, because they were attempting to do two things which were entirely inconsistent with each other, namely, to establish a government based on force and yet weaker than its subjects.

The Thirty, however, paid no attention to these criticisms, and for a long time they postponed the publication of the list of the Three Thousand and kept the names of the persons included to themselves; in fact, whenever they did decide to publish it, they at once began again to remove the names of some who had previously been included and added the names of some who were not on the list.

(37) At the beginning of the winter, Thrasybulus, together with the exiles, occupied Phyle. When the Thirty were defeated in an expedition which they had led against [the exiles], they decided to disarm the others and to do away with Theramenes. This they contrived in the following way: They laid two laws before the Council and ordered the Council to pass them. The first of these laws gave the Thirty full powers over life and death of all citizens who were not on the list of the Three Thousand; the second prohibited anyone from participating in political rights who either had taken part in the demolition of the fortifications of Eetionea or had in any way been in active opposition to the Four Hundred who had set up the previous oligarchic regime. Theramenes had done both, so that, when the laws had been passed, Theramenes was deprived of his political rights and the Thirty had full power to put him to death. When Theramenes was out of the way, they disarmed all people except the Three Thousand, and from then on became ever more cruel and wicked.

They also sent an embassy to Sparta to denounce Theramenes and at the same time asked for military assistance. Upon this request, the Lacedaemonians sent Callibius as harmost with about seven hundred men; and he, upon his arrival, occupied the Acropolis.

(38) Following this, the exiles from Phyle occupied Munichia and defeated the force sent by the Thirty to rescue the place. After this skirmish, the men from the city retreated. On the following day, they assembled in the market place and deposed the Thirty. Then they elected ten citizens with full powers to bring the war to an end. These men took over the government but did not do anything to achieve the ends for which they had been selected. On the contrary, they sent to

Sparta in order to ask for help and to borrow money. When those admitted to full citizenship showed their indignation over their actions, they [the Commission of Ten] were afraid lest they might be deprived of their office. They, therefore, decided to intimidate the others – in which action they were successful – and arrested one of the most outstanding citizens, Demaretus, and put him to death. From then on they had the power firmly in their hands, being supported by Callibius and the Peloponnesian forces which were in Athens, and also by some of the Knights. For some of this group of citizens were most anxious to prevent a return of the exiles from Phyle.

When, however, the party which was in possession of the Piraeus and of Munichia gradually gained the upper hand, since the whole people went over to their side, they [that is, the Three Thousand] deposed the board of Ten which they had elected originally and elected another board of Ten consisting of men who enjoyed the highest reputation. Thus the end of the civil strife was actually brought about while these men were in power and were sincerely doing whatever they could to help.

The most active members of this board were Rhinon of the deme Paeania and Phayllus of the deme Acherdus. For these men, even before the arrival of Pausanias, had undertaken missions to the men in the Piraeus, and after his arrival they did everything to promote the return of the exiles. For it was the Spartan king Pausanias who brought the peace and the reconciliation to completion, together with the ten mediators who arrived later from Sparta and whom he himself had requested to come. Rhinon and his associates were praised because of their good will toward the people. Though they had been entrusted with their duties under the oligarchy, they handed in their accounts under the democratic regime. Yet no one, either of those who had remained in the city or of those who returned from the Piraeus, brought any charge against them. On the contrary, Rhinon was at once elected General because of his aforementioned activities ...

(41) The events last mentioned happened at a somewhat later date. But immediately after the people had become masters of the state, they established the constitution which is still in force, in the archonship of Pythodorus.... And the people seemed to have a just claim to the control of the state since they had effected a return by their own efforts.

This was the eleventh of the changes of the constitution. The first change of the original state of things occurred when Ion and his companions came to dwell with them. For it was at this time that they were grouped together in the four Tribes and that the Tribe-kings were first established. The second change, and the first after this which implied something of a constitutional order, was the one which happened under Theseus. This was a slight deviation from the pure monarchy. After this came the constitution which prevailed under Draco, in which, for the first time, they drew up a code of laws. The third was the one under Solon, after the civil disturbances, from which democracy had its beginnings. The fourth was the tyranny under Pisistratus. The fifth was the constitution of Cleisthenes after the overthrow of the tyrants, a constitution more democratic than that of Solon.

The sixth was the one after the Persian War, when the Council of the Areopagus had the leadership. The seventh was the one which followed this constitution; it had been ancitipated to some extent by Aristeides, but was brought to completion by Ephialtes when he deprived the Areopagus of his power. Under this constitution, the greatest mistakes were committed by the nation under the influence of the demagogues and for the sake of the domination of the sea. The eighth was the establishment of the Four Hundred. After this, the ninth was the restored democracy. The tenth was the tyranny of the Thirty and the Ten. The eleventh was the one which came into being after the return of the exiles from Phyle and the Piraeus from which date [?] it continued to exist until it reached its present form, all the time adding to its grasp of arbitrary power for the people. For the people have made themselves masters of everything and administer everything through decrees of the Assembly and decisions of the law courts, in which they hold the power. For even the juridical functions of the Council have passed into the hands of the people. In this they appear to be right. For a small number of judges can be more easily corrupted by money and favour than the many.

At first, they refused to allow payment for attendance at the Assembly of the People. But when the people did not come and the Prytanes had tried many things to induce the people to attend for the sake of ratification of proposals by their vote, Agyrrhius first introduced a fee of one obol; afterwards, Heracleides of Clazomenae, with the surname 'King', a fee of two obols; and then again Agyrrhius a fee of three obols.

Aristotle *Constitution of Athens* 23–38; 41
tr. K. v. Fritz and E. Kapp *Aristotle's Constitution of Athens and Related Texts* (Hafner, New York 1950)

A3 A Realistic View of Political Affiliations

The speaker is addressing the jurymen, i.e. the citizens of Athens, probably soon after the restoration of democracy in 403.

Now, first of all, you should reflect that no human being is naturally either an oligarch or a democrat: whatever constitution a man finds advantageous to himself, he is eager to see that one established: so it largely depends on you whether the present system finds an abundance of supporters.

Lysias 25, 8

A4 The Debate on the Constitution

Herodotus (c. 484–c. 425) travelled extensively in Persia and Egypt as well as throughout the Greek world. His histories, which include geographical and anthropological digressions, trace the enmity of Europe and Asia from mythical times to the Persian Wars (490 and 480/79). This debate, which he implausibly puts into the mouth of Persian nobles in the sixth century, reflects the political debates of Greece in the mid-fifth century. See W. W. How and J. Wells A Commentary on Herodotus *(Oxford, Clarendon Press 1964).*

Five days later, when the excitement had died down, the conspirators met to discuss the situation in detail. At the meeting certain speeches were made – some of our own countrymen refuse to believe they were actually made at all; nevertheless – they were. The first speaker was Otanes, and his theme was to recommend the establishment in Persia of democratic government. 'I think,' he said, 'that the time has passed for any one man amongst us to have absolute power. Monarchy is neither pleasant nor good. You know to what lengths the pride of power carried Cambyses, and you have personal experience of the effect of the same thing in the conduct of the Magus. How can one fit monarchy into any sound system of ethics, when it allows a man to do whatever he likes without any responsibility or control? Even the best of men raised to such a position would be bound to change for the worse – he could not possibly see things as he used to do. The typical vices of a monarch are envy and pride; envy, because it is a natural human weakness, and pride, because excessive wealth and power lead to the delusion that he is something more than a man. These two vices are the root cause of all wickedness: both lead to acts of savage and unnatural violence. Absolute power ought, by rights, to preclude envy on the principle that the man who possesses it has also at command everything he could wish for; but in fact it is not so, as the behaviour of kings to their subjects proves; they are jealous of the best of them merely for continuing to live, and take pleasure in the worst; and no one is readier than a king to listen to tale-bearers. A king, again, is the most inconsistent of men; show him reasonable respect, and he is angry because you do not abase yourself before his majesty; abase yourself, and he hates you for being a superserviceable rogue. But the worst of all remains to be said – he breaks up the structure of ancient tradition and law, forces women to serve his pleasure, and puts men to death without trial. Contrast with this the rule of the people: first, it has the finest of all names to describe it – *isonomy*, or equality before the law; and, secondly, the people in power do none of the things that monarchs do. Under a government of the people a magistrate is appointed by lot and is held responsible for his conduct in office, and all questions are put up for open debate. For these reasons I propose that we do away with the monarchy, and raise the people to power; for the state and the people are synonymous terms.'

Otanes was followed by Megabyzus, who recommended the principle of oligarchy in the following words: 'In so far as Otanes spoke in favour of abolishing monarchy, I agree with him; but he is wrong in asking us to transfer political power to the people. The masses are a feckless lot – nowhere will you find more ignorance or irresponsibility or violence. It would be an intolerable thing to escape the murderous caprice of a king, only to be caught by the equally wanton brutality of the rabble. A king does at least act consciously and deliberately; but the mob does not. Indeed how should it, when it has never been taught what is right and proper, and has no knowledge of its own about such things? The masses have not a thought in their heads; all they can do is to rush blindly into politics and sweep all before them like a river in flood. As for the people, then, let them govern Persia's enemies, not Persia; and let us ourselves choose a certain number of the best men in the country, and give *them* political power. We personally shall be amongst them, and it is only natural to suppose that the best men will produce the best policy.'

Darius was the third to speak. 'I support,' he said, 'all Megabyzus' remarks about the masses, but I do not agree with what he said of oligarchy. Take the three forms of government we are considering – democracy, oligarchy, and monarchy – and suppose each of them to be the best of its kind; I maintain that the third is greatly preferable to the other two. One ruler: it is impossible to improve upon that – provided he is the best man for the job. His judgment will be in keeping with his character; his control of the people will be beyond reproach; his measures against enemies and traitors will be kept secret more easily than under other forms of government. In an oligarchy, the fact that a number of men are competing for distinction in the public service cannot but lead to violent personal feuds; each of them wants to get to the top, and to see his own proposals carried; so they quarrel. Personal quarrels lead to open dissension, and then to bloodshed; and from that state of affairs the only way out is a return to monarchy – a clear proof that monarchy is best. Again, in a democracy, malpractices are bound to occur; in this case, however, corrupt dealings in government services lead not to private feuds, but to close personal associations, the men responsible for them putting their heads together and mutually supporting one another. And so it goes on, until somebody or other comes forward as the people's champion and breaks up the cliques which are out for their own interests. This wins him the admiration of the mob, and as a result he soon finds himself entrusted with absolute power – all of which is another proof that the best form of government is monarchy. To sum up: where did we get our freedom from, and who gave it us? Is it the result of democracy, or of oligarchy, or of monarchy? We were set free by one man, and therefore I propose that we should preserve that form of government, and, further, that we should refrain from changing ancient laws, which have served us well in the past. To do so would lead only to disaster.'

Herodotus, 3, 80–82
tr. A. de Selincourt (Penguin 1954)

A5 The Political Debate on the Stage

Euripides's play The Suppliant Women *is probably to be dated to the Cold War period after the Peace of Nicias in 421. Theseus, the legendary king of Athens, is given the defence of democracy.*

HERALD: Who is dictator here?...
THESEUS: A bad start, my friend, to look for
a dictator here. This city
is free, not under one man's rule.
The people are sovereign, in annual rota
by turns. They do not allow the rich
supremacy. The poor have equal rights
HERALD: There's one point which gives me the best
of the game. The city I represent
has one man in command, not mob-rule.
No one can flatter it, varying
his policy to his own advantage,
buttering it up, then turning
and damaging it, evading the consequences
of his own mistakes by blaming others.
The people don't know how to weigh
arguments, or to keep a city straight.
Time is needed for wisdom, not off-the-cuff
judgments. A working man without money
may not be an utter fool, but his work
won't allow him to look at the common interest.
When a wretch with no background
uses slick talk to win position with the people,
it nauseates his betters.
THESEUS: Here's a herald too fond of his own views!
Well, you've asked for an argument.
Listen to me. You started it.
There's nothing worse for a city than a dictator.
In the beginning, when there are no established
laws, one man controls the law
in his own interest. There's no equality yet.
Once laws are framed the weak
and wealthy have an equal chance of justice.
Now a man of standing, badly spoken of,
is in the same case as his weaker brethren.

The little man with right on his side, defeats the great.
This is liberty: 'Who wishes to offer
the city good advice publicly?'
The man who responds wins renown. Those who won't
keep quiet. That's political equality.

Euripides *The Suppliant Women* 399–441

A6 A Right-wing View of Democracy

Among the works attributed in antiquity to Xenophon, the fourth-century writer, but certainly not by him, is a right-wing commentary on Athenian democracy. The author has come to be known as the Old Oligarch. The date may be as early as 443 (see G. W. Bowersock in Harvard Studies in Classical Philology *71, 1966) or as late as 415 (see A. W. Gomme* More Essays in Greek History and Literature *Blackwell 1962). A useful recent edition will be found in J. M. Moore* Aristotle and Xenophon on Democracy and Oligarchy *(Chatto 1975).*

1

1 My opinion about the Athenian constitution is this: I object to their choice of this form of constitution, because this first choice entails a second – to prefer the interests of the mob to those of respectable people; this is why I object to it. But since this is their decision, I shall prove that, even when the other Greeks think they are going about it the wrong way, they are in fact 2 employing the best means of preserving their constitution. First of all, I maintain that it is appropriate that in Athens the poor and the common people should seem to have more power than the noble and rich, because it is this class that provides the rowers for the fleet and on which the power of the city is based; for the steersmen, boatswains, under-boatswains, look-out men, shipwrights – these are the men on whom the power of the city is based, far more than the hoplites, the noble, and the respectable. Since this is so, it seems appropriate that they should all share in the offices of state by the processes of lot and election and that anyone of the citizens who wishes should have the right to 3 speak in the Assembly. Moreover, some offices can bring safety to the state as a whole when they are in respectable hands, danger when they are not; the common people do not require any share in these and do not think that they should stand a chance of becoming general or cavalry commander by process of lot. For they recognize that they derive greater benefit by not holding these offices themselves but by allowing the leading men of the state to do so. But they are eager to hold all those offices which involve the receipt of money and where there 4 is a chance of making a personal profit. Moreover, one thing that surprises some

people is that they regularly give more power to the mob, to the poor and the common people, than to the respectable, but you will come to see that even here their intention is to preserve the democracy. For, if the poor, the common people, and the lower classes do well and increase in number, they will increase the power of the democracy, but if the rich and respectable do well, all the common people
5 achieve is to increase the strength of their opponents. Throughout the whole world the aristocracy in a state is opposed to democracy; for the natural characteristics of an aristocracy are discipline, obedience to the laws, and a most strict regard for what is respectable, while the natural characteristics of the common people are an extreme ignorance, ill-discipline, and immorality. For their poverty, lack of education, and ignorance – itself in some cases resulting from lack of money – all tend rather to lead them to a form of behaviour that is far from
6 respectable. Some people may think that they were wrong in allowing everybody to speak in the Assembly and serve on the Council and that they should have restricted these rights to the ablest and best. But here too, by allowing even people from the mob to speak, the Athenians know their own business best. For if the respectable people spoke and served on the Council, this would be good for those like them but quite the opposite for the common people. But, as it is now, anyone who likes can get up and speak and, if he comes from the mob, he discovers what
7 is in his own interest and that of the rest of the mob. But how could a man like this recognize what was good for himself and for the common people? The Athenians recognize that for all his ignorance and immorality the good will of this man does them more good than the ill will of the respectable, however skilful and wise.
8 Such a way of life could never produce an ideal city, but it would be the best means of preserving a democracy. For what the common people want is not to be slaves in a law-abiding city, but to be free and in control – and they're not much worried about lawlessness. For what you consider lawlessness is in fact the basis
9 upon which the strength and freedom of the common people rests. But if you are looking for a law-abiding city, the first thing you will see is that the able make laws in their own interest; then, the respectable will punish the mob and will make their own plans for the city; they will not allow madmen to become members of the Council, nor to speak in the Assembly, not even to attend it. However excellent this might be, it would soon plunge the common people into slavery.

10 Now, as for the slaves and metics in Athens, they lead a most undisciplined life; one is not permitted to strike them there, and a slave will not stand out of the way for you. Let me explain why this happens in Athens. If the law permitted a free man to strike a slave or a metic or a freedman, he would often find that he had mistaken an Athenian for a slave and struck him, for, so far as clothing and general appearance are concerned, the common people
11 look just the same as the slaves and metics. Some people are also surprised that the Athenians allow their slaves to live in the lap of luxury and some of them indeed to live a life of real magnificence, but in this respect too I consider that they have reason on their side. For in a city based on naval power, the slaves

inevitably work for money so that we can take a share of their earnings and let them go free; and, where there are rich slaves, there is no longer any point in my slave fearing you. In Sparta, on the other hand, my slave would be afraid of you. But in Athens, if your slave is afraid of me, he is quite likely to avoid personal 12 danger by handing over some of his money. This is why in the matter of freedom of speech we have put slaves on equal terms with free men and metics with citizens, for the city needs metics because of all its industries and because of the fleet. This is why we have done right in establishing freedom of speech for metics too.

13 The old educational system, combining physical exercise and cultural interests, is now rejected by the common people; they disapprove of it because they know they cannot cope with it. On the other hand, they realize that, where it is a matter of providing choral or dramatic festivals or athletic contests or of equipping a trireme, it is the rich who put up the money while the common people enjoy their festivals and contests and are provided with their triremes. Whether it is taking part in the different kinds of festivals and contests or serving in the fleet, the common people constantly expects to receive money, so that its own wealth may grow and the rich may become poorer. And in the law courts they are more concerned with self-interest than with justice.

14 On the subject of the allies, it is well known that the Athenians sail out and bring false charges against the respectable elements among them and hate them, because they realize that the ruler is always hated by the subject, and that if the rich and powerful come to power in the allied cities, the empire of the common people of Athens will last only a very short time. This is why they deprive the respectable elements of their citizen rights, take away their money, drive them into exile, and kill them, while increasing the power of the mob. The respectable elements in Athens try to protect the respectable elements in the allied cities, because they recognize that it is in their own in-15 terest to protect the aristocracies in these cities. Some people may think that, if the allies were able to contribute money, this would strengthen the power of the Athenians. But the common people think it preferable that each individual Athenian should possess allied money and that the allies should keep just enough to live and work on, without being able to plot against them.

16 Again, people think that the Athenians are wrong to compel the allies to sail to Athens for justice. In reply the Athenians enumerate all the benefits accruing to the common people from this practice. First of all, the allies' legal deposits provide them with enough money to pay the jurymen each year; then, they can control the allied cities without the trouble of leaving home and going on a sea voyage. They make use of their law courts to protect those who belong to the common people and to ruin their opponents; whereas, if each of the allied cities had its own courts, they would show their dislike of the Athenians by ruining those of their number who seemed particularly well-17 in with the Athenian common people. Furthermore, the common people of

Athens derive the following benefits from the fact that the allies are tried in Athens. First, the 1 per cent duty levied at the Piraeus brings in more revenue to the state; then, if anyone had rooms to let, he makes a higher profit on

18 them; similarly, if a man has a carriage or a slave for hire. Then again, the heralds make a profit from the allies' stay in Athens. Furthermore, if the allies did not come to Athens for justice, they would honour only those Athenians who visited them – the generals, trierarchs, and ambassadors; but, as it is, each one of the allies is compelled to fawn on the common people of Athens, because he recognizes that he must come to Athens to have his case tried and that these are the very people who will decide it, for this is the law at Athens. And so he is compelled to employ a tone of wheedling entreaty in the courts and, when anyone enters, to grab his hand in supplication. By this means the allies' slavery to the common people of Athens is more firmly established.

19 Furthermore, because of their overseas possessions and the public offices which take them overseas, the Athenians and their attendants have learnt how to row almost without realizing it; for when a man often travels by sea he and his servant are bound to take an oar and learn the names of things

20 concerned with seamanship. Their experience in ships and their practice make them good steersmen. For some of them have practised as steersmen in boats, others in merchant ships, while yet others go on from there to a trireme. The majority can row as soon as they get aboard, since they have practised all through their life.

2

1 The Athenian hoplite force, which is not particularly good, is based on the following principle: the Athenians realize that they are inferior to their enemies in skill and number, but as compared with their allies, who pay tribute, they are the strongest by land as well as by sea; they consider they

2 have sufficient hoplites if they are superior to their allies. In addition, the following point has been found true. Those who are subject to a land power can concentrate the forces of small cities and fight in one body; but all those islanders who are subject to a sea power cannot unite their cities. For the sea is in-between, and their rulers control the sea. Even if the islanders could

3 secretly assemble on one island, they would inevitably die of starvation. As for all the mainland cities ruled by the Athenians, the large ones are ruled by fear and the small ones by sheer necessity. For no city can do without exports and imports, but it will not be permitted to trade unless it submits to the

4 rulers of the sea. Again, a sea power can ravage the lands of those more powerful than itself, something a land power cannot always do. For they can sail along until they reach a place where there is no enemy or only a few and, if the enemy approach, can embark and sail away. In this way it is less likely to

5 get into difficulties than a land army. Again, those who rule a naval empire can sail as far as they like from their own country, but those who rule a land empire cannot travel many days' journey from home. For the rate of progress

is slow, and it is not possible to carry provisions for a long time if one travels on foot; an army travelling on foot must either pass through friendly territory or fight its way through. On the other hand, a naval force can land where it has superior numbers and, where it has not, it need not put in but can sail on
6 until it comes to a friendly land or one that it can overpower. Again, diseases sent by Zeus against the crops affect land powers severely, but sea powers hardly at all; these diseases do not affect the whole world at once, and sea powers can have supplies brought in from unaffected areas.

7 To consider less important matters, the rulers of the sea visit various other lands and so have discovered their gastronomic specialities; thus, specialities from Sicily, Italy, Cyprus, Egypt, Lydia, Pontus, the Peloponnese, or anywhere else have been assembled in one place, – and all due to their com-
8 mand of the sea. Again, they listen to every kind of dialect, and take something from one, something from another. The Greeks in general tend to keep to their own dialect, way of life, and dress, whereas the culture of Athens is a medley of elements drawn from all parts of the Greek world and even from the barbarians.

9 Then there is the question of sacrifices, offerings, festivals, and sanctuaries; the common people are aware that individually the poor are quite unable to sacrifice and feast, to erect temples, or to build a great and beautiful city, but they have found a means of achieving this end. Publicly, as a city, they frequently make sacrifices, but it is the common people as individuals who
10 enjoy the feasts and who are allotted a share in the offerings. Some of the rich possess gymnasia, baths, and dressing rooms for their private use, but the common people build themselves many palaestras, dressing rooms, and public baths for their own use; and the rabble get more benefit from this than the wealthy minority.

11 They are the only people who possess the wealth that comes from trading overseas. Suppose, for example, that a city is rich in timber for shipbuilding; where can it dispose of it, except with permission from the ruler of the sea? The same is also true of a city rich in iron, copper, or flax. Now these are just the materials I need to build my ships; I get my timber from one source, iron
12 from another, and copper, flax and wax from yet others. In addition, the Athenians will not allow our competitors to take their produce elsewhere; if they try to, they will be barred from the sea. Thus, without producing anything from the land myself, I possess all these materials through our control of the sea. No other city possesses two of them; you will not find timber and flax in the same country, for, where a city is rich in flax, you will find that its territory is a treeless plain. Nor can you get copper and iron from the same city; in fact, no one city will provide you with two or three of these materials,
13 but you will find one of them here, another there. Yet again, all along the coast of the mainland there are headlands jutting out or islands lying just off shore or straits; so the rulers of the sea can anchor at these spots and inflict
14 harm on the inhabitants of the mainland. They have only one weakness; if, in

addition to their naval supremacy, the Athenians lived on an island, then, so long as they retained their control of the sea, they would be able, if they so wished, to harm other peoples without suffering anything in return; their land would not be ravaged, and no enemy could enter it. But, as it is, the farmers and the rich men of Athens are more inclined to make up to the enemy than are the common people, for the latter are quite well aware that it is not their property that is burnt and ravaged and so are quite confident and

15 without fear. In addition, they would be free of another fear, if they lived on an island. They would not need to worry about the possibility of the oligarchs betraying the city or opening the gates and suddenly letting the enemy in. (How could this happen if they lived on an island?) Again, there would be no chance of a counter-revolution against the common people, if they lived on an island. But, as it is, such a revolution would be based upon the expectation of bringing in the enemy – and that, of course, would be by land. But if they

16 lived on an island, they would have no grounds for fearing even this. Since nature has decreed that they do not live on an island, this is what they do; they deposit all their property in the islands, trusting their control of the sea, and accept the devastation of Attica, for they recognize that, if they are swayed by sentiment in this matter, they will on balance be the losers.

17 Moreover cities under oligarchic rule must of necessity abide by their alliances and agreements. If they do not, or if some injustice is committed, then among so few the names of those who voted for the proposal are well known. But when the common people make any agreement, they can always fix the blame on the individual who proposed the measure or who put it to the vote, and the rest of them can reject it, saying 'I wasn't there, and anyway I don't approve of it', when they find that it was agreed at a full meeting of the common people; if they decide that the policy should not be put into effect, they have countless reasons to hand for not doing what they have no wish to do. And if the common people decide on a course of policy which then turns out badly, they pick on a few individuals and fasten the responsibility on them, claiming that they have acted against the interests of the common people and thus ruined their plans; if the policy succeeds, of course, they claim the credit for themselves.

[Xenophon] *Constitution of Athens* 1, 1–2, 17
tr. Ken Hughes, Margaret and Martin Thorpe *Lactor 2* (1968)

A7 Isocrates Sums up Athenian Democracy

Isocrates, the fourth-century teacher and pamphleteer wrote the Areopagiticus, *perhaps in 355. It is a plea for a return to pre-Periclean democracy.*

To put it shortly, our forebears resolved that the people should have absolute power of appointing magistrates, exacting penalties from those who failed, and pronouncing judgment in disputed cases. Those citizens who had the time and income should engage in responsibility for the commonwealth as servants of the people. If they exercised office with justice they should receive a vote of thanks and be content with that honour. If their stewardship was unsatisfactory they should receive no mercy and be subject to the severest penalties. It would be impossible to find a democracy with a more satisfactory combination of stability and integrity than this in which the most competent are appointed to office and the commons exercise the ultimate authority over them.

Isocrates *Areopagiticus* 26–7

A8 The Operation of Democracy

*Aeschines, rival of Demosthenes, is attacking one of the latter's political associates named Timarchus under a law which excluded men of disreputable life from addressing the Assembly. The date is 345. According to Aristotle (*Constitution of Athens *28, 3), Cleon was the first orator to use extravagant language and gesture.*

Gentlemen, recognize the difference between Timarchus, and Solon and those earlier statesmen of whom I was just speaking. They had a sense of propriety which prevented them from speaking with their arms exposed. Timarchus recently – only the other day in fact – in the Assembly threw off his cloak and cavorted about like an athlete, stripped to the bone, except that drink and loose living had left his body in such a disgraceful condition that honourable men covered their eyes, in shame for our city if we allowed men like that to be our statesmen. The legislator had this sort of behaviour in mind when he explicitly defined who were and who were not to address the assembly. He does not exclude from the speaker's platform men with no record of office among their ancestors, or men who earn their daily bread by manual labour. On the contrary he gives them a warm welcome, and this is why he asks the repeated question, 'Who wishes to speak?'

Who are the men whom legislation excludes from speaking? Those whose lives are scandalous; it is these who are excluded from addressing the people. Where is this made clear? These are the words: 'Public Scrutiny of Statesmen. Any who does violence to father or mother, or neglects them or fails to support them, and seeks to address the Assembly' is forbidden to do so. And rightly in my opinion. Why? Because if a man behaves pettily to those whom he ought to honour equally with the gods, how will he behave towards those who do not belong to his own family, to the city as a whole? So the argument runs. Who else is debarred from speaking? 'The man who has failed to perform the military duties demanded of him, or who has thrown away his shield.' Rightly. Why? Sir, if you do not take up arms in defence of your country, if your cowardice prevents you from defending her, you have no right to be one of her counsellors. Who next? 'The man of loose sexual morals' it goes on. The man who has sold his own body in violation of decency is probably likely to sell his country's interests. Who fourthly? 'The man who has wasted his patrimony or inheritance.' Clearly the man who cannot keep his own house in order is not likely to handle public affairs any better; it is not likely in the legislator's view that the same man will prove a scoundrel in private life, and a useful citizen publicly, a statesman who does not practise what he preaches should not mount the dais. Any man of upright life, however clumsy his words, may have useful advice for his audience. Any man of loose life, anyone who abuses his own body, anyone who has wasted his patrimony, however eloquent his words, is not likely to have beneficial advice for his audience. So he debars them from the speaker's platform, and bans them from addressing the Assembly. If any person contrary to these enactments addresses the people, and goes on to irresponsible chicanery so that the citizens cannot stomach him any longer, the legislator rules: 'Any citizen who chooses and is not legally debarred may call him to submit to Public Scrutiny', and authorizes you the people to give your verdict in a court of justice. On this law I base my present case.

Aeschines *Against Timarchus* 26–32

A9 Attendance at the Assembly

A short passage from The Women in Parliament, *one of the last comedies of Aristophanes (c. 444–380). He refers to payment for attendance at the Assembly instituted at the beginning of the fourth century to encourage the poor to play their part in politics, and also to the custom of 'sweeping' the city centre with a robe drenched in vermilion at the time of the Assembly, staining those who were not doing their political duty.*

BLEPYRUS: Where have you sprung from?
CHREMES: The Assembly.
BLEPYRUS: What! Adjourned already?
CHREMES: Yes. It was very early.
Dear Zeus I laughed and laughed at
the vermilion spattered all about.
BLEPYRUS: Did you get your three obols?
CHREMES: I wish I had.
I arrived too late. It's a proper shame.
I've nothing but an empty purse.

Aristophanes *Ecclesiazusae* 376–82

A10 Audit

In addition to the democratic precautions about attaining office, the euthune or audit was the main protection against mismanagement in office. One Ctesiphon in 336 proposed that Demosthenes be awarded a golden crown for his services to the state. Aeschines opposed this as illegal, as indeed it was; one ground was that Demosthenes was Commissioner for Repair of the Walls and Superintendent of the Festival Fund and had not yet submitted to audit.

Our city has a long history of power. No one in it who has held public office is exempt from public audit. I will begin with examples which you would not expect. For example, the law insists that priests and priestesses are subject to audit collectively and individually. These are people who receive nothing but perquisites and whose function is to offer prayer on your behalf. Their accountability extends not just to individuals but collectively to clans, the Eumolpidae, the Ceryces and the others.

Again the law insists that trierarchs are subject to audit. No public money has passed through their hands. They have no opportunities to withdraw large sums of public money and repay small ones, or to claim to be making donations when they are repaying your rightful money. We know that they spend their own family resources in honour of serving you.

It is not only the trierarchs. The highest political committees come under judgment in the courts. The law requires the Council of the Areopagus to place its accounts with the auditors and to submit to audit . . . Again the legislator makes the Council of Five Hundred subject to audit. And so strong is the distrust of those liable to audit that the legislator begins, 'The official who is still liable to audit may not leave the country.' 'Good God!' someone may exclaim. 'Just because I've been in office may I not leave the country?' No – in case you are escaping with the profits of your public activities.

Aeschines *Against Ctesiphon* 17–21

A11 The Duties of the Rich

We do not know the defendant for whom Lysias wrote this speech. He was born in 429–8, and in the eight years after he reached eighteen he claims to have spent over ten talents on public service, more than four times the amount normally expected. These public services were called liturgies. In Demosthenes's time there were ninety-seven in an ordinary year and 118 once every four years in a Panathenaic year. See N. Lewis 'Leitourgia and related terms' Greek, Roman and Byzantine Studies *3 (1960) 175–84; 6 (1965) 226–30; J. K. Davies 'Demosthenes on Liturgies: A note'* Journal of Hellenic Studies *87 (1967) 33–40.*

I came of age when Theopompus was in office. I was appointed to produce tragedies and spent thirty minas, and at the festival of Thargelia two months later on won a victory with a male chorus at a cost of 2,000 drachmas. When Glaucippus was in office I spent 800 drachmas on producing a war dance for the Great Panathenaic festival. In the same year I won a victory with a male chorus at the Festival of Dionysus, spending in all, including the dedication of the tripod, 5,000 drachmas. With Diocles in office I spent 300 drachmas on dancing in the round at the Lesser Panathenaic festival. In the meantime I was equipping warships – for seven years – and spent six talents on that. Despite all these contributions, and my readiness to face daily danger abroad on your behalf, I have made contributions of thirty minas and of 4,000 drachmas to special funds. On my return, with Alexias in office I moved straight into producing sports for the festival of Prometheus, and won a victory; the cost was twelve minas. Subsequently I was charged with producing a chorus of boys, which cost more than fifteen minas. In Euclides's term of office I produced comedies for Cephisodorus, winning a victory, the cost including the dedication of the set was sixteen minas. At the Lesser Panathenaic festival I produced a war dance with beardless dancers at a cost of seven minas. I have won a victory with a warship in the race at Sunium; the cost was fifteen minas. I have been responsible for religious spectacles, for the procession of the Errephoria and so on, which have cost more than thirty minas. If I had limited myself to my legal obligations it would not have come to a quarter of the sum.

Lysias 21, 1–5

A12 The Citizens as Judges

Aristophanes produced The Wasps *in 422, satirizing the dicasts, the citizens who sat as jury or judges (the offices were combined) in large numbers (to prevent bribery), with payment introduced by Pericles and raised by Cleon (to enable the poor to serve without loss of wages). Aristophanes caricatures the jurymen as 'wasps'. Six of the Archons presided over civil courts; the Eleven were in charge of criminal jurisdiction. The Concert-Hall was used for food distribution. The officers charged with the upkeep of walls were chosen from the dicasts.*

CHORUS: Examine us closely, you'll readily find
our ways of behaviour resemble the wasp.
For first when aroused there's no creature alive
more fierce or relentless than we are.
In other ways too we behave like the wasp.
We gather in swarms, like the wasps in their nests,
some with the Archon, some with the Eleven,
some at the courts in the Concert-Hall, some
crammed by the walls, bowed to the earth,
hardly able to move, like the grubs in their nests.
We've always an eye to new means of resource.
We'll sting any man to increase our income.
Of course we have drones sitting among us,
stingless, wanting to consume the product
of our revenues, for which they haven't worked.
This annoys us most, when someone who hasn't served
with spear, or a blister on his hand
for his country, pinches our dues.
In brief I propose for the future for all citizens
'No sting, no three obols.'

Aristophanes *Wasps* 1101–21

A13 A Criticism of Periclean Democracy

Plato wrote his philosophical works in the form of dialogues, in which his own theories are expressed by Socrates. The early dialogues are perhaps nearer to the historical Socrates's own thinking. Plato uses other historical characters to express differing philosophical arguments, giving them at times a more extreme position than they would really have held. The Republic *and* The Laws *are a culmination of Plato's criticism of Athenian democracy; in them he presents a detailed plan for his ideal state. For a general book on Plato see I. M. Crombie* An Examination of Plato's Doctrines *(2 vols) (Routledge and Kegan Paul 1962–3).*

SOCRATES: Allow me to recall to you the names of those whom you were just
d now mentioning, Pericles, and Cimon, and Miltiades, and Themistocles, and ask whether you still think that they were good citizens.

CALLICLES: I do.

SOCRATES: But if they were good, then clearly each of them was making the citizens better instead of worse?

CALLICLES: Yes.

SOCRATES: And therefore, when Pericles first spoke in the Assembly, the Athenians were worse than at the time of his last speeches?

CALLICLES: Very likely.

SOCRATES: Nay, my friend, 'likely' is not the word; for if he really was a good citizen, the inference is certain.

e CALLICLES: And what difference does that make?

SOCRATES: None; only I should like further to know whether the Athenians are supposed to have been made better by Pericles, or, on the contrary, to have been corrupted by him; for I hear that he was the first who gave the people pay, and made them idle and cowardly, and encouraged them in the love of talk and of money.

CALLICLES: You heard that, Socrates, from our pro-Spartan pugilists.

SOCRATES: But what I am going to tell you now is not mere hearsay, but well known both to you and me: that at first, Pericles was held in high esteem and his character was unimpeached by any verdict of the Athenians – this was during the time when they were not so good – yet afterwards, when they had been made good and noble by him, at the very end of his life they convicted him
516 of theft, and almost put him to death, clearly regarding him as a malefactor.

Plato *Gorgias* 515c–516a
tr. B. Jowett (Oxford 1953)

A14 A State Emergency

This justly celebrated passage from Demosthenes's greatest speech gives a vivid picture of the Assembly in emergency session. The time is September 339. Philip of Macedon, in a sudden show of force in central Greece, has just seized Elatea, near the border of Boeotia, directly threatening Thebes, and perhaps also Athens. The Prytaneis were members of the committees of fifty.

It was evening, when a messenger came to tell the prytaneis that Elatea had fallen. At this some of them leaped to their feet in the middle of dinner, and began to drive the men in the city-centre away from their stalls and used the wickerwork for beacon-fires. Others sent for the Generals and called for the alarm to be sounded. The city was filled with consternation. Next day as dawn broke, the prytaneis convoked the Council in their Chamber, you made your way to the Assembly, and before the Council could come to a decision over a draft, the whole commons were in their places on the hill. Next the Council appeared, the prytaneis announced the news they had already received, producing their informant to tell his story. The herald made the proclamation: 'Who wishes to address the Assembly?' No one came forward. He repeated the proclamation time and again. Still no one rose to his feet. All the Generals were present, all the politicians. Athens was calling with a single voice for someone to speak and save her. For the voice of the herald, raised in the solemn form prescribed by law, must be considered our country's voice.

Demosthenes *On the Crown* 169–70

A15 Punishment of the Leaders of the Oligarchic Revolution

In 411 the oligarchy which had come to power as a result of the Sicilian disaster was overthrown. We have the record of a decree passed against two of their number. It appears in a treatise falsely ascribed to Plutarch, a Greek writing in Roman times.

Archeptolemus, son of Hippodamus, of Agryle, and Antiphon, son of Sophilus, of Rhamnus, being present in court, were found guilty of treason. Sentence was passed on them that they be handed over to the Eleven for execution, that their property be confiscated, a tithe being reserved for the Goddess, that their houses be demolished and boundary-stones set upon the sites with the inscription 'Property of Archeptolemus and Antiphon, traitors', that their demarchs publish an inventory of their property, that it be forbidden to give burial to Archeptolemus and Antiphon in Athens or in territory controlled by Athens, that Archeptolemus and Antiphon be disfranchised together with their descendents, legitimate and illegitimate, and that if any man adopt a descendent of Archeptolemus or Antiphon, the adopter is to be disfranchised. This is to be published on a pillar of bronze and erected where the decrees relating to Phrynichus stand.

[Plutarch] *Lives of the Ten Orators* (*Moralia* 834A–B)

A16 Draco's Law on Homicide

When the news of the military disaster in Sicily reached Athens they appointed ten Special Commissioners. There was a general desire to ensure that traditions were maintained, and committees were charged with searching out old enactments. As a product of this operation, this law on homicide was republished in 409–8. It is on a marble column somewhat damaged. The previous history of the legislation concerned is highly controversial. It purports to go back to the noted legislator Draco in 621–0, and on the whole this is the most likely account. See R. S. Stroud Drakon's Law on Homicide *(University of California Publications: Classical Studies 3; University of California Press 1968). The text is in R. Meiggs and D. Lewis* Greek Historical Inscriptions *(Oxford 1969) no. 86.*

Secretary: Diognetus (deme: Phrearrioi). Archon: Diocles. Resolution of the Council and Assembly. Tribe in Office: Acamantis. Secretary: Diognetus. President: Euthydicus. Proposer of the motion: . . . . . .

The Recorders of the Laws are required to make a public record on a stone column, of the Laws of Draco on Homicide, taking the text from the Royal Archon, with the Assistance of the Secretary to the Council, and to set it up in front of the Royal Stoa. The Revenue Officers are required to put the contract out to tender in accordance with the law, and the Treasury Officials to make payment.

First clause.
Even if a person commits homicide without intention to do so, the sentence is exile. The Royal Archons are to adjudge the responsibility for homicide between . . . . . . and the person who took the original decision. The Homicide Jurors are to give the verdict. Where there is a father or brother or sons, a decision to pardon must be unanimous; a single negative voice acts as veto. If none of these is living, the right to pardon extends to cousins and their sons, but must be unanimous; a single negative voice acts as veto. If not even one of these is alive, and the homicide was unintentional, and the fifty-one Homicide Jurors resolve that the homicide was unintentional, then ten members of the clan are permitted to admit him to the country if they so resolve. It is for the fifty-one to select these according

to seniority. This ordinance applies to cases of homicide retrospectively. Relatives as far as the degree of cousins and their sons are required to make a denunciation in the city-centre of the man responsible for the homicide. The prosecutors must include cousins and their sons, sons-in-law, fathers-in-law and members of the clan . . . . . . responsible for homicide . . . . . . the fifty-one . . . . . . If anyone take the life of the man guilty of homicide while he is avoiding a frontier market, games or the Amphictyonic festival, he is to be dealt with under the laws affecting one who has taken life of an Athenian citizen. The Homicide Jurors responsible for the verdict . . . . . . he is a free man. And if in defending himself against a person who is carrying off his property illegally by means of force, he takes that person's life, the dead man is to receive no recompense . . . . . .

Second clause . . . . . .

A17 The Dictatorship of the Thirty

After the defeat of Athens by Sparta in 404 a dictatorship of thirty, known as the Thirty Tyrants, was established in Athens. See also Aristotle's Constitution of Athens *34–40 (see no. A2). Xenophon wrote in the fourth century on subjects ranging from philosophy to horsemanship. This passage comes from his history which he started where Thucydides left off.*

(a)

At Athens the Thirty were elected directly after the demolition of the Long Walls and the walls of Piraeus. Though they were elected to frame laws for a new constitition they kept on putting things off. No laws were framed or published, and meanwhile they appointed members of the Council and other magistrates just as they saw fit. Their first measure was to arrest and put on trial for their lives all who were generally known to have made a living during the time of the democracy by acting as informers and had made a practice of attacking the aristocrats. The Council was glad enough to condemn these people to death and no objections were raised by the public in general – or at least not by those who had no guilty consciences in the matter themselves. Next, however, the Thirty began to consider how they could get the power to do exactly what they liked with the state. They sent Aeschines and Aristoteles to Sparta to persuade Lysander to support their request that a Spartan garrison should be sent just until, so they said, they had got rid of 'the criminals' and had established a new constitution; and they undertook to pay for the garrison themselves. Lysander agreed, and helped them to secure the sending of a garrison with Callibius to act as governor. Then, when they had got their garrison, they made themselves as agreeable as they possibly could to Callibius so as to get him to approve of everything they did. He gave them troops to go with them and they began to arrest all whom they wished to arrest. And now it was no longer a question of the so-called 'criminals' or of people whom no one had heard of. Those arrested now were the people who, in the view of the Thirty, were the least likely to submit to being pushed out of politics and who could count on the greatest support if they chose to take action.

At first Critias and Theramenes shared the same views and were personal friends. But when Critias, acting as one who had himself been exiled by the democracy, began to show this lust for putting people to death, Theramenes opposed him. 'There is no sense,' he said, 'in putting a man to death simply because he has been honoured by the democracy and when he has done the aristocracy no harm at all.' . . .

So more and more people were put to death, and put to death unjustly, and it became clear that many citizens were getting together in opposition and were wondering what the state was coming to. Theramenes then spoke again and expressed the view that the oligarchy could not possibly survive, unless they brought in a reasonable number of others to share in the government.

By this time Critias and the rest of the Thirty were alarmed, and they were particularly afraid of Theramenes, in case the citizens might turn to him as a leader. So they enrolled a body of 3,000 citizens who, according to them, were to be associated in the government. Theramenes, however, objected to this move too. . . .

The Thirty, however, proceeded to hold a review under arms. The Three Thousand paraded in the market place and the other citizens in various other parts of the city. The order was given to pile arms, and when the men were off duty, the Thirty sent their Spartan troops and other people who were on their side, seized the arms of all who were not included among the Three Thousand, carried them up to the Acropolis and stored them in the temple. Once this was done they considered that they were now free to act exactly as they liked, and they began to put people to death in great numbers, some because they were personal enemies, some for the sake of their money. It was necessary, too, to find money to pay the Spartan garrison, and so they decided that each one of them should arrest one of the resident aliens, put him to death and confiscate his property.

Xenophon *Hellenica* 2, 3, 11–21
tr. R. Warner (Penguin 1966)

(b) *Another version from Plutarch's parallel lives of famous Greeks and Romans written much later about AD 100. Lysander was the Spartan commander, the date of the change of government September 404.*

After the Athenians had finally given way to all Lysander's demands, he sent for a great company of flute girls from the city and collected all those who were in his camp. Then to the sound of their music, he pulled down the walls and burned the ships, while the allies garlanded themselves with flowers, rejoiced together, and hailed that day as the beginning of freedom for Greece. Next, without any delay,

Lysander set about making changes in the constitution, and established a council of thirty in Athens and ten in the Piraeus. He also posted a garrison in the Acropolis and appointed Callibius, a Spartan, to be its military governor. It was Callibius who once raised his staff to strike Autolycus the wrestler . . . When Autolycus gripped him by the legs and threw him to the ground, Lysander showed no sympathy with Callibius's rage, but actually reprimanded him and told him that he did not know how to govern free men. However, the Thirty soon afterwards put Autolycus to death, to please Callibius.

Plutarch *Lysander* 15
tr. I. Scott-Kilvert (Penguin 1960)

A18 Grant of Citizenship to Resident Aliens

During the dictatorship of the Thirty, Thrasybulus, an exiled democrat, led a company of seventy to seize the border-fortress of Phyle. Recruits flocked to him and he was able to enter Piraeus and secure the high ground of Munychia. He was joined by foreign residents, spurred on partly by their ill treatment and partly by the promise of citizenship. This decree, datable to 401–0, fulfils the promise. The list of names appended is interesting and at times mysterious. We have not included the further fragments, found in Aegina, giving more names, some clearly non-Greek. See D. Hereward 'New Fragments of IG *II² 10'* Annual of the British School at Athens *47 (1952) 102–17.*

Secretary: Lysiades. Archon: Xenaenetus. Decree of the Council and Commons. Tribe in office: . . . . . . Secretary: Lysiades. Chairman: Demophilus. Proposal moved by: . . . . . .

Decided: that the resident foreigners who joined in the return from Phyle share in the benefaction offered to the returning citizens . . . . . . decreed by the Athenians. They and their descendants are to enjoy citizenship, choosing their own tribe, deme and clan. Those in office shall apply the same laws to them as to the Athenians, because . . . . . . they fought with the Athenians in the battle of Munychia . . . . . . when the agreement was reached and they carried out their orders . . . . . . just like the Athenians, and they . . . . . .

Chaeredemus, farmer
Leptines, cook
Demetrius, carpenter
Euphorion, muleteer
Cephisodorus, butcher
Hegesias, gardener

Bendiphanes, digger
Emporion, farmer
Paedicus, baker
Socias, fuller
Psammis, farmer
Egersis

. . . . . .
Phrynichus
. . . . . . ysias
Zoilus
Timaeus
Lenaeus

Epamenon, donkey driver
. . . . . . opus, olive . . . . . .
Glaucias, farmer
. . . . . . on, nut . . . . . .
Dionysius, farmer

Ona . . . . . .
Eucolion, hired labourer
Callias, statuary
. . . . . .
Aigeis
Athenogiton

Euathlus
. . . . . .

IG II^2 10

A19 Proposal for a Peasant Democracy

After the restoration of democracy there was a proposal to restrict citizenship to peasant-owners. This was frustrated by a radical democrat, name unknown, for whom Lysias wrote 'Against a proposal to destroy the ancestral constitution in Athens'. *For secondary discussions see: J. Pečirka 'Land Tenure and the Development of the Athenian* Polis', Studies G. Thomson *(Prague 1963) pp. 183–201; R. Goossens 'République des paysans',* Mélanges F. de Visscher *(Brussels 1950) pp. 551ff;* Euripide et Athènes *(Brussels 1962) pp. 556–8 and 645–6; Cl. Mossé* La fin de la démocratie athénienne *(Paris 1962) pp. 251–3; M. I. Finley* Studies in Land and Credit, *pp. 56–8.*

When the people had returned from Peiraieus, although they had passed a decree which brought about a reconciliation with the men of the city and established a general amnesty, there was a fear that the common people, having recovered their former power, would again harass the rich. Many speeches were made on this subject. Phormisios, one of those who had returned with the people, introduced a proposal to the effect that once the exiles had come back citizen rights should not be given to all, but should be restricted to those who owned (the) land; this is also what the Lacedaimonians wanted. Had this decree been voted some 5,000 Athenians would have been deprived of their civic rights.

Dionysius of Halicarnassus *On Lysias* 34
tr. M. M. Austin and P. Vidal-Naquet *Economic and Social History of Ancient Greece* (B. T. Batsford 1977) pp. 266–7

A20 Athenian Law against Dictatorship

On 3 May 1952 American excavators in the Agora found a magnificent pillar of Pentelic marble 1·57 m in height, and 0·41 to 0·43 m in width, with a sculptured relief showing Democracy crowning the Athenian People, and an inscription datable to the summer of 336, containing a law against dictatorship. After the restoration of the democracy in 403 Athenian politics in the first half of the fourth century had proved remarkably stable, but after Philip of Macedon's conquest of Greece there was fear that he might impose a dictator to foster Macedonian policies. The inscription was published and discussed by B. D. Meritt in Hesperia *21 (1952) pp. 355–9.*

Archon: Phrynichus. Prytany: ninth, held by Leontis ...... Secretary: Chaerestratus, son of Ameinias from Acharne. Vote moved by Menestratus of Aexone, presiding officer. Proposer of the motion: Eucrates, son of Aristotimus from Piraeus.

Blessing on the People of Athens.

Resolved by the legislative committee.

If anyone assail the Assembly with a view to establishing dictatorship or conspire for the establishment of dictatorship, or subvert the Assembly of the Athenian people or the democracy at Athens, anyone who kills the guilty person is to be sacrosanct. If the Assembly or the democracy at Athens be overthrown it is not permitted for any member of the Council of the Areopagus to go up to the Areopagus, to sit in Council or to transact any Council business. If the Assembly or the democracy at Athens be overthrown and if any member of the Council of the Areopagus go up to the Areopagus or take his seat in the Council, or attempt to transact any Council business, he is to be disfranchised together with his posterity, and his possessions are to be publicly confiscated, a tithe being given to the Goddess. The Secretary of the Council is to have this law inscribed on two stone pillars and to have one copy erected on the approach to the Areopagus by the entrance to the Council Chamber, and the other in the Assembly. The Treasurer of the Commons is to issue twenty drachmas from the moneys duly authorized for public expenditure to cover the cost of the inscriptions.

A21 Law against 'Hybris'

Hybris *is not easy to define. In a recent article* 'Hybris *in Athens'* Greece and Rome *23 (1976) 14–31, Douglas MacDowell argues that* hybris *is always bad, always voluntary, often but not always has its roots in youth, wealth, over-indulgence, is not (contrary to general opinion) primarily a religious matter, often involves a victim. It consists in having energy or power and misusing it self-indulgently. It becomes a legal matter when there is a victim. For a criticism see N. R. E. Fisher* 'Hybris *and Dishonour'* Greece and Rome *23 (1976) 177–93. The date of the law is uncertain but may belong to the sixth century (a different version of the law appears in Aeschines 1, 16, but this is certainly a forgery). I append a passage from Aristotle, which is designed to guide forensic pleaders.*

(a)

If any commit *hybris* against another whether child, woman or man, slave or free, or commit any unlawful act against any such, any citizen of Athens who so desires, being properly qualified, may indict him before the magistrates, and the magistrates are required to bring him before the People's Court within thirty days from the lodging of the indictment, unless some public business interpose, or else at the earliest possible date. In the event of condemnation the Court shall determine on the spot the appropriate fine or other penalty. Any who lodges a personal indictment in accordance with the law, and fails to prosecute or on prosecution to obtain one fifth of the votes shall pay 1,000 drachmas to the public treasury. If the penalty for the *hybris* is a fine, the offender is to be imprisoned, provided the offence was against a free citizen, until he pays.

Demosthenes *Against Meidias* 47

(b)

To commit *hybris* is another form of slight. *Hybris* consists in words or actions which damage the victim's reputation, not for personal advantage but for pleasure. Retaliation is punishment, not *hybris*. Those who commit *hybris* receive pleasure from the thought that their capacity to do harm to another implies superiority. It is found particularly among the young and wealthy, who think that it shows their superiority. Dishonour is characteristic of *hybris*, and dishonour is a form of slight.

Aristotle *Rhetoric* 2, 2, 5–6, 1378b 23–31

B IMPERIALISM AND INTER-STATE POLITICS

The so-called Delian Confederacy came into being in 478 as a result of some Aegean states' rejection of Spartan leadership in the campaign to free Ionia from Persian domination. The Athenians accepted an invitation to provide the executive leadership (hegemonia) of a military league ('Athens and her Allies') in which the 'synod' (a Congress consisting of representatives of all the member states, except Athens, on a basis of one state one vote which met on the island of Delos) and the Athenian state each had an equal share in policy-making.

The objectives of the League were triumphantly realized, mainly under the energetic command of Cimon, son of Miltiades, the victor at Marathon: piracy, which had been rife in the Aegean, was eliminated, resulting in an enormous growth in trade and prosperity for the commercial states, particularly Athens; while the victory both by land and sea of Athens and her allies at the mouth of the River Eurymedon in c. 469 BC virtually guaranteed the freedom of all Asia Minor Greek states from Persian domination. Athens now wielded a thalassocracy in the Aegean, which made her just as powerful as Sparta was in mainland Greece; after showing some unease at this challenge to her traditional leadership of Greece, Sparta had, apparently by c. 475 BC, decided to acquiesce in the emergence of a rival: for one thing the constant threat of the helots of Messenia and the nature of her closed society made Sparta unfit for waging overseas campaigns; for another thing initial Spartan suspicion was to some extent allayed when Athens ostracized the anti-Spartan adventurer Themistocles, and replaced him by the pro-Spartan conservative Cimon.

However a gradual transformation had been taking place in the nature of the Confederacy, away from an equal partnership between the 'hegemon' and her allies, towards authoritarian rule (arche) over subjects (see no. B3). From the start any attempt to secede from the League had been prevented, by force if necessary, but this can be excused on the grounds that the original oath of allegiance had been sworn 'in perpetuity'. Some states were forced to join against their wishes (see no. B2), but this too can be justified, at least while Persia still posed a threat, on the grounds both that there was a risk of the Persians seizing a neutral state as a base, and that such states were 'free-riders', i.e. deriving the benefits of having the Persians ejected from the Aegean, without contributing to the effort required to do it. The transfer of the Treasury of the League from the tiny island of Delos to Athens (see no. B5) which is often conjecturally dated to 454 BC, looks at first sight blatantly imperialistic; but Plutarch recounts a story that it was the Samians who proposed the transfer, and the date could easily be much earlier, before the

Eurymedon Campaign, in which case the motive may have been solely concern for the safety of the Treasury.

After 449 BC it is difficult to deny that the Confederacy of Delos had become the Athenian Empire, for whether one believes in the existence of a formal Peace Treaty (the so-called Peace of Callias) or merely a tacit agreement between Athens and Persia, the fact is that hostilities between them finally ceased in that year. There is even a story, probably apocryphal, that the Athenians summoned a Panhellenic Congress, apparently to discuss the use of the tribute money now that hostilities had ceased, but the invitation was spurned by the Peloponnesians. There is also a gap in the Tribute List at about this point which some scholars have taken as evidence that Athens ceased to collect tribute in the year 449/8, but there is no proof that the gap is anything more than an accident, or that the year is 449/8. At any rate Athens's right to maintain this Empire, by force if necessary, and to discipline her subjects, was formally recognized by Sparta and the Peloponnesian League in the Thirty Years' Peace of 446 BC, in return for Athens's guarantee to respect Spartan predominance in mainland Greece.

Until 1954 scholars unanimously accepted Thucydides's view that by 431 the Athenian Empire had come to be regarded throughout Greece as a tyranny, which Athens maintained by the open use of force solely for her own benefit against the wishes of her subjects (see no. B1), and that the Spartans fought the Peloponnesian War in order to liberate Greece from Athens's tyranny. This view was questioned by de Ste. Croix in an article 'The Character of the Athenian Empire' (*Historia* 3, 1954, 1–41), in which he points out that much of the factual evidence, as presented in Thucydides's own account, is at variance with his general conclusion, in that many allied states voluntarily supported Athens, even to the bitter end in 404 BC (e.g. no. B25). His conclusion is that though no allied city welcomed a diminishing of its autonomy, for the mass of the population in each state full freedom was not a real choice; the only choice lay between subjection to their own oligarchic factions, or acceptance of some interference by Athens in order to preserve democracy, and most chose the latter as the lesser of two evils. The authoritative work on this subject is R. Meiggs *The Athenian Empire* (Oxford University Press 1972) in which he steers a middle course between the two more extreme viewpoints. An outstanding work on the rivalry between the Athenian and Spartan power blocs, and the events leading to the Peloponnesian War (Thucydides's so-called Pentacontaetia or Fifty Year Period i.e. 478–431) is G. E. M. de Ste. Croix *The Origins of the Peloponnesian War* (Duckworth 1972).

B1 A Pragmatic Defence of Imperialism

Athenians: So far as the favour of the gods is concerned, we think we have as much right to that as you have. Our aims and our actions are perfectly consistent with the beliefs men hold about the gods and with the principles which govern their own conduct. Our opinion of the gods and our knowledge of men lead us to conclude that it is a general and necessary law of nature to rule wherever one can. This is not a law that we made ourselves, nor were we the first to act upon it when it was made. We found it already in existence, and we shall leave it to exist for ever among those who come after us. We are merely acting in accordance with it, and we know that you or anybody else with the same power as ours would be acting in precisely the same way. And therefore, so far as the gods are concerned, we see no good reason why we should fear to be at a disadvantage. But with regard to your views about Sparta and your confidence that she, out of a sense of honour, will come to your aid, we must say that we congratulate you on your simplicity but do not envy you your folly. In matters that concern themselves or their own constitution the Spartans are quite remarkably good; as for their relations with others, that is a long story, but it can be expressed shortly and clearly by saying that of all people we know the Spartans are most conspicuous for believing that what they like doing is honourable and what suits their interests is just. And this kind of attitude is not going to be of much help to you in your absurd quest for safety at the moment.

Thucydides 5, 105
tr. R. Warner (Penguin 1954)

B2 Early Athenian Imperialism

This episode is placed by Herodotus in the year 480 after the Greeks had defeated the Persians at Salamis; it is no doubt told with some hindsight relating to the later nature of Athenian imperialism.

The Greeks took the decision not to pursue the Persian navy further, and not to sail to the Hellespont to break down the bridge. Instead they surrounded Andros with a view to capturing it. Andros was the first island to reject Themistocles's request for money. Themistocles adduced the argument that the Athenians had come with the support of two mighty gods, Persuasion and Necessity, and that in consequence the citizens of Andros could not avoid paying up. To this they replied: 'We can well understand that Athens is great and prosperous with the blessing of such practical gods. We in Andros have one supreme gift, lack of land. We have two totally impractical gods who love our island and never abandon it, Poverty and Impotence. We in Andros rely on the power of these gods in rejecting the request for money. The power of Athens can never overrule our lack of power.'

Herodotus 8, 111

B3 The Growth of Athenian Power

Cimon was the leading aristocratic statesman of the second quarter of the fifth century.

He (Cimon) did not bring force to bear upon any of the Greeks and he accepted money or empty ships from all those peoples who were unwilling to serve abroad. In this way he let the allies yield to the temptation of taking their ease and attending to nothing but their private affairs, until they had lost all their military qualities and become unwarlike farmers and traders through their own folly and love of comfort. On the other hand he obliged a large part of the Athenian population to take turns in manning their ships and hardened them on his various expeditions, and thus in a short while, using the funds the allies had contributed, he made the Athenians the rulers of the very men who paid them. Those Greeks who did no military service came to fear and even to flatter men who were regularly at sea or constantly training or under arms, and so before they knew it, they had sunk into the position of tributaries and subjects instead of allies.

Plutarch *Cimon* 11
tr. I. Scott-Kilvert (Penguin 1960)

B4 Casualty List of the Erechtheid Tribe, 460 or 459 BC

This inscription shows the remarkable activity of the Athenians overseas at this time. The names of the dead which follow on the inscription, approximately 195 in three columns, have not been included here. The inscription is in R. Meiggs and D. Lewis Greek Historical Inscriptions *(Oxford 1969) no. 33.*

Of the Erechtheid tribe
these died in the war in Cyprus, in Egypt,
in Phoenicia, in Halieis, in Aegina, in Megara
in the same year.

B5 The Treasurers of the Greeks

The treasury of the confederacy of Delos was in the hands of magistrates called Hellenotamiae or the Treasurers of the Greeks. They were Athenians, ten in number, with their headquarters in Delos from 477 to the transfer of the treasury to Athens, probably in 454. The office was abolished in 404. Their work was evidently severely scrutinized, as this extract from a speech delivered perhaps in 420 suggests, though it is oddly circumspect about an event which must have fallen within living memory. The Eleven were the police responsible for condemned criminals.

All but one of the Treasurers of the Greeks were once executed on a false charge of peculation, a verdict given in the heat of the moment. The truth later came to light. The sole survivor, whose name apparently was Sosias, had been condemned to death but not in fact executed; he had actually been handed over by the commons to the Eleven when the true explanation of the money's disappearance came out. He was released, but the others, innocent though they were, had already been executed. I expect that some of the older among you recall the incident; younger citizens, like myself, know it by hearsay.

Antiphon 5, 69–71

B6 Tribute Lists

The Athenians transferred the treasury of the Confederacy of Delos from Delos to Athens, probably in 454. Records of tribute collected from the allies survive in more or less fragmentary form from that year down to the last year of such exactions, 406–5, with some gaps. Under the impact of war there was a drastic reassessment, almost quadrupling the figure in 425. The lists have naturally been much studied: see B. D. Meritt, H. T. Wade-Gery, M. F. McGregor The Athenian Tribute Lists *(4 vols) (Harvard University Press, Cambridge, Mass. 1939–53). For the reassessment see B. D. Meritt and A. B. West* The Athenian Assessment of 425 BC *(Ann Arbor 1934) together with the modifications in R.*

Meiggs and D. Lewis Greek Historical Inscriptions *(Oxford 1969) pp. 193–9. The sample which follows is the list for the Hellespontine cities for 441–0* IG I^2 *204. The figures are drachmas and obols.*

Hellespontine Tribute

5		Harpagion	5		Neapolis from Athens
200		Arisbe	288		Tenedos
100		Dardanus	16	4	......
16	4	Sigeion	1000		Perinthus
8	2	Palaipercote	33	2	Neandreia
16	4	Castle Daunion	16	4	Paisos
16	4	Castle Didymon	400		Abydos
1200		Lampsacus	8	2	Priapus
900		Chalcedon	100		Campsa
16	4	Lamponeia	33	2	Artace
900		Cyzicus	8	2	Sestos
300		Proconnesus	8	2	Madytos
100		Chersonese Market	8	2	Limnai
16	4	Astacus	50		Elaious
1507	4	Byzantium	33	2	Parion
500		Selymbria	......		Zeleia

B7 Improvements in Efficiency of Tribute Collection

This inscription may date from 447. Cleinias who died in battle in 446 is perhaps the father of Alcibiades. The inscription is in G. F. Hill Sources for Greek History *(Oxford [2] 1951) no. 46.*

O Gods:
Resolution of the Council and the Dēmos, in the prytany of the tribe Oineis, when Spoudias was Secretary, and ...... ōn was epistatēs; Cleini[as proposed this motion:

Th]e Council and the arch[ontes in] the cities and the [episco]poi are to ensure that the tribute is collected each year and brought to Athens.

They are to arrange seals for the cities in order to make it impossible for those bringing the tribute to defraud. The cities are to record on a tablet the tribute which it is sending, and after sealing (the tribute) with the seal, it is to send it to Athens. Those who bring it are to hand over the tablet in the Council to be read when they pay the tribute.

The prytaneis are to hold an Assembly after the Dionysia for the Hellenotamiae to report to the Athenians which cities have pai[d their tribute i]n full, and, separately, which have defaulted.

The Athenians are to choose fo[ur men and send them to] the cities to give a receipt for the [tribute which has been paid and] to demand the un[paid tribute from those which have defaulted]; two shall sail in a fast trireme to [the cities of the Islands and of Ionia, and two to those on the Hellespont and] towards Thrace. [The prytaneis are to introduce this subject before the] Council and the [dēmos immediately after the Dionysia and] are to discuss this [continually until the matter is settled.]

If any Athenian [or ally commits an offence in respect of the] tribute which [the cities] ought [to send to Athens after they have written it on a tablet] for those who are bringing it, any Athenian or ally who wishes may prosecute him before [the prytaneis. The pryta]neis are to bring before the Council [any prosecution which] may be made, [or else] each of them is to be liable at his euthūnai [to a fine of 1,000 drachmae] for bribery. The [Council shall not] have the authority [to decide the penalty for any man it] convicts, but shall send the case [at once to the Hēliaea.] When a man is found guilty, the prytaneis are to recommend the punishment or fine they think he should receive.

If anyone commits an offence over the bringing of the cow or [of the panopl] y, he shall be prosecuted, [and the penalty] shall be in accordance with these same principles.

The [Hellenotamiae are to record on] a whitened notice-board [and are to display both the assessment] of the tribute and [the cities which have paid up in full, and] are to record . . . . . .

Lacuna of about 10 lines

. . . . . . the incoming Council also [is to discuss the men who bring the tribute. The Council] is to report to the dēmos, [for each city in turn,] those amongst the men bring[ing (the tribute) to Athens] who have been recorded [on the notice-board in the Council] as owing money.

If any of the cities [disputes the pay]ment [of the tribute], saying that it has paid . . . . . . the people (koinon) of the city . . . . . . the cities and the. . . . . . but it may not prosecute . . . . . . but the prosecutor shall be obliged to pay [the defendant's fine if he is acquitted.] The trial is to take place [before the Polemarch in the month of Gamē] - lion (January/February). If anyone [disputes . . . . . .] summons, after the Council has deliberated, it shall . . . . . . the [eisagōgeis] are to bring [before the Hēliaea in turn those who owe] the tribute to the Athenians [according to the notice-b]oard for information [. . . . . . of the present] tribute and of last year's [tribute . . . . . . and after the Council] has framed a preliminary decree (probouleuma) it is to introduce . . . . . . on about the next day [to the dēmos . . . . . .] to discuss . . . . . . of the choice . . . . . .

IG I² 66
tr. LACT Ancient History Group *Lactor 1* AE 146

B8 Appointment of Tribute Collectors

The decree dates from 426. Cleonymus appears often in Aristophanes who attacks him as greedy, cowardly and crooked; the vigour of the attack shows that he was a statesman to be reckoned with. The reading at ll 21–5 is uncertain, but refers to indemnity payments. The Greek is in R. Meiggs and D. Lewis Greek Historical Inscriptions *(Oxford 1969) no. 68.*

2. ...... tribute:

(1) Resolution of the Council and the [Dēmos] in the prytany of the tribe Cecropis, when Polemarchus was Secretary, and Onasos was epistatēs; Cleōnymus [proposed this motion:

All] the cities that bring tribute for the Athenians [are to choose eklogeis (collectors) of tribute] in each city, [so that all the tribute may be collected for the Athenians] from all quarters, or else [the eklogeis are to be held responsible (hypeuthūnoi) ......]

Lacuna

... It is enjoined that whichever prytany is in office [(?) 10 days after the] Dionysia shall ...... and read [out in the Assembly the] cities that pay their [tribute, those that] do not pay and those that pay [in part.] Five men are to be sent to the cities which owe money, to exact the tribute.

The Hellenotamiae are to record on a public notice-board the [cities that default in payment] of tribute and ...... of the men who bring it; they are to put up the notice on each occasion in front of [(?) the Metrōon.]

It is to be lawful for Samos and Thera [to pay by instalments the] money which they owe [and of which payment must be made, through the agency of the men who come to them, and it is to be lawful for] any other city that has agreed to pay money to Athens.

The prytany of the tribe Cecropis is to set up this decree on a stēlē on the Acropolis.

P ...... critos moved this amendment to the decree of Cleōnymus:— So that the Athenians may endure the war in the best and easiest manner, these things are to be brought before the dēmos and an Assembly [is to be held] on the following morning.

(2) Resolution of the [Council and the Dēmos] in the prytany of the tribe Cecropis, when Polemarchos was Secretary, and Hygiainōn was epistatēs; [(?)Cleōnymus proposed this amendment] to the foregoing [decree:

Lacuna

...] They are to choose epimelētai (financial officials) to be in charge of the [other cases concerning] Athenian moneys in accordance [with the ......] decree, and [to appoint one] of the Generals to sit alongside them whenever [a case] about any of the [cities is to be judged]. If anyone acts fraudulently [so as to prevent] the

Tribute Decree [from being effective or to prevent] the tribute from being brought to Athens, then anyone from that city [who wishes] may indict him before the epimelētai [on a charge of treason.] The epimelētai are to bring the case to court within a month of the return of the summoners (klētēres). The [klētēres must be] two in number, otherwise whoever wishes may indict them. If it convicts anyone, the court is to decide the punishment or fine that he should receive.

All the heralds [who are elected] by the prytaneis together [with the Council,] are to be sent to the cities during the prytany [of the tribe Cecropis,] so that the men to collect the tribute may be chosen and [be recorded in the] Council Chamber. [The pōlētai] are to put out a contract for the stēlē.

Eklogeis of the tribute
from the cities.

IG I² 65
tr. LACT Ancient History Group *Lactor 1* AE 148

B9 Reassessment of Tribute

The reassessment of tribute carried through by Cleon in 425–4 is not mentioned by Thucydides. The inscription is fragmentary but its general purport is not in doubt. The only two surviving district totals are given, together with the grand total (with some restoration), and the assessment of the Island District. The figures in square brackets are restorations: those in ordinary brackets are the previous assessment. The inscription will be found in R. Meiggs and D. Lewis Greek Historical Inscriptions *(Oxford 1969) no. 69. The eisagogeis seem to have been magistrates specially charged with the raising of taxes. See further B. D. Meritt and A. B. West* The Athenian Assessment of 425 BC *(Ann Arbor 1934).*

O Gods:
Ass[essme]nt [of Tr]i[bute:]
(1) Resolution of the [Council and the Dēmos, in the] pr[ytany of the tribe Leontis, when . . . . . .] ōn was Sec[retary, and . . . . . . was epi]statēs; Thoudi[ppos proposed this motion:

Heralds chosen] from the [. . . . . . are to be sent, as the Council shall] ele[ct, to the] cities, two [to Ionia and Caria], two to [Thrace, two] to the I[slands, and two to the Hellesp] ont. They [are to declare in the] Assembly (koinon) of e [ach ci]ty [that representatives are to] pre [sent themselves (in Athens) during the month Mai] maktērion (November/December).

[(?)Thirty] eisagōgeis [are to be chosen by lot and they are to appoint a secre]tary and an assis[tant secretary from among their number]. The C[ouncil is to choose ten m] en [to assess the tribute. Within five day]s from that on which [they are chosen,] these men [are to record] (the names of) the cities, [or else pay a fine of 1,000 drachmae] each for each day of default. [The Assessors (taktai) are to be sworn in] by the commissioners for oaths [on the same day that they] are [elected, or else each commissioner shall be liable to the] same fine. The eisag[ōgeis are to be responsible for legal proceedings concerned with the tribute, according as] the [dēmos may de] cree. [One of the eisagōgeis, selected by l]ot, and the Polemar[ch are to prepare the cases for trial in] the Hēliaeā, [as with o]ther [cases] brought before the jurymen of the Hēliaea. [And if the Assessors fail to assess the] cities in accordance [with the outcome of the legal proceedings, they shall each] face a fine of 10,000 drachmae at their examination (euthūnai) [according to the law.]

The [Thesmo] thetai are to establish a new [court] of a th[ousand jurymen.

The present assessments of the tribute, since] it has become too little, [are to be] assessed jointly by the jurymen and the Council, [and, as in the la]st administrative period, assessments [on all the cities in due] proportion (are to be completed) within the month Posideion (January /February). The bu[siness is to be conducted daily] from the beginning of the month in the [same way, so that the assessment of] the tribute may be completed in the [month] Po[sideion: The Council in full session is to] conduct the business [of assessments without interruption until] they are completed, unless [the dēmos passes any decree to the contrary.] No c[ity is to be assessed for] the tribute [at a rate less] than that [which they have previously paid,] unless a [shortage] be [proved such that it is] impo[ssible for more to be paid from] the country's [total resources.

This] motion [and this decree and the tri] bute assessed [for each city are to be re] corded by the Se[cretary of the Council on two] stone stēlai, [of which one is to be set up in the Council] Chamber and the other [on the Acropolis.] The pōlētai [are to let out the contract for this work and] the kolakretai [are to provide the money.

In future, a declaration is to be made to the ci]ties about the tr[ibute before the] Great [Panathenaea. Whichever prytany] happens to be in office is to in[troduce the subject of assessments at the time of the] Panathenaea. [If the prytaneis do not introduce the business] of the [tribute at that time] before the dēmos a [nd the Council and the jury c]ourt [and do not at once conduct the business] within their own term of office, [each of the prytaneis shall be liable to] pay [100 sacred drachmae] to Athena and a h [undred] to the public treasury [and shall face a fine of 1,] 000 drachmae [at his examination (euthūnai)]. If anyone else [votes] that the assessments [for the cities should n]ot be made [at the time of] the [Great Panathena]ea in the prytany [which is fir]st in office, he is to lose his citizen rights (atīmia) and his pr[operty] is to be confiscated [with a ten]th given to the Goddess.

The prytany of the tribe [(?) Oineis] is to introduce this subject before the dēmos compulsorily on the second day after the exped [ition returns immediate]ly after [the sacri]fices. And if it is [not c]ompleted on this day, this subject is to be the first business of the next day [and is to be conducted continu]ously until it is completed in the prytany of [the tribe (?) Leontis]. If they do not introduce the subject before [the dēm]os or do not complete the business within their own term of office, each of the [prytaneis] shall [face a fine of] 10,000 dr[achmae at his euthūnai for] preventing the contri[bution of tri]bu[te for the] military expeditions. Those summone[d to tr]ials are to be [brought] by the public summoners (klētēres), [so that] the Council [may pass judgment immediately] if they appear to be failing to [perform their duties correctly].

[The ro]utes for the heralds [who are to set out are to be prescribed by] the Asses[sors (taktai) in accordance with] their oath, [indicating to what point they shall] proceed, so that they shall not [proceed (?) on their own initiative without instructions. The heralds are compulsorily to announce] the assessments to the c[ities] wherever [the archontes] judge best: [The dēmos is to] pass a decree [concerning what] must be said [to the cities ab]out the assessments and [about the decree] and any [other urgent matter the prytaneis may introduce.

The Generals are to see that] the cities pay [the tribute as soon] as [the Council jointly determines] the assessment of tribute, in order that [the dēmos] may have [sufficient money for the] wa[r. The Generals] shall be obliged to give con[sideration annually to the tr]ibute [after first investigating by land and] sea what sum]s need [to be spent on military expeditions or on anything else. They are always to introduce cases concerning] this subject at the fir[st session] of the Council, [without reference to the Hēliaea or] the other jury-courts, unless, after a pre[vious judgment by the jurymen, the] dēm[os decrees that they are to be introduced. The kōlakretai are to] hand over [the pay] for the heralds who are to set out.

...... moved this amendment to the Council's probouleuma:

The [assessments] which [are made on the individual] c[ities are to be declared to] the jury-court when it is dealing with assess[ments, by the pr]ytaneis who happen to be in office at the time and by the Secret[ary of the Council, in order that the jurymen in their turn may approve them.]

(2) Resolution of the Council and the Dēmos, in the prytany of the tribe A[egeis, when Phil]ip[pos was Secretary, and ......] oros was epistatēs; Thoudippos proposed this motion:

[The ci]ties [assessed] for tribute [in the year when Pleisti]as was for the first time Secretary of the Council, in the archonship of Stratocles (425/4 BC), are all [to bring to] the G [reat Panath] enaea a co[w and a panop]l[y.] They are to take part in the procession [in the same manner as colo]n[ists.

This is the record of the assess] ment of tri[bute for] the cities by the Council, for which Pleistias of the deme ...... was for the f [irst time Secretary, in] the archonship of Stratocles, in the term of office of the eisagōgeis, for whom Ca ...... of the deme ...... was secretary.

	Minimum	: Maximum
Hellespontine District Total:	250 T.	300 T.
Thracian District Total:	310 T.	350 T.
GRAND TOTAL:	1,460 T.	1,500 T.

Tribute from the Island District

30 T.	Parians	(18 T.)
15 T.	Naxians	($6\frac{2}{3}$ T.)
15 T.	Andrians	(6 T.)
15 T.	Melians	—
9 T.	Siphnians	(3 T.)
15 T.	Eretrians	(3 T.)
5 T.	Therans	—
10 T.	Ceians	(4 T.)
5 T.	Carystians	(5 T.)
10 T.	Chalcidians	(3 T.)
6 T.	Cythnians	(3 T.)
10 T.	Tēnians	(2 T.)
2 T.	Styrians	(1 T.)
[2 T.]	Mykonians	(1 T.)
[2 T.]	Seriphians	(1 T.)
[1 T.]	Ians	($\frac{1}{2}$ T.)
[1 T.]	Dians	($\frac{1}{3}$ T.)
1 T.	Athenitai	($\frac{1}{3}$ T.)
1 T.	Syrians	($\frac{1}{4}$ T.)
$\frac{1}{3}$ T.	Grynchians	($\frac{1}{6}$ T.)
$\frac{1}{6}$ T.	Rhēnaians	(300 dr.)
$\frac{1}{3}$ T.	Diakrians from Chalcis	(800 dr.)
$\frac{1}{6}$ T.	Anaphaians	—
$10\frac{1}{2}$ dr.	Ceria	—
$\frac{1}{3}$ T.	Pholegandros	—
300 dr.	Belbina	—
$\frac{1}{6}$ T.	Cimolos	—
$\frac{1}{6}$ T.	Sikinians	—
100 dr.	Posideion in Euboea	—
$1\frac{1}{3}$ T.	Diakrians in Euboea	—
4 T.	Hephaistians in Lemnos	(3 T.)
[blank	Myrinaians]	($1\frac{1}{2}$ T.)
[1 T.	Imbrians]	(1 T.)
[Island District Total:	163 T. $410\frac{1}{2}$ dr.]	

IG I[2] 63
tr. LACT Ancient History Group *Lactor 1* AE 137

B10 Athenian Decree about Erythrae

The original, dating from the 450s, was found on the Acropolis but is now lost. Erythrae was a city on the Asia Minor coast. Athens was beginning her imperial policy of imposing her will on her 'allies'. The decree was usefully discussed by R. Meiggs 'The Growth of Athenian Imperialism' Journal of Hellenic Studies *63 (1943) 21–33. Only the central section of the decree was legible, and not all of that.*

The Erythraeans are to bring to the Great Panathenaic Festival food to a value not less than three minas; the superintendent of the Festival is to dispense to those Erythraeans present . . . . . . If they bring less than three minas' worth, they must purchase food in accordance with their undertakings, and the commons . . . . . . Those of the Erythraeans so desirous may . . . . . .

There is to be a Council of 120 men chosen by lot; . . . . . . within the Council; an alien may not serve, nor may anyone under the age of thirty. Any offence against these provisions is subject to legal action. No one shall serve on the Council more than once in a period of four years. The Administrator and Commanding Officer shall cast lots and determine the composition of the Council at this time; hereafter the Commanding Officer and the Council itself shall do so, not less than thirty days before the Council relinquishes office. They shall take an oath by Zeus, Apollo and Demeter, laying a curse of annihilation upon those who swear falsely and upon their children . . . . . . together with a sacrifice. The Council shall offer in burnt offering not less than . . . . . ., or else be liable to a fine of one thousand drachmas . . . . . . the commons shall offer no less as a burnt offering.

The oath of the Council runs as follows: 'To the best and highest of my ability, as Councillor I will serve the democracy of Erythrae and of Athens, and of the Allies. I will not revolt against the democracy of Athens and of the Allies, either by personal initiative or through another's inducement . . . . . . either by personal initiative or through another's inducement . . . . . . I will not, either by personal initiative or through another's inducement, receive back a single exile from those who deserted to Persia, without the authority of the Council and Commons of Athens. I will not expel any of those who remain, without the authority of the Council and Commons of Athens.'

If any citizen of Erythrae kill another citizen of Erythrae, he shall be put to death if adjudged guilty . . . . . . adjudged guilty shall be exiled from the whole Athenian Confederacy, and his property shall revert to the state of Erythraeans. And if any citizen is caught betraying the city of the Erythraeans to dictators he shall be put to death and the children of his loins with him. . . . . . !

IG I^2 10

B11 Athenian Economic Imperialism

At some uncertain date, perhaps in the early 440s, though the matter is highly controversial, the Athenians passed a decree prescribing the use of Athenian currency, weights and measures throughout the Confederacy; it is not quite clear whether the decree applied to the more powerful 'independent' allies, Chios, Lesbos and Samos. Fragments of the decree have been found at Aphytis, Cos, Siphnos, Smyrna and Syme. Aristophanes parodies this decree in The Birds *1040–1. The text is in R. Meiggs and D. Lewis* Greek Historical Inscriptions *(Oxford 1969) no. 45. The implications are briefly discussed in A. French* The Growth of the Athenian Economy *(London 1964).*

...... (3) If any, whether citizen or alien, within the cities, apart from the Administrators, acts contrary to the statutes, he is to be disfranchised, and his property confiscated, a tithe belonging to the goddess. If there are not Athenian Administrators, the magistrates in the several cities are to enforce the provisions of this decree; if they do not act in conformity with the decree they are to be prosecuted at Athens with a view to disfranchisement.

In receiving the silver money in the mint the officials shall convert not less than half into Attic coin ...... They shall exact a fee of three drachmas a mina ......

...... (8) If anyone proposes or votes in this matter that it is legitimate to use foreign coinage or make a loan therein he is to be reported to the Eleven without delay. The Eleven shall pass sentence of death. If he plead 'Not Guilty', they shall bring him to trial.

The Commons are to appoint heralds ...... the statutes, one to the Islands, one to Ionia, one to the Hellespont, one to the area around Thrace. The generals shall make arrangements for their travelling expenses and dispatch them; if they fail to do so, they shall be liable to a fine of 10,000 drachmas each.

The Administrators in the cities shall publish the decree by inscribing it on a pillar in every city centre, and the officials shall publish a copy in front of the mint. If they refuse, the Athenians shall see that it is done, but the herald who is sent shall require of them what the Athenians command.

The secretary of the Council shall in future add the following words to the Council oath: 'If anyone in the cities strikes silver coins and does not use the currency, weights and measures of the Athenians, but foreign currency, weights and measures, I will exact penal retribution in conformity with the earlier decree of Clearchus.'

Everyone is authorized to hand in the foreign currency in his possession and exchange it on the same terms whenever he wishes, and the city will give him Attic currency in exchange. Each shall bring his own currency to Athens and deposit it at the mint. The officials shall record the several deposits and set up a marble pillar in front of the mint for anyone who wants to see. They shall set down the total sum of foreign currency, silver and gold separately, and the total sum of Attic silver . . . . . .

B12 The Athenians Colonize Brea

The Athenians established a number of overseas settlements in the middle of the fifth century. This inscription, probably to be dated to 446–5, relates to one of the lesser-known ones, at Brea in Thrace, and is the only contemporary inscription relating to a foundation. It is thus of great interest. For a useful discussion see H. B. Mattingly 'Athenian Imperialism and the Foundation of Brea' Classical Quarterly *16 (1966) 172–86. The passage dealing with the decision to establish the settlement is missing. Phantocles's addendum confines the colonists to the two poorest classes of citizen and gives him the right to further representations.*

. . . . . . The founders of the colony are to provide for sacrifices on behalf of the colony to the extent they deem right. Ten men are to be selected to allocate the land, one from each tribe. These are to make the allocations. Democleides has full authority to establish the settlement so far as in him lies.

The consecrated precincts are to remain as at present, and no others are to be consecrated. They are to offer an ox and a full set of armour at the Great Panathenaic Festival, and a phallus at the festival of Dionysus.

If anyone raises a military expedition against the settlers' territory, the cities are to come to the rescue with all speed in accordance with the conventions established in relation to the cities in Thrace when . . . . . . was secretary.

These enactments are to be inscribed on a pillar and published in the Acropolis. The settlers are to provide for the pillar at their own expense. If anyone moves a vote in contravention of the pillar, or if any politician speaks in favour or presses a proposal to abandon or abolish any of its provisions, he is to be disfranchised together with his progeny, and his possessions are to be publicly forfeit, a tithe going to the Goddess, except that the settlers may register a petition.

Those of the soldiers who on their return to Athens apply to be colonists, are to be at Brea as prospective settlers within thirty days. The colony is to emigrate within thirty days. Aeschines is to accompany them as paymaster.

Phantocles moved: In support of Democleides's motion about the colony at Brea, the prytany of the tribe Erechtheis is to present Phantocles at the first session of the Council. Also that the settlers going to Brea shall be drawn from the thetes and zeugitae.

IG I^2 45

B13 A Diplomatic Initiative

This account from Plutarch's Life of Pericles, *which occurs only in this late source, ostensibly refers to events about 449 seemingly designed to stimulate international opinion into accepting the Athenian Confederacy. The language, however, suggests the fourth century rather than the fifth, and there is reason to think that it may pertain to Athenian initiatives to soften the impact of their renewed imperialism at that time, and that the episode was a judicious invention.*

When the Spartans began to be vexed by the growing power of Athens, Pericles, by way of encouraging the people to cherish even higher ambitions and making them believe themselves capable of great achievements, introduced a proposal that all Greeks, whether living in Europe or in Asia, in small or in large cities alike, should be invited to send delegates to a congress at Athens. The subjects to be discussed were the Greek sanctuaries which had been burned down by the Persians; the sacrifices owed to the gods on behalf of Hellas to fulfil the vows made when they were fighting the Persians; and the security of the seas, so that all ships could sail them without fear and keep the peace. Twenty men were chosen from the citizens above fifty years of age to convey this invitation. Five of these invited the Ionian and Dorian Greeks in Asia and the islands, as far as Lesbos and Rhodes; five visited the regions on the Hellespont and those of Thrace as far as Byzantium; five others proceeded to Boeotia, Phocis, and the Peloponnese, passing from there by way of the Ozolian Locrians to the neighbouring mainland, as far as Acarnania and Ambracia, while the rest travelled through Euboea to the Oetaeans and the Maliac gulf, and to the Achaeans of Phthia and the Thessalians, urging them all to attend and join in the deliberations for the peace and well-being of Greece. However, nothing was achieved, and the delegates never assembled because of the covert opposition of the Spartans; at least this is the reason generally given, since the Athenian overtures were first rejected in the Peloponnese. I have mentioned this episode, however, as an illustration of Pericles' lofty spirit and of the grandeur of his conceptions.

Plutarch *Pericles* 17
tr. I. Scott-Kilvert (Penguin 1960)

B14 Athenian Resources

Reported words of Pericles to the Athenians in face of the prospect of war in 431. For a detailed examination of the figures see A. W. Gomme's commentary. W. Kolbe Thukydides in Lichte d. Urkunden *(Stuttgart 1930), though outdated in some regards, remains an important treatment of the economy.*

They were to keep firm control of the Allies; their power depended on the income from the Allies' payments; and victory in war generally depended on a combination of sound judgment and capital resources. They could take courage from the fact that Athens received an annual income of something like six hundred talents from tribute from the Allies, apart from the rest of the revenue. On the acropolis there were still reserves of six thousand talents of silver coin. (There had originally been 9,700 talents, from which money had been withdrawn for the Propylaea and other buildings on the acropolis, and for Potidaea.) In addition there was uncoined gold and silver from private and public offerings, the sacred vessels for the processions and games, the spoils from the Persians, and the like, to the quantity of at least five hundred talents. There were also the treasures from the other temples, which were not negligible and could be used; if they were absolutely forced to do so, they could use the goddess's gold decorations: the statue had a weight of forty talents of gold and it was all detachable. This could be used in an emergency, though it would have to be repaid with interest. Economically there were grounds for optimism. They could put 13,000 heavy infantry into the field, apart from the 16,000 on guard and garrison duty...... There were 1,200 cavalry, including mounted archers, and three hundred seaworthy warships.

Thucydides 2, 13

B15 The Real Cause of the Peloponnesian War

The openly expressed grounds of complaint, or formal reasons for breaking the truce, seem to be the conflicts over Corcyra and Potidaea. There has been some controversy over the second half of passage (a). The phrase in question literally means 'the most true reasons for the war were also the most hidden'; yet Thucydides himself mentions Athenian imperialism as a cause put forward by others in several passages. According to G. E. M. de Ste. Croix (The Origins of the Peloponnesian War *Duckworth 1972), although fear of Athenian imperialism had been mentioned by Sparta's allies many times yet it was not mentioned by*

Sparta herself as a formal cause for breaking the truce and initiating war. A. Andrewes in his article 'Thucydides on the Causes of the War' Classical Quarterly *53 (1959) thinks Thucydides is inconsistent here. For another interpretation see the translation by R. Warner in the Penguin edition.*

(a)

The (Peloponnesian) war began when the Athenians and the Peloponnesians broke the thirty-year truce which had been drawn up between them after the capture of Euboea. I have already given first the grounds of complaint and the differences for which they broke the truce, so that no one will ask for what reasons such a great war befell the Greeks. In my opinion, the truest explanation, though it was least publicized, was that the Athenians, becoming great and instilling fear into the Spartans, compelled them to go to war; but the openly expressed grounds of complaint on each side, for which they broke the truce and declared war, are as follows.

Thucydides 1, 23, 6
tr. after G. E. M. de Ste. Croix

(b)

The Spartans voted that the treaty had been broken, and that war should be declared not so much because they were influenced by the speeches of their allies as because they were afraid of the further growth of Athenian power, seeing as they did, that already the greater part of Hellas was under the control of Athens.

Thucydides 1, 88
tr. R. Warner (Penguin 1954)

(c)

It was only a few years later that there took place the events already described – the affair of Corcyra, the affair of Potidaea, and the other occurrences which served as causes for the war between Athens and Sparta. The actions of the Hellenes against each other and against foreign Powers which I have just related all took place in a period of about fifty years between the retreat of Xerxes and the beginning of this present war. In these years the Athenians made their empire more and more strong, and greatly added to their own power at home. The Spartans though they saw what was happening did little or nothing to prevent it and for most of the time remained inactive, being traditionally slow to go to war unless they were forced into it and also being prevented from taking action by wars in their own territory. So finally the point was reached when Athenian strength attained a peak plain for all to see and the Athenians began to encroach upon Sparta's allies. It was at this point that Sparta felt the position to be no longer tolerable and decided by starting this present war to employ all her energies in attacking and, if possible, destroying the power of Athens.

Though the Spartans had already decided that the truce had been broken by

Athenian aggression, they also sent to Delphi to inquire from the god whether it would be wise for them to go to war. It is said that the god replied that if they fought with all their might, victory would be theirs, and that he himself would be on their side, whether they invoked him or not.

Thucydides 1, 118
tr. R. Warner (Penguin 1954)

B16 A Political Commentary from 425

In 426 Aristophanes presented The Babylonians, *and was attacked by the radical Cleon.* The Acharnians *was presented at the Lenaea in January–February 425, before (as we might say, though it is wartime) the tourist season. In 432 before the Peloponnesian war actually broke out Pericles proposed economic sanctions against Corinth's ally Megara. Aristophanes is suggesting that this was gross provocation to Sparta and the Peloponnesians. The passage is notable for: (a) the thumbnail sketch of the wrath of Pericles, portrayed as Zeus; (b) the very realistic picture of life at Athens in an emergency; (c) the humane pacifism of the poet. For Aspasia (Pericles's mistress) see no. G13.*

DICAEOPOLIS: Members of the audience, please don't be cross,
If a down and out like me has the nerve here in Athens,
to make a political speech in a comedy.
Comedy has a sense of justice too.
It's justice I shall lay before you, unpalatable justice.
Cleon on this occasion won't be able to malign me
for criticizing my country in the presence of foreigners.
We're here on our own; it's the Lenaea.
No foreigners present. The allied soldiers
and the financial contributions haven't yet arrived.
Here we are, pure wheat without chaff
(counting the resident aliens with the citizens – as bran).
I heartily loathe the Spartans.
I'd like to see Poseidon, God of Taenarus,
have an earthquake and turn all their houses upside down.
They chopped my vineyards to bits like yours.
But look – we're all friends here –
why blame the Spartans for all this?
What about our own people? I don't mean Athens:
kindly note that I do not mean Athens.
What about those useless creatures, those corrupt

debased, dishonourable, un-Athenian types
who denounced the import of little woollen jackets from Megara?
They've only to see a cucumber, rabbit,
pig, a clove of garlic, a lump of salt
and it's 'Megarian contraband!' and instant confiscation.
Minor matters. Purely domestic.
But now some of our young heroes got sloshed, sent
to Megara and kidnapped a tart named Simaetha.
That put Megarian hackles up all right.
They pinched a couple of tarts from Aspasia's pantry.
That sparked off world war in Greece –
all for three whores.
Olympian Pericles in wrath
thundered and lightened and had Greece in a whirl,
laying down laws like barrack-room ballads.
'The people of Megara have no right to live on earth
in market-places, on the seas, or in the skies!'
Meanwhile the people of Megara were steadily starving,
and asked the Spartans to annul
that hoary old decree.
Time and again they pressed us. We said 'No!'
The Spartans started beating the war-drum
'They didn't oughter done it!' What did they oughter done?
Suppose some Spartan set out in a launch to Seriphos,
saw a mongrel there and had it sold as contraband,
would you have sat tight at home? You would not!
You'd have acted promptly, put out to sea
with three hundred ships, Athens would have been pack-a-jam,
what with troops shouting, captains finding a crew,
wages paid, figureheads painted,
crowds in the public places, rations allocated,
wineskins, oar-loops, pots for sale,
garlic, olives, strings of onions,
chaplets, sardines, flute-girls, black eyes.
Down at the docks they're planing spars,
hammering rivets, fitting oar-loops,
and it's music while you work.
Oh yes, that's what you'd have been up to! So why not
the Spartans? We've none of us any sense.

Aristophanes *Acharnians* 496–556

B17 A Special Levy

In 428 Mytilene revolted from Athens and was besieged. Some scholars think that the collection was arrears of the normal tribute, but A. W. Gomme A Historical Commentary on Thucydides *(Oxford, Clarendon Press) II p. 279, more probably identifies it as a special levy imposed on the allies to match their own contributions.*

The Athenians were short of money for the siege and for the first time made a special levy of two hundred talents. At the same time they sent twelve ships under the command of Lysicles and four others to collect money from the allies. After sailing all round and collecting the rest of the money he went up country from Myus in Caria through the plain of the Maeander as far as Mt Sandius. There the Carians and Anaeitans set upon them and killed Lysicles and many of his troops.

Thucydides 3, 19

B18 The Hazards of Rebellion

Mytilene was captured by the Athenians in the following year. The date is 428; the siege that of Mytilene. Thucydides (3, 36–49) has a vivid picture of how the Athenians passed a motion one day condemning to death all the male inhabitants and next day rescinded the sentence. The reprieve arrived just in time. The next sentence is sometimes forgotten.

The rest of the men whom Paches had sent to Athens as holding the largest responsibility for the uprising were executed by the Athenians on a motion by Cleon to the number of rather more than a thousand, and the walls of Mytilene were dismantled and their navy taken over.

Thucydides 3, 50

B19 Agreement with Mytilene

After the revolt of Mytilene had been crushed, Athenian settlers were sent out; the decree seems to refer to disputes between the settlers and the Mytilenians being resolved in the latter's favour. The best edition of the inscription is by P. H. Davis in American Journal of Archaeology *30 (1926) 177–9.*

The Mytile[nians:
When . . . . . . was Secret]ary:
O Gods:
[Resolution of the Council and the Dēmos in the prytany of the tribe Acama]ntis, [when . . . . . . was Secretary and . . . . . .] thos was epistatēs; . . . . . . proposed this motion:– . . . . . . if it is resol[ved, and to reply also to] the [Mytilen]-ians that . . . . . . the Athenians dēmos and . . . . . . and it is resolved that they (i.e. the Mytilenians) shall be autonomous [and keep all] their own property . . . . . . the Athenians order . . . . . . granting to the Athenians reciprocal rights at law in accordance with the former symbolai, and anything which they sold to the *cleruchs* before [the land] was handed over to them by the Generals and the soldiers [is to be handed over] by those Mytilenians who now hold it.

These things are to be recorded by the Secretary of the Council on a stone stēlē and are to be set up on the Acropolis at the expense of the [Mytilenians.

These] things are to be recorded and [the embassy] of the Mytilenians is to be invited to [be entertained at the Town Hall (*prytaneion*)] tomorrow; to the cleruchs . . . . . . of the land . . . . . . is to be restored again [(?) to the Mytilenians . . . . . .]

Resolution of . . . . . .

IG I² 60
tr. LACT Ancient History Group *Lactor 1* AE 168

B20 Cleruchies

The cleruchies or settlements of colonists were one of the most unpopular aspects of Athenian imperial rule. The play dates from 422.

STREPSIADES: What's this?
STUDENT: Geometry.
STREPSIADES: What use is that?
STUDENT: Land-measurement.
STREPSIADES: You mean for cleruchies?

When the Athenians conquered a piece of enemy territory and evicted the occupants they would send out some of their own citizens and allocate the land among them.

Aristophanes *Clouds* 201–3 with Scholiast

B21 The Twelve-months Truce of 423

See A. W. Gomme A Historical Commentary on Thucydides *(Oxford, Clarendon Press, vol. III, 1956). The document seems reliable, though it will not have been recorded on stone, and Thucydides probably did not see it until 403.*

'With regard to the temple and oracle of the Pythian Apollo we agree that all who wish should have the right to consult the oracle without fraud and without fear, according to the established laws of each man's country. This has been agreed by the Spartans and by the allies present, and they undertake to send heralds to the Boeotians and Phocians and to do their best to persuade them to subscribe to the agreement.

'With regard to the treasure belonging to the god we agree to take measures to find out those who have been guilty in respect of this treasure, both we and you proceeding with justice and equity according to our own laws; and that all others who wish to do so, may do the same, each according to the law of his country. On the above points the Spartans and their allies are agreed.

'On the following points also the Spartans and the other allies are agreed, if the Athenians are prepared to make a treaty. It is proposed that each side should remain in its own territory, holding what it now holds: the troops in Coryphasium are to remain within Buphras and Tomeus: the troops in Cythera are to enter into no communication with the Peloponnesian League, neither we with them, or they with us: the troops in Nisaea and Minoa are not to cross the road leading from the gates of the temple of Nisus to the temple of Poseidon and from there straight on to the bridge at Minoa: the Megarians and the allies are also bound not to cross this road: the Athenians are to retain the island which they have taken, but there is to be no communication between it and the allies or the allies and it: in the territory of Troezen each side is to keep what it now holds, according to the agreement made with the Athenians.

'With regard to travel by sea, in respect of their own coastline and that of their allies, the Spartans and their allies may travel in any ship rowed by oars and not exceeding a tonnage of 500 talents. They may not travel in ships of war. That all heralds and embassies, with their appropriate staffs, who are dealing with the ending of the war and the settlement of claims are to be guaranteed a safe conduct, going and coming, to Peloponnese or to Athens, by land and by sea.

'That during the truce neither side is to receive deserters, whether free men or slaves.

'That claims made by us against you and by you against us are to be settled in accordance with the laws of our countries, and points in dispute are to be submitted to arbitration, without recourse to war.

'The above articles have been agreed upon by the Spartans and their allies. But if you have any better or fairer proposals to make, we invite you to come to Sparta and inform us of them. Neither Sparta nor her allies will reject any just suggestion that you make. But if you send delegates, let them come with full powers, as you have asked us to do. The armistice is to last for one year.

'Approved by the people.

'The tribe of Acamantis held the prytany. Phaenippus was secretary, Niciades chairman. Laches proposed the motion, in the name of the good fortune of the Athenians, that an armistice should be made on the terms offered by Sparta and her allies and approved by the people; that the armistice should last for one year, beginning on that very day, the fourteenth of the month of Elaphebolion; that during the period of the armistice ambassadors and heralds should go between the two countries to discuss means for reaching a permanent peace settlement; that the generals and prytanes should call an assembly of the people, so that the Athenians should first be able to discuss the terms on which an embassy to negotiate a final settlement should be admitted; that the embassy now present should at once pledge itself before the people to abide by the terms of this truce for one year.'

Thucydides 4, 118
tr. R. Warner (Penguin 1954)

B22 The Peace of Nicias 421

This is the fifty-year peace treaty (wishful thought) that brought to an end the first phase of the war between Athens and Sparta. As far as Athens was concerned the defence of her empire had been successful; she fell later through expansionist policies in the west. For the moment, militarists like Lamachus and Demosthenes were ready to sign alongside the more peaceable Nicias and Laches. Plutarch Nicias *9, 7–9 records the general approval in Athens of the end of fighting. See A. W. Gomme* A Historical Commentary on Thucydides *(Oxford, Clarendon Press, vol. III, 1956).*

The Athenians, the Spartans and their allies made a treaty and swore to it, city by city, as follows:

'With regard to the Panhellenic temples, everyone who wishes, according to the customs of his country, to sacrifice in them, to travel to them, to consult the oracles, or to attend the games shall be guaranteed security in doing so, both by sea and by land. At Delphi the consecrated ground and the temple of Apollo and the Delphians themselves shall be governed by their own laws, taxed by their own state, and judged by their own judges, both the people and the territory, according to the custom of the place.

'The treaty is to be in force between the Athenians, with their allies, and the Spartans, with their allies, for fifty years without fraud or damage by land or sea.

'It shall not be lawful to take up arms with intent to do injury either for the Spartans and their allies against the Athenians and their allies, or for the Athenians and their allies against the Spartans and their allies, in any way or by any means whatever. If any dispute should arise between them, they are to deal with it by law and by oath, as may be agreed between them.

'The Spartans and their allies are to give back Amphipolis to the Athenians. In the case of all cities given back by the Spartans to the Athenians, the inhabitants shall have the right to go where they please taking their property with them.

'These cities are to pay the tribute fixed by Aristides and are to be independent. So long as they pay the tribute, it shall not be lawful for the Athenians or their allies to take up arms against these cities, once the treaty has been made. The cities referred to are Argilus, Stagirus, Acanthus, Scolus, Olynthus and Spartolus. These cities are to be allied neither to Sparta nor to Athens. If, however, the Athenians persuade the cities to do so, it shall be lawful for the Athenians to make them their allies, provided that the cities themselves are willing.

'The Mecybernaeans, the Sanaeans and Singaeans shall inhabit their own cities, as shall the Olynthians and Acanthians. The Spartans and their allies shall give back Panactum to the Athenians. The Athenians shall give back Coryphasium, Cythera, Methana, Ptelium and Atalanta to the Spartans; also all Spartans who are in prison in Athens or in any prison in the Athenian dominions.

'The Athenians shall let go the Peloponnesians besieged in Scione and all others in Scione who are allies of Sparta, and those whom Brasidas sent in there, and any other allies of Sparta who are in prison in Athens or in any other prison in the Athenian dominions. The Spartans and their allies shall in the same way give back all Athenians or allies of Athens whom they have in their hands. With regard to Scione, Torone, Sermyle, and any other cities in Athenian hands, the Athenians may act as they think fit.

'The Athenians shall take an oath to the Spartans and their allies, city by city. The oath taken shall be the most binding one that exists in each city, and seventeen representatives on each side are to swear it. The words of the oath shall be these: "I shall abide by the terms of this treaty honestly and sincerely." In the same way the Spartans and their allies shall take an oath to the Athenians. This oath is to be renewed annually by both sides. Pillars are to be set up at Olympia, Pythia, the Isthmus, in the Acropolis at Athens, and in the temple at Amyclae in Lacedaemon.

'If any point connected with any subject at all has been overlooked, alterations may be made, without any breach of oath, by mutual agreement and on due consideration by the two parties, the Athenians and the Spartans.

'The treaty comes into effect from the 27th day of the month of Artemisium at Sparta, Pleistolas holding the office of ephor; and at Athens from the 25th day of the month of Elaphebolium, in the archonship of Alcaeus.

'Those who took the oath and poured the libations were as follows: For the Spartans, Pleistoanax, Agis, Pleistolas, Damagetus, Chionis, Metagenes, Acanthus, Daithus, Ischagoras, Philocharidas, Zeuxidas, Antiphus, Tellis, Alcinadas, Empedias, Menas and Laphilus. For the Athenians, Lampon, Isthmonicus, Nicias, Laches, Euthydemus, Procles, Pythodorus, Hagnon, Myrtilus, Thrasycles, Theagenes, Aristocrates, Iolcius, Timocrates, Leon, Lamachus and Demosthenes.'

Thucydides 5, 18–19
tr. R. Warner (Penguin 1954)

B23 Different Outlooks of Rich and Poor

The city poor would often be employed as oarsmen, the rich might have to spend money on fitting out ships; war meant devastation and neglect of the land.

PRAXAGORA: Must the ships be launched? The poor say yes,
but the rich and the farmers say no.

Aristophanes *Ecclesiazusae* 197–8

B24 Proxenia

Some thirty-odd inscriptions survive relating to the office of Proxenos, but this is the only one complete. The Proxenos was a citizen of another state who looked after the interests of Athenians in that state. The office often stayed in a single family, and harm done to them was regarded as if committed against Athenian citizens. This dates from 408–7. The decree will be found in R. Meiggs and D. Lewis Greek Historical Inscriptions *(Oxford 1969) no. 90.*

Gods

Decree of the Council and Commons. Tribe in office: Antiochis. Secretary: Euclides. President: Hierocles. Archon: Euctemon. Proposer of the motion: Dieitrephes.

Since Oeniades of Old Skiathos is a loyal supporter of Athens, eager to help in any way he can, and is valuable to Athenians visiting Skiathos, he is to receive official approbation and to be recorded as Proxenos and benefactor of Athens, together with his children. The Council for the year, the Generals, and whoever is in office at Skiathos at any given time, are to ensure that no wrong is done to him. The Secretary of the Council is to record this decree on a stone pillar to be erected on the Acropolis. Oeniades is further to be invited to dinner at the City Hall tomorrow.

Amendment to the Council's decree proposed by Antichares: The wording of the resolution to be altered to read 'Oeniades of Old Skiathos' rather than 'Skiathos'.

B25 Decree in Honour of Samos

Samos was a loyal ally of Athens throughout the Peloponnesian War and the centre from which democracy was restored at Athens in 410. The island stood by Athens even after her final defeat at Aegospotami. The decree was moved in 405 but not publicly recorded until 403 or 402 after the second restoration of democracy. The Greek text is in R. Meiggs and D. Lewis Greek Historical Inscriptions *(Oxford 1969) no. 94.*

Cēphisophōn from the deme Paeania was Secretary: All the Samians who were on the side of the Athenian dēmos: Resolution of the Council and the Dēmos, in the prytany of the tribe Cecropis, when Polymnis from the deme Euōnymōn was Secretary, and Alexias was archon, and Nikophōn from the deme Athmonōn was epistatēs; proposal of Cleisophos and his fellow-prytaneis: –

The Samian envoys now present and those who came earlier and the Council and generals and the rest of the Samians are to be commended for their loyalty and their eagerness to perform such loyal service as they are able, and because in their deeds they seem to have acted in the true interests of Athens and Samos, and in return for their loyal services to the Athenians, for the high regard in which they hold them, and for their loyal proposals.

The Council and the Dēmos have resolved that the Samians are to become Athenian citizens, with whatever form of government they themselves want. So that this may be put into effect as conveniently as possible for both sides, as the Samians themselves propose, joint discussion of the remaining details shall take place when peace is made.

The Samians are to be autonomous and follow their own laws, and in all other respects shall act in accordance with the oaths and treaties which have been agreed between Athens and Samos.

On the question of the prosecutions which may be brought by one side against the other, the Athenians and the Samians are to grant reciprocal rights at law in accordance with the existing symbolai.

If any emergency arises on account of the war, and earlier about the form of government, they are to deliberate and to act for the present, as the envoys themselves propose, in whatever way seems to be best. As for the question of peace, if it is to be made, it shall be made on the same terms for the present inhabitants of Samos, as for the Athenians. If warfare is necessary, the Samians are to make preparations to the best of their ability, keeping in contact with the Generals. Whenever the Athenians send an embassy to any place, they are also to send with it any of the Samians present whom they choose, and are to give whatever good advice they can.

The Samians shall be given the use of the triremes now at Samos, provided that they themselves equip them in such manner as they think fit. The envoys are to record for the Secretary of the Council and for the Generals the names of the trierarchs to whom these ships were assigned. Any [debts] recorded in the public treasury against their names for having taken possession of the triremes are to be totally [cancelled] by the dockyard-superintendents, but the equipment [is to be collected as quickly as possible] for the public treasury and those who have [any] shall be obliged to return it [in full.

Proposals of Cleisophos and] his fellow-prytaneis, as an amendment to the decree of the Council:–

As they themselves request, [an honorary gift is to be made to those of the Samians] who have come, and they are [at once] to be distributed equally [amongst the demes and the] 10 tribes.

[The Generals shall provide] a safe passage [for the envoys a] s quickly as possible, and Eumachus and [all the other Samians who have come with Eumachus] are to be commended for their [loyalty to Athens. Eum] achus is to be invited to dine at the Town Hall (prytaneion) [tomorrow.]

The Secr[etary of the Coun] cil, together with the [Generals, is to record this decree on a stone stēlē and set] it up on the Acropoli [s, and the Hellen] otamiae [are to provide the money. It is to be recorded at Sa]mos on the same terms at [their expen] se.

tr. LACT Ancient History Group
Lactor 1 AE 160

B26 The Fate of Prisoners of War

These events belong to 405, at the end of the Peloponnesian War. According to Plutarch (Lysander *13), 3,000 Athenians were killed.*

Many charges were pressed against the Athenians, for crimes already committed and for what they had voted to do if they had won the battle, e.g. to cut off the hands of all prisoners of war – in addition to the fact that they had captured two warships, one from Corinth and one from Andros, and thrown the whole of the crews overboard. This massacre was due to the Athenian admiral Philocles. Many other allegations were made, and the decision was taken to execute all the Athenian prisoners except Adeimantus, who had raised a solitary voice in the Assembly against the motion to cut off the hands.

Xenophon *Hellenica* 2, 1, 31–2

B27 The News of the Disaster at Aegospotami Reaches Athens

In 405 the Athenian navy was finally destroyed by the Spartans at Aegospotami.

It was at night that the *Paralus* arrived at Athens. As the news of the disaster was told, one man passed it on to another, and a sound of wailing arose and extended first from Piraeus, then along the Long Walls until it reached the city. That night no one slept. They mourned for the lost, but more still for their own fate. They thought that they themselves would now be dealt with as they had dealt with others – with the Melians, colonists of Sparta, after they had besieged and conquered Melos, with the people of Histiaea, of Scione, of Torone, of Aegina and many other states. Next day they held an Assembly at which it was decided to block up all the harbours except one, to repair and man the walls, and take all other measures to put the city into a state of readiness for a siege.

Xenophon *Hellenica* 2, 2, 3–4
tr. R. Warner (Penguin 1966)

B28 Alliance between Boeotia and Athens

In 395 Athens, recovering from the Peloponnesian War, joined in a coalition with Boeotia, Argos and Corinth against Sparta. This is part of the consequent treaty.

Gods
Alliance between the Boeotians and Athenians in perpetuity.
If anyone commits military aggression against the Athenians by land or sea, the Boeotians shall come to their help in full strength, conforming to the best of their abilities with the Athenian request. If anyone commits military aggression against the Boeotians by land or sea the Athenians shall come to their help in full strength, conforming to the best of their abilities with the Boeotian request. If the Athenians and Boeotians in joint council agree to any addition or curtailment ......

W. Dittenberger *Sylloge Inscriptionum Graecarum* 122+ (Leipzig[3] 1915)

B29 Payment for Fortifying Piraeus

*In 404 the Long Walls of Athens and the fortifications of Piraeus were destroyed. Rebuilding began after Athens's alliance with Thebes in 395 with the help of Boeotian workmen, and was greatly speeded up by Conon, the Athenian admiral, when he returned to Athens with Persian money and put his sailors on to the job. These are records of payments (*IG *II^2 1656–7) from 395–4 and 394–3.*

Archon: Diophantus. Month: Scirophorion. Payments for day work, hiring fee for oxen to haul stone: 160 dr. Hire of tools: 53 dr.

Archon: Eubulides. Beginning from the marked spot as far as the façade of the gates near the shrine of Aphrodite on the right as you go out: 750 dr. Contractor for the transport of the stone: Demosthenes from Boeotia.

B30 The King's Peace 387–6

The King's Peace, which brought the Corinthian War to an end, was remarkable – and widely resented – because it was the first time a Persian King had arbitrated the affairs of Greece, and because it abandoned the Greek cities in Asia to Persian domination.

King Artaxerxes thinks that justice is done if (a) the cities in Asia Minor and Clazomenae and Cyprus among the islands are his possessions, (b) the remainder of the Greek cities, whether large or small, should be independent except for Lemnos, Imbros and Scyros, and (c) these last shall be Athenian possessions as in the past. If either party does not accept these terms of peace, I shall make war on them in alliance with those who do approve these terms, by land and sea, with ships and money.

Xenophon *Hellenica* 5, 1, 31

B31 The Formation of the Second Athenian Confederacy

This magnificent inscription was found in the Agora at Athens. It is a record of the terms of the Second Athenian Confederacy formed in 377. In forming this league against the Spartans Athens is careful not to antagonize the Great King. It ends with a list of present members, new members being added at later dates. The text is in M. N. Tod Greek Historical Inscriptions *II (Oxford 1948) no. 123. For a Commentary see S. Accame* La Lega Ateniese del sec. IV a.c. *(Rome 1941). Another fragmentary decree of Aristoteles appears at the foot of the pillar.*

In the archonship of Nausinicus
Callibios, son of Cephisophon, from Paeania, secretary.
In the seventh prytany held by Hippothontis.
The Council and Commons decreed as follows, with Charinus from Athmone in the chair, on a motion by Aristoteles.

Blessings on the Athenians and the Athenian Allies; that the Spartans may allow the Greeks to live in peace, free and autonomous, in secure possession of their territories, and that the Common Peace sworn by the Greeks and the Great King in treaty may last for ever, the Commons decreed:

If any, Greeks or non-Greeks, from the mainland or the islands, not being subjects of the Great King, wishes to be allied to Athens and her allies, they may do so, while retaining their freedom and autonomy, under whatever constitution they choose, without submitting to a garrison or receiving a Governor or paying tribute, on the same terms as Chios, Thebes and the other allies. For those who join in alliance with Athens and with her allies, the Commons remit any possessions privately or publicly held by Athenians within the territory of those joining in alliance, and give them a pledge to that effect. If there should exist at Athens any inscription unfavourable to those making alliance with the Athenians, the Council in office at any time has authority to destroy it. After the archonship of Nausinicus it shall not be lawful for any of the Athenians, publicly or privately, to acquire as possession in the territory of their allies, either house or land, whether by purchase, as security, or in any other way. If anyone buys or takes possession of or acquires such in any other way, it is legitimate for any of the allies who will to report him to the delegates of the Allies. The delegates are to confiscate his property and give half to the informer and the rest is to be the common property of the Allies. If anyone makes war by land or sea upon those joining in this alliance, the Athenians and the Allies are to give the latter the utmost possible support by land and sea. If anyone, whether a state official or private citizen, proposes or moves contrary to this decree a motion to abrogate any of its terms, he is to lose his citizenship, his property is to be subject to state confiscation with a tithe for the goddess, he is to be tried before the Athenians and the Allies on the charge of seeking to annul the alliance and subject to a sentence of death or banishment from Athenian or Allied dominions; if the sentence is death, he is not to receive burial in Attica or in Allied territory.

The secretary of the Council is to have this decree inscribed on a stone pillar and set up by the sanctuary of Zeus the Liberator. The treasurers of the goddess are to allot sixty drachmas from the ten talents for the inscription on the pillar. There is to be inscribed on this pillar the name of the Allied cities, and of any future Ally. All this is to appear in the inscription. The Commons are to appoint without delay three delegates to visit Thebes and persuade the Thebans to such good as is within their power.

The following were chosen: Aristoteles from Marathon, Pyrrhandrus from Anaphlystus, and Thrasybulus from Collytus.

The following cities are Allies of the Athenians, Chios, Mytilene, Methymna, Rhodes, Byzantium, Thebes.

(additions early 377) Chalcis, Eretria, Arethusa, Carystus, Icus.

(late 377) Perinthus, Peparethus, Sciathus, Maroneia, Dion.

(c. 376) Pallene . . . . . . Paros, Athenae.

(c. 375) the Zacynthians in Nellos, the democracy of Corcyra, Acarnania, Pronnoi in Cephallenia, Alcetas, Neoptolemus, Jason *(the last deleted c. 371),*

Abdera, Thasos, the Chalcidians of Thrace, Ainos, Samothrace, Dicaeopolis.

(c. 374–3) Andros, Tenos, Hestiaea, Myconos, Antissa, Eresos, Astraeusa. On Ceos: Ioulis, Carthaea, Coresus, Elaeus, Amorgos, Selymbria, Siphnos, Sicinos, the Dians from Thrace, Neapolis.

IG II[2] 43+

B32 The Working of the Confederacy

Some details of the working of the Confederacy are found in Diodorus who wrote his World History in the first century BC. Important inscriptional evidence will be found in IG *II*[2] *40–45, 82, 95–101. The Athenians were at pains not to repeat some of their earlier errors. For the colonists or cleruchs see Diodorus 15, 23, 4: 'The Athenians were unpopular with the other Greeks because of their policy of imposing colonists on conquered territories.'*

The first to respond to the invitation to secession from Sparta were Chios and Byzantium, then Rhodes, Mytilene and some of the other islands. The movement steadily gained momentum all through Greece, and a large number of city-states acceded to Athens. The democracy, elated by the support of these cities, established a General Council representing all the allied states and designated representatives from each. There was general agreement that the Council should meet in Athens, that every city-state, whatever its size, should be equally represented by a single vote, and that all should retain their independence, allowing the Athenians to exercise leadership. . . .

The Athenians . . . took a decision to restore the land settled by colonists to its former owners, and carried a law that no Athenians should own farmland outside Attica.

Diodorus Siculus 15, 28, 3–4; 29, 1

B33 The Confederacy Deals with Paros

An important fragment, found on the Acropolis, containing the end of a decree of the Athenian Council and Commons, and the beginning of a decree of the Parliament of the Allies. The date is established as the summer of 372. There has evidently been trouble on Paros, and the islanders are required to put things right with the gods, and to establish law and order themselves. The decree was originally published by J. H. Oliver in American Journal of Archaeology *40 (1936) 461 ff, and more fully with full discussion by S. Accame* La lege ateniese del sec IV a.c. *(Rome 1941) 229 ff.*

. . . . . . in accordance with ancestral tradition, and to present at the Panathenaic festival an ox and a full set of armour, and at the festival of Dionysus an ox and a phallus as a memorial since they are colonists of the Athenian democracy. This decree is to be recorded in an inscription together with the settlement made by the Allies with the people of Paros, and the pillar is to be erected on the Acropolis.

The Treasurer of the Commons is to issue twenty drachmas for the cost of inscribing the pillar. The ambassadors from Paros are to be invited to receive hospitality in the Prytaneion tomorrow.

Archon: Asteios. Date: last day of Scirophorion. Mover of the resolution ...... of Thebes.

Resolution of the Allies:

No one is to be deprived of house or land. No violence is to be done contrary to this decree. In the event of murder the Assembly and Commons are to pass the sentence of death on those responsible in obedience to the established laws. If in contravention of the established laws and of this decree, any one expels or exiles another, he is himself to be disfranchised ......

B34 The Athenian Navy

Athenian power depended primarily on the navy. The basic warship was the trireme and a liturgy called the trierarchy was undertaken by wealthy citizens; it involved the direction and upkeep of a warship for a year, the state paying the crew and providing some of the equipment, which had to be returned in good order. A number of inscriptions relating to naval affairs have been found in Piraeus, as might be expected; this (about 372) is an extract from one of them. We cannot be certain about all the equipment mentioned; the curtains seem to have been to protect the oarsmen. Apollodorus is known from other sources as a man of great wealth. The ships have feminine names. Naucratis is a Greek port in Egyptian territory and also means 'Mistress of the Sea'.

The Protectress. Trierarchs: Apollodorus of Acharne, Timocrates of Crioa. Issued with: a complete equipment in wood provided by Archestratus of Alopeke; for rigging, a sail provided by Stephanus of Euonymon, white curtains, anchors (2) provided by Apollodorus of Acharne, a curtain of woven hair, undergirding, a tarpaulin screen returned by Phil ...... of Acharne, cables returned by Pasion of Acharne. During our period of office this ship was ...... sheets; a sail provided by Na......

Warships sailing out under the command of Euctemon of Lusia and Euthius of Sunium. Purpose: to found a cleruchy. *The Dorian Girl.* Trierarchs: Apollodorus of Acharne, Timocrates of Crioa. Equipment in wood: ladders (2), poles (2), mast stays (2). *Leadership.* Trierarchs: Philinus of Lamptrae, Demomeles of Paeania. No equipment issued to them in our period of office. *Culture.* Trierarchs: Phanostratus of Cephisia, Dorotheus of Eleusis. No equipment issued to them in our period of office. *Victory.* One of the new ships, built by Pistocrates. Trierarchs: Deinias of Erchia, Leochares of Pallene. No equipment issued to them in our period of office. *Leadership.* One of the new ships built by Lysicrates.

Trierarch: Chabrias of Aexone. Oars (200). He is responsible for returning full oarage. *Renown*. Trierarch: Callippus of Aexone. Issued with full equipment in wood and rigging. In charge of the customs-officers. *The Bacchante*. One of the new ships built by Hierophontus. Trierarch: Aristaichmus of Cholleidae. Issued with: complete rigging; of equipment in wood, oars (200) (he is responsible for returning full oarage), mast, large size (1). *The Naucratis*. One of the new ships, built by Xenocles. Trierarchs: Timotheus of Anaphlystus, Theoxenus of Euonymon. Issued with: rigging, sail, undergirding, tarpaulin screen, sheets, anchor cables; equipment in wood: oars (200). The last-named is responsible for returning full oarage. *Fine Day*. One of the new ships, built by Aristocles. Trierarchs: Charicleides of Myrrhinus, Callistratus of Aphidna. Issued with: full rigging, full equipment in wood except for one boatsail, and oars (200), not full oarage. Responsible for returning full oarage. *Perfect*. Trierarchs: Philippus of Colonus, Polycles of Anagyrus. Issued with: full rigging; equipment in wood: mast, large (1); sails, large; ladders; oars (200). Responsible for returning full oarage. (Returned: rigging apart from cables, undergirdings: oarage complete.) *Rose of Rhodes*. Trierarchs: Cleotimides of Atene, Cephalion of Aphidna. Issued with: full rigging; equipment in wood: boom, large; ladders.

IG II^2 1609 83–110

B35 Athens and Ceos

Things were not always smooth in the Second Athenian Confederacy. An important decree found on the Acropolis, and dated securely to 362, records trouble with the four cities on the island of Ceos. All four asserted their independence, and exiled collaborators. This uprising was quelled and the exiles restored. Ioulis tried again on its own. A number of pro-Athenians lost their lives. The first part of the decree provides for the punishment of those responsible, and for an economic settlement. The last part, here translated, throws more general light on the relation between Athens and her allies. The events are reconstructed and discussed by Richard Laqueur Epigraphische Untersuchungen zu den griechischen Volksbeschlüssen *(Leipzig and Berlin 1927) 179 ff.*

. . . . . . The following agreements were reached and ratified on oath by the Generals of the Athenians and the Allies in relation to the cities on Ceos. 'I will hold past events on Ceos against no man. I will not execute or exile any citizen of Ceos who observes these oaths and agreements. I will admit them to the Confederacy on the same terms as the other Allies. If anyone engages in revolutionary activity on Ceos in contravention of these oaths and agreements, by whatever device or stratagem, to the best of my ability I will not allow him. If anyone wishes not to live on Ceos, I will permit him to live wherever in allied territory he wishes in enjoyment of his possessions. I swear by Zeus, Athene, Poseidon and Demeter not to break this oath. May I be blessed in observing it, cursed in forswearing.'

Oaths and agreements of the cities on Ceos in relation to the Athenians and their Allies, and to those citizens of Ceos whom the Athenians restored. 'I will be an ally of the Athenians and their Allies, I will not revolt from the Athenians and their Allies by my personal act, or under another's compulsion so far as in me lies. I will make all civil suits involving Athenian citizens and a sum in excess of 100 drachmas subject to appeal in accordance with the agreements. If any do criminal injury to the restored citizens of Ceos or to the Athenians or to any of the Allies in contravention of the oaths and agreements, by whatever device or stratagem, I will not allow him, and will defend them with all my power so far as in me lies. I swear by Zeus, Athene, Poseidon and Demeter not to break this oath. May I be blessed in observing it, cursed in forswearing.'

The following oaths were sworn by the citizens of Ceos restored by the Athenians. 'I will hold past events against no man ......'.

W. Dittenberger *Sylloge Inscriptionum Graecarum* 1, 173 (Leipzig[3] 1915)

B36 Economic Monopoly in the Confederacy

Ruddle, or red ochre, was used as a pigment and in drug preparations. According to Theophrastus (Minerals *8, 52*), *Ceos provided the best quality, though later authorities (Strabo 12, 2, 10; Pliny* Natural History *33, 111 ff; 35, 30 ff) speak favourably of the varieties from Sinope and Lemnos. Some authorities have supposed that the Athenian monopoly here mentioned was for military purposes associated with the painting of ships; this is not supported by evidence. This inscription, found on the Acropolis, is an Athenian copy of decrees passed by the cities of Ceos. Economic interests explain Athenian anxiety about Ceos (compare no. B35). The decree is fragmentary.*

...... Proposer of the motion: Theogenes. Resolution of the Council and Commons at Coresus. On the report of the delegation from Athens, ruddle is to be exported to Athens on the same terms as previously. To maintain the validity of the previous decrees of Athens and Coresus on the subject of ruddle, export is permitted solely in a ship nominated by the Athenians. The operators are to pay the shipowners one obol per talent of ochre as freight-charge. If anyone exports ruddle in any other vessel, he is to be liable ...... This decree is to be inscribed on a stone pillar and set up in Apollo's Temple, and this enactment is to have the same validity as previous enactments. Charges of infringement are to be laid with the police-magistrates, who are to bring the issue to court within thirty days. The person from whom information is received is to be awarded half ...... If he be a slave belonging to the exporters, he is to receive his freedom, and a third share; if a slave belonging to someone else, his freedom and ...... An informer has the right of appeal to Athens. If the Athenians pass new legislation on the subject of ruddle protection their enactments are valid on arrival. The operators are to pay the collector a 2 per cent tax. The Athenians are to be invited to receive hospitality in the prytaneum tomorrow.

Resolution of the Council and Commons of Ioulis. On the report of the delegation from Athens the Council and Commons of Ioulis resolved that from this day the export of ruddle shall be exclusively for Athenian import. If anyone exports it anywhere else his ship and all its cargo are to be confiscated. A half-share is to be given to the person from whom information is received. If the informant be a slave, he is to be granted his freedom and ...... of the property. The exporter is to export ruddle from Ceos in a ship nominated by the Athenians. If anyone exports ruddle in any other vessel, he is to be liable ...... If the Athenians pass new legislation on the subject of ruddle ...... their enactments are to be valid. There is to be exemption from ...... after the month of Hermaeon. The Athenians are to be invited to the prytaneum for hospitality. Charges of infringement are to be laid with the Eleven at Athens or the leading citizens at Ioulis. If anyone is found guilty of exporting in contravention of the law, half of his property is to go to the Commons of Ioulis, and half to the informant. The Council is to be responsible for having the decree inscribed and set up at the harbour.

The following were selected: Andron from Cerameis, Lysia ...... from Phyla, Euphrosynus from Paeania.

IG II^2 1128

B37 A Defence of Athenian Imperialism

Isocrates in extreme old age wrote a last patriotic tribute for the Panathenaic Festival of 342. Illness supervened, and it was not completed before 339 in his ninety-eighth year.

If they have anything to say about our exaction of tribute we shall be ready with our answer. We shall show that our predecessors acted to the advantage of those cities which paid tribute; the Spartans did not. In the first place, the payment was not imposed by us, but made in the knowledge that they had invited us to take command of the seas. Secondly, their contributions were directed not to our defence, but to the maintenance of their own democratic liberties and protection against the disasters arising from the establishment of oligarchy: they experienced this under the rule of Ten when the Spartans were dominant. Further their contributions came not from their own resources but from resources which they owed to us. It did not require much reflection to show a proper gratitude for this. When we took over their cities they were in some instances totally destroyed by the Persians, in others they had been sacked. We advanced them to a stage where the small proportion of their wealth which they contributed to us left them no less prosperous than the Peloponnesian states which were subject to no tribute at all.

Isocrates *Panathenaicus* 67–9

B38 Epitaph on Athenian Dead at Chaeronea

In 338 Philip of Macedon defeated the allied Greeks at Chaeronea. The epitaph survives in a fragmentary form in an inscription (M. N. Tod Greek Historical Inscriptions *(Oxford 1948) no. 176) and in an edited form in* Palatine Anthology *7, 245.*

Time, Power watching men in all they do,
proclaim to the world our fate;
in seeking to save Greece, holy soil, we brought
glory in death to Boeotia's fields.

B39 Peace of 338–7

After Philip of Macedon's victory at Chaeronea, a peace congress was held at Corinth. All the Greek states except Sparta signed the Peace. The inscription is in M. N. Tod Greek Historical Inscriptions *II (Oxford 1948) no. 177.*

I swear by Zeus, Earth, Sun, Poseidon, Athena, Ares, and all the gods and goddesses that I will keep the Peace, and I will not break the treaties with Philip of Macedon. I will not bear arms with hostile intent by land or by sea against those who keep the oaths, nor will I attack in war by any device or stratagem any city, fort, or harbour which belongs to anyone who shares in the Peace. I will not oppose the kingship of Philip and his offspring nor those constitutions that were in effect in each city when it swore the oath of peace. I will not do anything against the oath, and will prevent anyone else from doing so as far as I can. If anyone does anything against the oath, I will aid in so far as possible those who have been wronged in the way they want me to. I will fight whoever transgresses the common peace in so far as it seems best to the common council and the leader's orders. I will not abandon . . . . . .

IG II[2] 236+
tr. J. Wickersham and G. Verbrugghe *Greek Historical Documents, the Fourth Century BC* (Hakkert, Toronto 1973)

C WORK AND TRADE

Athens was the great trading centre of the Greek world; she could not survive without importing corn (see no. C3) and evidence of her exports (e.g. oil, vases) has been found throughout the ancient world. Foreign merchants were encouraged to settle at Piraeus and business enterprises seem mostly to have been in their hands.

The philosophers may have condemned manual work, because it interfered with the cultivated leisure necessary for a man to undertake civic duties (see nos. C9, C10), but most Athenian citizens worked for a living despite the existence of slaves. The real indignity was to work for someone else, thus most landholdings and workshops were on a very small scale.

Important general studies include: F. M. Heichelheim *An Ancient Economic History* (3 vols. Leiden 1958); H. Michell *The Economics of Ancient Greece* (Cambridge University Press 1957); M. I. Finley *The Ancient Economy* (Berkeley and Los Angeles 1973); C. Mossé *The Ancient World at Work* (London University Press 1969); A. Burford *Craftsmen in Greek and Roman Society* (Thames and Hudson 1972).

C1 The Natural Advantages of Athens

Xenophon's little book Ways and Means *contains his formula for improving the public revenues at Athens, principally through offering more favourable terms to resident aliens, or metics, including the right to own house-property. It begins with an account of the natural advantages enjoyed by Athens. The date is about 355–4.*

I always held it for a certain maxim, that governments resembled their governors, and that the prosperity or declension, the vigour or decay of all states, was derived from the virtues and vices, the abilities or weakness of their rulers: but since it is generally alleged in vindication of the Athenian ministry, that they understand the common principles of justice as well as the rest of mankind, but that they are compelled by the necessities of the common people to oppress their confederate cities with unreasonable tributes and taxes: I have attempted to examine whether this apology is well grounded, and whether they are not capable by native riches, and revenue of the state of Athens, to maintain the whole body of our people, which is the justest and most honourable provision can be thought of: for I imagine if such a design could be compassed, that the wants of the people would be more effectually relieved, and the jealousies and suspicions of our neighbours would be quieted.

Upon a general view of the whole matter, it appeared to me that the Athenian territory is capable of affording a mighty income and revenue, the truth of which assertion may be easily evinced by a brief survey of the state and nature of the country.

The fruits of the earth, and native products of our soil, are a proof of the temperature of our climate and the mildness of our seasons; for we have plants which bear in great abundance in our country, which will never grow in others; and our sea, as well as land, abounds in all things necessary for life, or luxury: add to this, that all the blessings which the gods have made peculiar to the different seasons of the year, begin earlier, and end later with us, than in any part of the world.

Besides the vast plenty we enjoy of perishable goods, our soil affords us some staple and permanent commodities, such as our noble quarries of marble, out of which are drawn the best materials for the building and ornamenting of temples, and for the altars and statues of the gods, and which both the Greeks and barbarous nations set a high value upon.

And where the soil is too barren to receive the common improvements of husbandry, it contains hidden treasures, which will feed a much greater number of mouths than any arable lands can do: for the Divine Bounty has bestowed upon us inexhaustible mines of silver, and advantages which we enjoy above all our neighbouring cities by sea and land, who never yet could discover one vein of silver ore in all their dominions.

We have reason likewise to believe that Athens is seated in the centre of Greece, and the habitable world; for all nations are incommoded with more intense degrees of heat or cold in proportion to their (northern or southern) distance from us; and that we lie in the heart of Greece is evident, for all travellers, that pass by sea or land, from one extremity of Greece to the other, must take Athens in their way.

And though Attica is no island, yet we have the same benefit of trading with all winds, for we are bounded on two sides by the sea, and by being joined to the continent we have the convenience of driving on an inland traffic.

Other cities lie exposed to the fury of barbarous nations, but we are so far from having so ill a neighbourhood, that the states which border immediately upon us, lie at a remote distance from them.

To all those advantages which conspire to the felicity and greatness of our state, and which we owe to the happy situation, and the native wealth of our country, a mighty improvement might be made by the institution of public laws, in favour of strangers who establish themselves among us; for besides the general benefits derived to all cities from numbers of people, our strangers would be so far from living on the public, and receiving pensions from the state as our own citizens do, that they would maintain themselves, and be the foundation of the noblest branch of our revenue by the payment of the aliens' duties.

Xenophon *Ways and Means* 1, 1
tr. W. Moyle (Bangs, Brother and Co., New York 1855)

C2 Trade

Athenaeus has a useful section in which he cites fifth- and fourth-century writers about trade. Plainly the evidence of comic dramatists has to be treated with care, but it remains evidence. Hermippus uses Homeric parody. The last passage is in fact from Eubulus.

That witty writer Antiphanes lists the particular products of individual cities as follows:

Cooks from Elis, cauldrons from Argos,
wine from Phlius, coverlets from Corinth,
fish from Sicyon, flute-girls from Aegion,
cheese from Sicily . . . .
perfume from Athens, eels from Boeotia.

So Hermippus:

Tell me now, Muses that live in your palace on Olympus,
all the blessings which Dionysus brought to mankind in dark ships
since he made his trip over the wine-faced sea.
From Cyrene stalks of silphium and hides of oxen,
from the Hellespont mackerel and salted fish of all kinds,
from Thessaly puddings and ribs of beef,
from Sitalces, an itch to bring the Spartans up to scratch,
from Perdiccas, fleets of ships with a cargo of lies,
from the Syracusans, pigs and cheese,
and God damn the Corcyreans and their
hollow ships, because they will sit on the fence.
Those cities, these products. From Egypt, rigging
for sails and papyrus, from Syria frankincense,
from glorious Crete cypress for the gods,
from Africa ivory in plenty at a price,
from Rhodes raisins and dried figs bringing sweet dreams,
from Euboea pears and well-fleeced apples,
from Phrygia slaves, from Arcadia mercenaries,
from Pagasae servants with a brand-mark on them,
from the Paphlagonians Zeus's own acorns and glossy

almonds, the adornments of a dinner,
from Phoenicia the fruit of the palm and fine flour,
from Carthage carpets and bright-coloured cushions.

Pindar in the Pythian ode to Hieron writes:

From Taygetus comes the Spartan
hound for hunting, swiftest of all animals in the chase.
The goats of Scyros
are exceptional for their milk.
Arms from Argos, chariots from Thebes, but look
to fertile Sicily for carefully built carriages.

So Critias:

Cottabos is the principal product of Sicily,
a target for wine-shooting.
Also from Sicily the best-looking and most expensive carriages.

. . . .

Thessalonica provides ceremonial chairs, comfortable to sit on,
but the best beds for sleep
are from Miletus, and Chios, Oenopion's city by the sea.
Etruria is first for gold cups,
and all bronze household utensils for any purpose.
The Phoenicians invented letters to record words.
Thebes was the first to form the structure of a chariot,
the Carians, stewards of the sea, cargo-boats.
The city which raised the glorious trophy at Marathon
invented the best-known domestic pottery
offspring of earth and oven, and the wheel to make.

In fact Attic pottery has a high reputation. Eubulus speaks of:

Pots from Cnidos, pans from Sicily, jars from Megara.

and Antiphanes:

From Cyprus mustard and convolvulus-juice,
from Miletus cress, onions from Samothrace,
stalks of silphium from Carthage,
silphium and thyme from Hymettus,
marjoram from Tenedos.

Athenaeus 1, 27d–28d

C3 Athenian Imports of Corn

Of course you know that we of all people are most dependent on imported corn. So any boat arriving from any other harbour is expected to bring corn from Pontus as an import. Naturally. Corn is exceedingly plentiful in that region, and Leucon was responsible for granting exemption from duty for those who brought it to Athens, and for publishing an agreement that those sailing to Athens have priority in loading.

Demosthenes *Against Leptines* 31

C4 An Attack on Corn Dealers

Their interests are diametrically opposed to those of the rest of us. They make their highest profit when bad news pushes up the price of corn. They smile to see your disasters; they are the first to hear of them – or they invent them. Perhaps it is shipwreck in the Black Sea, or capture on the outward voyage by the Spartans, or the blockade of the ports, or the imminent abrogation of the truce. Their hostility has reached the point where they and your enemies are plotting against you simultaneously. When you need grain most urgently, they corner it and refuse to sell till we will not haggle over the cost, but be content to buy at any price. Sometimes they put us in a state of siege even in time of peace. The city has long been aware of their malicious villainy and appointed for this operation alone corn-supervisors, where general market-supervisors check all the dealings. Several times, too, you have exacted the supreme penalty from these officials allowing their villainy to get the better of you.

Lysias 22, 14–16

C5 A Trading Fraud

Some of the details are not clear. It looks as if Theodorus and Lampis offered lower terms than the plaintiff. The general nature of the fraud is clear enough. For the return journey, Phormio was accused of overloading the ship with 1,000 hides, which led in fact to its loss.

Gentlemen, I lent the defendant Phormio twenty minas for the voyage to and from Pontus, on the security of goods twice that value, and deposited a contract to that effect with Cittus the banker. This contract required him to load on his ship goods to the value of 4,000 drachmas. He now committed a major crime. Without informing us he secured a further loan in Piraeus from Theodorus the Phoenician, amounting to 4,500 drachmas, and another of 1,000 from Lampis the shipowner. He was in duty bound to purchase in Athens a cargo valued at 115 minas, if he was to fulfil his contractual obligations to all his creditors. But the value of the cargo he invested in was only 5,500 drachmas, including provisions. His debts were seventy-five minas! This was the beginning of his criminal activity, gentlemen. He did not provide security. He did not, despite the explicit terms of the contract, load a cargo of proper value on the ship.

Demosthenes *Against Phormio* 6–7

C6 Banking and Industry

Pasion, a former slave, had made a fortune as a banker. He passed on his business to a former slave of his own, Phormio, to hold jointly with the eldest son, Apollodorus, in the interests of the younger. There was a division of property.

Gentlemen, as soon as they had set my client free from liability under the lease, they divided the bank from the shield-factory. Apollodorus had the choice and chose the shield-factory in preference to the bank. If he had had private capital in the bank, why on earth should he have made the factory his first preference? The income was not larger; as a matter of fact it was smaller by a talent to a hundred minas. It wasn't a more attractive prospect, if he had capital in the bank. He did not. That is why he was prudent in choosing the factory. The factory is a safe investment, the bank offers a hazardous income from other people's money.

Demosthenes *For Phormio* 11

C7 Banking Procedures

It is the general practice of bankers that when a private individual makes a monetary deposit with the instructions that it be paid to a particular person, they begin by writing the name of the depositor and the sum of money involved, and then write alongside thus 'to be paid to X'. If they know by sight the person to whom payment is to be made, it suffices to write the name of the payee; if they do not, they add the name of a person who will identify and introduce to them the person who is to receive the money.

Demosthenes *Against Callippus* 4

C8 An Athenian Law on Silver Coinage

In 1970 an important inscription was found in the agora datable to 375–4. Apparently there was a sudden distrust of Athenian coinage, for what reason we do not know. The first publication was by R. S. Stroud in Hesperia *43 (1974), pp. 157–88; cf. A. Giovannini 'Athenian Currency in the Late Fifth and Early Fourth Century BC'* Greek, Roman and Byzantine Studies *16, 2 (Summer 1975), pp. 185–95. The document is important not least for the information about the tester* (dokimastes), *a public slave with an important official position.*

It was resolved by the *nomothetai,* in the archonship of Hippodamas (375–374); Nikophon moved: let Attic silver currency be accepted when [it is shown to be] of silver and bears the official [type]. Let the public tester sitting among the tables test (the coins) according to these regulations every [day except] when payments of money are made; at that time let him test in the [council] chamber. If anyone brings to him [. . .] which bear the same type as the Attic [. . .], let (the tester) return it to the one who brought it to him. If it has a core [of copper], or of lead, or is counterfeit, let him cut it across [. . .] and let him consecrate it to the Mother of the Gods and [deposit] it with the council. If the tester does not hold session or test (coins) according to the law, let the *syllogeis* of the people strike him with fifty blows of [the whip]. If anyone refuses to accept the silver currency which has been tested by the tester let him be deprived of the value of what he has sold [that] day. Let denunciations for offences in the [corn market] be made before the commissioners of the grain trade (*sitophylakes*), for offences committed in the *agora* and in the rest of the city before the *syllogeis* of the people, and for those committed in the commercial port and in Peiraieus before the inspectors of the commercial port (*epimeletai tou emporiou*) except for those in the corn market which should be made before the commissioners of the grain trade (*sitophylakes*). For all denunciations which do not exceed ten drachmae, let the magistrates have authority to give a verdict, but for those which exceed ten drachmae let them introduce them to the law court. Let the *thesmothetai* assign them a court drawn by lot whenever they request one or let them be fined [. . .] drachmae. Let the informer receive one-half if [the culprit] is convicted. If the seller is a male or female slave let him or her receive fifty blows of the whip from [the magistrates] dealing with each particular case. If any magistrate does not act in accordance with the written rules, let any Athenian who wishes and who is qualified bring him before the council. If he is convicted, let him be deposed from office and in addition let the council impose on him a fine of up to 500 drachmae. So that there should be a tester in Peiraieus for the benefit of the [ship] owners and the merchants and [all] the others, let the council appoint one from among the public slaves [. . .] or let it purchase one, and let the receivers (*apodektai*) [set aside] the required sum. Let the inspectors of the commercial port see to it that he sits near the stele of Poseidon and observes the law in the same way as was specified for the tester in the city. Let this law be inscribed on a stone stele and a copy be placed in the city among the tables, and another copy in Peiraieus in front of the stele of Poseidon. Let the secretary of the council report the price to the sellers (*poletai*). Let the sellers communicate it to the council. Let the salary for the tester in the commercial port be paid to him, in the archonship of Hippodamas (375–374) from the moment of his appointment and let the receivers set aside for him a sum equivalent to that for the tester in the city, and in future let his salary come from the same source as for the workers in the mint. If there is any decree inscribed anywhere on a stele which contravenes this law, let the secretary of the council pull it down.

tr. M. M. Austin and P. Vidal-Naquet
Economic and Social History of Ancient Greece
(B. T. Batsford 1977) pp. 328–30

C9 Occupations Suitable for Citizens

It clearly follows that in the state which is best governed and possesses men who are just absolutely, and not merely relatively to the principle of the constitution, the citizens must not lead the life of mechanics or tradesmen, for such a life is ignoble and inimical to virtue. Neither must they be husbandmen, since leisure is necessary both for the development of virtue and the performance of political duties.

Aristotle *Politics* 7, 1328b–1329a
tr. B. Jowett (Oxford 1921)

C10 A Philosophical View of Industrial Employment

Socrates is speaking. He is not attacking manual work as such, since he accepts it for agriculture and war.

'People in our states criticize the so-called mechanical skills and understandably hold them in no great esteem. They damage the physique of those who practise them and their supervisors by compelling them to sit indoors, sometimes stooping over a fire all day. Their bodies become flabby, their minds are seriously impaired. Further, these so-called mechanical skills leave no free time for friends or politics; their practitioners are no use for supporting their friends or their country. In some states, especially those with a military reputation, citizens are not permitted to engage in mechanical employment.'

'What forms of skill do you recommend us to take up, Socrates?'

'We needn't be ashamed to emulate the King of Persia, need we? He is said to reckon agriculture and war as two professions which combine usefulness and respectability, and to hold strongly to those.'

Xenophon *Oeconomicus* 4, 2–3

C11 Vocation

It was not possible to direct everyone to the same work, because of differences of circumstances. Our forebears therefore directed each individual to work appropriate to his means. They directed the less affluent to farming and trade in the knowledge that idleness leads to indigence and indigence to crime. They thought that to eliminate the source of evil was to eliminate the resulting crimes. Those who possessed private means were directed to riding, athletics, hunting and philosophy, in the observation that these activities keep people out of trouble where they do not foster excellence.

Isocrates *Areopagiticus* 44–5

C12 Making a Living

The examination of wealth-getting is of philosophical interest because it involves the conduct and role of citizens who are also those who must have enough leisure to run the state.

(a)

Let us now inquire into property generally, and into the art of getting wealth, in accordance with our usual method, for a slave has been shown to be a part of property. The first question is whether the art of getting wealth is the same with the art of managing a household or a part of it, or instrumental to it; and if the last, whether in the way that the art of making shuttles is instrumental to the art of weaving, or in the way that the casting of bronze is instrumental to the art of the statuary, for they are not instrumental in the same way, but the one provides tools and the other material; and by material I mean the substratum out of which any work is made; thus wool is the material of the weaver, bronze of the statuary. Now it is easy to see that the art of household management is not identical with the art of getting wealth, for the one uses the material which the other provides. For the art which uses household stores can be no other than the art of household management. There is, however, a doubt whether the art of getting wealth is a part of household management or a distinct art. If the getter of wealth has to consider whence wealth and property can be procured, but there are many sorts of property and riches, then are husbandry, and the care and provision of food in general, parts of the wealth-getting art or distinct arts? Again, there are many sorts of food, and therefore there are many kinds of lives both of animals and men; they must all have food, and the differences in their food have made differences in their ways of life. For of beasts, some are gregarious, others are solitary; they live in the way which is best adapted to sustain them, accordingly as they are carnivorous or herbivorous or omnivorous: and their habits are determined for them by nature in such a manner that they may obtain with greater facility the food of their choice. But, as different species have different tastes, the same things are not naturally pleasant to all of them; and therefore the lives of carnivorous or herbivorous animals further differ among themselves. In the lives of men too there is a great difference. The laziest are shepherds, who lead an idle life, and get their subsistence without trouble from tame animals; their flocks having to wander from place to place in search of pasture, they are compelled to follow them, cultivating a sort of living farm. Others support themselves by hunting, which is of different kinds. Some, for example, are brigands, others, who dwell near lakes or marshes or rivers or a sea in which there are fish, are fishermen, and others live by the pursuit of birds or wild beasts. The greater number obtain a living from the cultivated fruits of the soil. Such are the modes of subsistence which prevail among those whose industry springs up of itself, and whose food is not acquired by exchange and retail trade – there is the shepherd, the husbandman, the brigand, the fisherman, the hunter. Some gain a comfortable maintenance out of two employments, eking out the deficiencies of one of them by another: thus the life of a shepherd may be combined with that of a brigand, the life of a farmer with that of a hunter. Other modes of life are similarly combined in any way which the needs of men may require. Property, in the sense of a bare livelihood, seems to be given by nature herself to all, both when they are first born, and when they are grown up. For some animals bring forth, together with their offspring, so much food as will last until they are able to supply themselves; of this the vermiparous or oviparous animals are an instance; and the viviparous animals have up to a certain time a supply of food for their young in themselves, which is called milk. In like manner we may infer that, after the birth of animals, plants exist for their sake, and that the other animals exist for the sake of man, the tame for use and food, the wild, if not all, at least the greater part of them, for food, and for the provision of clothing and various instruments. Now if nature makes nothing incomplete, and nothing in vain, the inference must be that she has made all animals for the sake of man. And so, in one point of view, the art of war is a natural art of acquisition, for the art of acquisition includes hunting, an art which we ought to practise against wild beasts, and against men who, though intended by nature to be governed, will not submit; for war of such a kind is naturally just.

Of the art of acquisition then there is one kind which by nature is a part of the management of a household, in so far as the art of household management must either find ready to hand, or itself provide, such things necessary to life, and useful for the community of the family or state, as can be stored.

. . . And so we see that there is a natural art of acquisition which is practised by managers of households and by statesmen, and what is the reason of this.

Aristotle *Politics* 1, 1256a1–1256b39
tr. B. Jowett (Oxford 1921)

(b)

And we have found the answer to our original question, Whether the art of getting wealth is the business of the manager of a household and of the statesman or not their business? – viz. that wealth is presupposed by them. For as political science does not make men, but takes them from nature and uses them, so too nature provides them with earth or sea or the like as a source of food. At this stage begins the duty of the manager of a household, who has to order the things which nature supplies; – he may be compared to the weaver who has not to make but to use wool, and to know, too, what sort of wool is good and serviceable or bad and unserviceable. Were this otherwise, it would be difficult to see why the art of getting wealth is a part of the management of a household and the art of medicine not; for surely the members of a household must have health just as they must have life or any other necessary. The answer is that as from one point of view the master of the house and the ruler of the state have to consider about health, from another point of view not they but the physician; so in one way the art of household management, in another way the subordinate art, has to consider about wealth. But, strictly speaking, as I have already said, the means of life must be provided beforehand by nature; for the business of nature is to furnish food to that which is born, and the food of the offspring is always what remains over of that from which it is produced. Wherefore the art of getting wealth out of fruits and animals is always natural.

There are two sorts of wealth-getting, as I have said; one is a part of household management, the other is retail trade: the former necessary and honourable, while that which consists in exchange is justly censured; for it is unnatural, and a mode by which men gain from one another. The most hated sort, and with the greatest reason, is usury, which makes a gain out of money itself, and not from the natural object of it. For money was intended to be used in exchange, but not to increase at interest. And this term interest, which means the birth of money from money, is applied to the breeding of money because the offspring resembles the parent. Wherefore of all modes of getting wealth this is the most unnatural.

Aristotle *Politics* 1, 1258a17–1258b9
tr. B. Jowett (Oxford 1921)

C13 Occupations

(a)

Examples of groupings of the commons include farmers, or technicians, or those engaged in buying and selling, or those whose livelihood depends on the sea (subdivided into the navy, merchantmen, those concerned with passenger shipping, and fishermen, each prominent in several areas, e.g. fishermen at Tenedos and Byzantium, the navy at Athens, merchant-traders in Aegina and Chios, passenger-transport at Tenedos), or again manual workers who lack the substance for leisure.

Aristotle *Politics* 4, 1291b18–27

(b) *A line from Philyllius's* The Cities, *an early fourth-century comedy, lists some trades and professions. The coal was charcoal. Pollux was a grammarian who wrote in the second century AD on the meaning of Greek words.*

(Coal-seller), sieve-maker, gardener, barber.

Pollux *Onomasticon* 7, 110

(c) *Nicophon in* The Handbelly-fillers *(i.e. manual workers) has another list:*

Sprat-sellers, coal-sellers,
Fig-sellers, leather-sellers,
Corn-sellers, spoon-sellers,
Book-sellers, sieve-sellers,
Bun-sellers, seed-sellers.

Nicophon fr. 19K
J. M. Edmonds *The Fragments of Attic Comedy* I,
(Leiden 1957) p. 937

C14 Early-rising Professions

A passage in Aristophanes lists the early-rising professions. The lyre-turning armourer is a profiteer with a double profession.

PISTHETAERUS: The cock was so strong, great and mighty that still,
so great is his power of old, when he calls 'Sunrise',
all jump to their job – smiths, potters, tanners,
cobblers, bath-attendants, corn-merchants, lyre-turning armourers.
On with their shoes and off in the dark.

Aristophanes *Birds* 487–91

C15 Work for Money

In Aristophanes's last play Wealth *Chremylus and his slave Cario are persuading Wealth of his influence.*

CHREMYLUS: Every skill and every invention
mankind has discovered is owing to you.
For you one of us sits making shoes.
CARIO: Another works in bronze another in wood.
CHREMYLUS: Another moulds the gold received from you.
CARIO: Another is a cutpurse, another a burglar.
CHREMYLUS: Another a fuller.
CARIO: Another washes skins.

CHREMYLUS: Another a tanner.
CARIO: Another sells onions.

Aristophanes *Plutus* 160–67

C16 Specialization

In small towns the same person makes beds, doors, ploughs, tables; he's often a builder too; and even so he is delighted if he finds enough work to keep him going. And of course a jack of all trades is master of none. In large cities there are plenty of customers for any one branch of industry, and one branch of industry or even a subdivision of it is enough to support an individual. So one worker specializes in male footwear, another in female. In some places one man earns his living by stitching shoes, another by cutting them out, another simply by sewing the uppers together, another without any specialized skill except rounding the job off. So anyone who is proposing to concentrate on a highly-specialized job is bound to be supremely good at it.

Xenophon *Education of Cyrus* 8, 2, 5

C17 The Farmer's Prayer

We will pray to the gods
to grant the Greeks wealth,
that we may all harvest
barley in plenty and plenty of wine
        and figs to devour,
that our wives may give birth,
that we may gather again
the blessings we've lost
        and that red war may end.

Aristophanes *Peace* 1320–28

D SLAVES

Slavery was a universal and accepted feature of ancient Greek society. Conditions in Athens varied greatly. Many ordinary citizens kept one or two slaves to work alongside them, while in larger commercial concerns in which citizen workers were not involved, slaves could rise to positions of responsibility and wealth. It was possible for some slaves to purchase their freedom, but others had to exist in brutal conditions, for example in the silver mines at Laurion. For the subject generally, see the papers in M. I. Finley (ed) *Slavery in Classical Antiquity: Views and Controversies* (Heffer 1960).

D1 Slaves and Free

Those who can do so buy slaves to share their work with them.

Xenophon *Memorabilia* 2, 3, 3

D2 The Value of Slaves

(a)
'Antisthenes,' he said, 'can you set a value on a friend as you can of a slave? One servant may perhaps be valued at two minas, another at less than half a mina, another at five, another at as much as ten. Nicias, Niceratus's son, is said to have paid a talent for a slave to manage his silver-mine.'

Xenophon *Memorabilia* 2, 5, 2

(b) *These slaves were the property of a man convicted of irreligious profanation in 415–4. The Greek text is in R. Meiggs and D. Lewis* Greek Historical Inscriptions *(Oxford 1969) no. 79A. This is part of the first column; for three more examples of sales of property see no. K8.*

Property of Cephisodorus, a resident alien living in Piraeus.

165 dr.	Thracian woman	144 dr.	Scythian
135	Thracian woman	121	Illyrian
170	Thracian	153	Colchian
240	Syrian	174	Carian boy
105	Carian	72	Carian infant
161	Illyrian	301	Syrian
220	Thracian woman	151	Maltese (?)
115	Thracian	85	Lydian woman

tr. N. Lewis
Greek Historical Documents (Hakkert, Toronto 1971)

D3 Two Paths to Slavery

Although this passage comes from tragedy, and refers to a palace, it represents an attitude which fifth-century Athenians would understand.

OEDIPUS: Answer my questions. Were you at one time in Laius's service?
SERVANT: Yes, born and bred in the palace, not bought in the slave-market.

Sophocles *Oedipus the King* 1122–3

D4 A Stage Slave

Euripides was liable to side with the underdog, and to put words favourable to slaves into his plays. Here a slave is speaking.

MESSENGER: It's low not to feel with your masters,
laugh with them, and sympathize in their sorrows.
Born to service as I am, I would be
numbered among the noble
slaves, unfree in name,
free in mind. Better this than for one man
to be doubly cursed – a slave in mind
as well as slave in the words of his fellows.

Euripides *Helen* 726–33

D5 The Slave as Property

Solon knew that many sales take place in Athens, and established a law which everyone agreed to be just, to the effect that liability for losses and offences committed by slaves rests with the owner for whom the slave is working at the time. It was a reasonable provision, for any benefit or profit produced by a slave belonged to his owner.

Hyperides *Against Athenogenes* 22

D6 Torture of Slaves

Slaves could only give evidence under torture.

Menexenus found the slave here in the city, and having seized him demanded that he give testimony under torture about both the deposit and the charge brought by his master. Pasion, however, reached such a pitch of audacity that he secured the release of the slave on the ground that he was a freeman and, utterly devoid of shame and of fear, he claimed as a freeman and prevented the torture of a person who, as he alleged, had been stolen from him by us and had given us all that money. But the crowning impudence of all was this – that when Menexenus compelled Pasion to give security for the slave before the Polemarch, he gave bond for him in the sum of seven talents.

(To the Clerk) Let witnesses to these facts take the stand.

WITNESSES

After he had acted in this way, men of the jury, Pasion, believing that his past conduct had clearly been in error and thinking he could rectify the situation by his subsequent acts, came to us and asserted that he was ready to surrender the slave for torture.

Isocrates *Trapeziticus* 13–15
tr. G. Norlin (Loeb Classical Library, Heinemann 1928)

D7 Hiring Slaves

Xenophon, writing in about 355–4, is referring to the previous century.

Nicias, Niceratus's son, had in his possession a thousand mine-workers. Sosias the Thracian hired them from him at one obol per day per man; Sosias had to replace any who fell by the wayside. Hipponicus similarly offered 600 slaves on hire on similar terms; his income was a mina per day. Philemonides with 300 received half a mina. Others owned slaves in proportion presumably to their capital. But why bother about the past? Today many slaves in the mines are let out for hire in the same way.

Xenophon *Ways and Means* 4, 14–16

D8 Slaves in Industry

Lysias had a shield-factory with his brother Polemarchus, which was confiscated by the dictators in 404. The work force of 120 is the largest known.

(a)
They took 700 of our shields, a large quantity of silver and gold, bronze, accoutrements, implements and women's clothes they could never have expected to get, and 120 slaves, keeping the best of these for themselves, and handing the remainder over to the public treasury.

Lysias 12, 19

(b)
Gentlemen of the jury, my father left two factories, each doing good business. One was a sword-factory, employing thirty-two or thirty-three slaves, mostly valued at five or six minas and none at less than three. From this he received a net income of thirty minas a year. The other was a bed-factory, employing twenty slaves, offering a security of forty minas, and bringing in a net income of twelve minas.

Demosthenes *Against Aphobus* 9

D9 Runaway Slaves

In 413 the Peloponnesians occupied the Athenian border-fortress of Decelea and remained there all the year round.

Since Decelea had been first fortified during that summer by the whole army, and subsequently occupied by garrisons from the allied states relieving one another at regular intervals in rotation, it had done the Athenians a great deal of harm. They were deprived of the use of their whole territory, and suffered desertion by more than twenty thousand slaves, for the most part manual labourers.

Thucydides 7, 27

D10 The Slave as Slave of Fortune

Anaxandrides was a writer of Middle Comedy in the fourth century. This is from Anchises. *Sunium was evidently a deme for new citizens.*

> Slaves have no city, my dear fellow.
> Fortune shifts their bodies here and there.
> There are many today not free,
> and in Sunium tomorrow, and next day
> shopping in the city-centre. The divine
> power controls their helm.

Anaxandrides in Athenaeus 6, 263

D11 A Utopia without Slaves

Crates in The Wild Animals, *a fifth-century comedy, imagines a technological universe with no need for slaves.*

A: Then won't anyone own a slave, male or female?
Will each poor old fellow have to do for himself?
B: Not at all. I'll give everything the gift of locomotion.
A: What good will that do them?

B: All the furniture
will come when called for. 'Table, lay yourself.'
'Frying-pan, at the ready.' 'Trencher, knead the dough.'
'Decanter, pour – where's that cup? Please wash yourself out.'
'Loaf, rise.' 'Meat-dish, it's time you served the beef.'
'Fish, get a move on!' 'But my other side's not brown.'
'Then turn over and take some oil and a pinch of salt.'
A: Hold it! I'll help you, I'll begin
by getting my people hot baths
from the pipes, straight out of the sea,
just like the hospital, and they'll all
have it straight into the bath, saying 'On with the water.'
The bath-oil will come directly of its own accord; so will the sponge and slippers.

Crates in Athenaeus 6, 267e–f

D12 A Philosophical Analysis of Slavery

Aristotle tries to give a basis in nature to some part of slavery, but he also considers the position of those who are brought to slavery by circumstance. His discussion draws on the distinction between Nomos and Physis (on which see also nos. F10, a–d; F11).

Seeing then that the state is made up of households, before speaking of the state we must speak of the management of the household. The parts of household management correspond to the persons who compose the household, and a complete household consists of slaves and freemen. Now we should begin by examining everything in its fewest possible elements; and the first and fewest possible parts of a family are master and slave, husband and wife, father and children. We have therefore to consider what each of these three relations is and ought to be: – I mean the relation of master and servant, the marriage relation (the conjunction of man and wife has no name of its own), and thirdly, the procreative relation (this also has no proper name). And there is another element of a household, the so-called art of getting wealth, which, according to some, is identical with household management, according to others, a principal part of it; the nature of this art will also have to be considered by us.

Let us first speak of master and slave, looking to the needs of practical life and also seeking to attain some better theory of their relation than exists at present. For some are of opinion that the rule of a master is a science, and that the management of a household, and the mastership of slaves, and the political and royal rule, as I was saying at the outset, are all the same. Others affirm that the rule of a master over slaves is contrary to nature, and that the distinction between slave and freeman exists by law only, and not by nature; and being an interference with nature is therefore unjust.

Property is a part of the household, and the art of acquiring property is a part of the art of managing the household; for no man can live well, or indeed live at all, unless he be provided with necessaries. And as in the arts which have a definite sphere the workers must have their own proper instruments for the accomplishment of their work, so it is in the management of a household. Now instruments are of various sorts; some are living, others lifeless; in the rudder, the pilot of a ship has a lifeless, in the look-out man, a living instrument; for in the arts the servant is a kind of instrument. Thus, too, a possession is an instrument for maintaining life. And so, in the arrangement of the family, a slave is a living possession, and property a number of such instruments; and the servant is himself an instrument which takes precedence of all other instruments. For if every instrument could accomplish its own work, obeying or anticipating the will of others, like the statues of Daedalus, or the tripods of Hephaestus, which, says the poet, 'of their own accord entered the assembly of the Gods'; if, in like manner, the shuttle would weave and the plectrum touch the lyre without a hand to guide them, chief workmen would not want servants, nor masters slaves. Here, however, another distinction must be drawn: the instruments commonly so called are instruments of production, whilst a possession is an instrument of action. The shuttle, for example, is not only of use; but something else is made by it, whereas of a garment or of a bed there is only the use. Further, as production and action are different in kind, and both require instruments, the instruments which they employ must likewise differ in kind. But life is action and not production, and therefore the slave is the minister of action. Again, a possession is spoken of as a part is spoken of; for the part is not only a part of something else, but wholly belongs to it; and this is also true of a possession. The master is only the master of the slave; he does not belong to him, whereas the slave is not only the slave of his master, but wholly belongs to him. Hence we see what is the nature and office of a slave; he who is by nature not his own but another's man, is by nature a slave; and he may be said to be another's man who, being a human being, is also a possession. And a possession may be defined as an instrument of action, separable from the possessor.

But is there any one thus intended by nature to be a slave, and for whom such a condition is expedient and right, or rather is not all slavery a violation of nature?

There is no difficulty in answering this question, on grounds both of reason and of fact. For that some should rule and others be ruled is a thing not only necessary, but expedient; from the hour of their birth, some are marked out for subjection, others for rule. . . .

. . . Nature would like to distinguish between the bodies of freemen and slaves, making the one strong for servile labour, the other upright, and although useless for such services, useful for political life in the arts both of war and peace. But the opposite often happens – that some have the souls and others have the bodies of freemen. And doubtless if men differed from one another in the mere forms of their bodies as much as the statues of the Gods do from men, all would acknowledge that the inferior class should be slaves of the superior. And if this is true of the body, how much more just that a similar distinction should exist in the soul? but the beauty of the body is seen, whereas the beauty of the soul is not seen. It is clear, then, that some men are by nature free, and others slaves, and that for these latter slavery is both expedient and right.

But that those who take the opposite view have in a certain way right on their side, may be easily seen. For the words slavery and slave are used in two senses. There is a slave or slavery by law as well as by nature. The law of which I speak is a sort of convention – the law by which whatever is taken in war is supposed to belong to the victors. But this right many jurists impeach, as they would an orator who brought forward an unconstitutional measure: they detest the notion that, because one man has the power of doing violence and is superior in brute strength, another shall be his slave and subject. Even among philosophers there is a difference of opinion. The origin of the dispute, and what makes the views invade each other's territory, is as follows: in some sense virtue, when furnished with means, has actually the greatest power of exercising force: and as superior power is only found where there is superior excellence of some kind, power seems to imply virtue, and the dispute to be simply one about justice (for it is due to one party identifying 'justice with goodwill', while the other identifies it with the mere rule of the stronger). If these views are thus set out separately, the other views have no force or plausibility against the view that the superior in virtue ought to rule, or be master. Others, clinging, as they think, simply to a principle of justice (for law and custom are a sort of justice), assume that slavery in accordance with the custom of war is justified by law, but at the same moment they deny this. For what if the cause of the war be unjust? And again, no one would ever say that he is a slave who is unworthy to be a slave. Were this the case, men of the highest rank would be slaves and the children of slaves if they or their parents chance to have been taken captive and sold. Wherefore Hellenes do not like to call Hellenes slaves, but confine the term to barbarians. Yet, in using this language, they really mean the natural slave of whom we spoke at first; for it must be admitted that some are slaves everywhere, others nowhere. The same principle applies to nobility. Hellenes regard themselves as noble everywhere, and not only in their own country, but they deem the barbarians noble only when at home, thereby implying that there are two sorts of nobility and freedom, the one absolute, the other relative. The Helen of Theodectes says: 'Who would presume to call me servant who am on both sides sprung from the stem of the Gods?' What does this mean but that they distinguish freedom and slavery, noble and humble birth, by the two principles of good and evil? They think that as men and animals beget men and animals, so from good men a good man springs. But this is what nature, though she may intend it, cannot always accomplish.

We see then that there is some foundation for this difference of opinion, and that all are not either slaves by nature or freemen by nature, and also that there is in some cases a marked distinction between the two classes, rendering it expedient and right for the one to be slaves and the others to be masters: the one practising obedience, the others exercising the authority and lordship which nature intended them to have. The abuse of this authority is injurious to both; for the interests of part and whole, of body and soul, are the same, and the slave is a part of the master, a living but separated part of his bodily frame. Hence, where the relation of master and slave between them is natural they are friends and have a common interest, but where it rests merely on law and force the reverse is true.

Aristotle *Politics* 1, 1253a40–1254a24; 1, 1254b26–1255b15
tr. B. Jowett (Oxford 1921)

E EDUCATION AND SCHOLARSHIP

Formal education in Athens was for boys and young men: girls were taught household skills at home. Schools gave an elementary education based on learning the poets, especially Homer, by heart, reading, writing, music and physical education. There was no formal secondary education. The Sophists fulfilled that role, teaching various skills associated with the art of being an effective citizen. The higher education given by the Sophists was a major innovation in the mid-fifth century, and there was considerable debate about the aims and effects of their teaching, especially in anti-democratic and traditionalist writers.

Useful secondary treatments are: K. J. Freeman *Schools of Hellas* (repr. Kannikat Press 1969); W. Jaeger *Paideia* (English translation, 3 vols., Blackwell 1939); F. A. G. Beck *Greek Education 450–350 BC* (London University Press 1964).

E1 Education

Aristotle outlines the normal Greek practice in education.

There are more or less four traditional subjects of education, reading and writing, PE, music, and sometimes drawing makes a fourth. Reading and writing, and drawing are of practical use, physical education is directed to toughness. There can be more than one opinion about music. At the present day it is mostly a source of personal enjoyment. But those who originally included it in the system of education did so because, as I am always saying, nature aims at a healthy use of leisure as well as a sound approach to work . . .

So our forebears introduced music into education not as a necessity (it is nothing of the sort) nor for its practical utility (as reading and writing are of practical utility in business, household management, study, and a variety of political activities, or drawing is perhaps of practical utility in the finer appreciation of the work of craftsmen), nor with a view to building up physical health and strength, as with PE (since we can see that these are not the result of music). The remaining possibility is that it is directed to our leisure activities, and this was evidently the object of its introduction – a leisure activity fit for free men.

Aristotle *Politics* 8, 1337b 23–33; 1338a 13–23

E2 Education for Body and Mind

Since this is so, certain of our ancestors, long before our time, seeing that many arts had been devised for other things, while none had been prescribed for the body and for the mind, invented and bequeathed to us two disciplines; physical training for the body, of which gymnastics is a part, and, for the mind, philosophy, which I am going to explain. These are twin arts – parallel and complementary – by which their masters prepare the mind to become more intelligent and the body to become more serviceable, not separating sharply the two kinds of education, but using similar methods of instructions, exercise, and other forms of discipline.

Isocrates *Antidosis* 181–2
tr. G. Norlin (Loeb 1928)

E3 Illiteracy

Literacy was not universal; witness a character in Cratinus The Laws. *A useful article is F. D. Harvey 'Literacy in the Athenian Democracy'* Revue des Etudes Grecques *79 (1966) 585–635.*

Good God! I don't know how to read or write.
But I can put it into words; I've a good memory.

Cratinus in *The Suda*

E4 A Literary Education

Before printing and the days of easy reference libraries, verbal memories were more highly developed. It is astonishing to see the detailed literary parodies which the comic dramatists used. The Iliad *and* The Odyssey *together number about 27,000 lines, and perhaps 190,000 words. They were regarded not only as literary masterpieces but as the storehouse of gathered wisdom, what Gilbert Murray called 'the inherited conglomerate'. 'Good' is ambiguous between moral and socially effective.*

'Niceratus,' he said, 'it's your turn. Tell us what kind of knowledge you take most pride in.'

He answered, 'My father was concerned to make a good man of me, and made me learn off the whole of Homer. Even today I could repeat by heart all the *Iliad* and *Odyssey.'*

Xenophon *Symposium* 3, 5

E5 Homer as Educator

Homer was considered a compendium of all wisdom, not just of military skill. Niceratus knew Homer off by heart (see no. E4). The references are to The Iliad *3, 179; 23, 334–7; 11, 630.*

Niceratus at this point remarked: 'You might like to hear the value of my company. I hardly need to say that Homer with his reputation for supreme wisdom has written about almost every human activity. So any of you wanting to master domestic economy, or political leadership, or military strategy, or to rival Achilles, Ajax, Nestor or Odysseus should come to me. I have all the answers.'

'Really?' said Antisthenes. 'Do you mean that you've mastered kingship just because you know that Homer praised Agamemnon as "a noble king and mighty warrior"?'

'Of course,' he replied. 'I also know that in a racing-chariot you must scrape the turning post

> and lean lightly to the left within
> the well-built car, whipping the horse
> on the right with a shout, and loosing his reins.

I've another piece of knowledge besides, which you can try out for yourselves on the spot. There's a phrase of Homer: An onion too gives flavour to the drink. If someone will fetch an onion, you can receive the benefit of this advice here and now. You'll enjoy your drink more.'

'Fellows,' said Charmides. 'Niceratus wants to go home smelling of onions, so that his wife can be quite sure that no one would even have dreamed of kissing him.'

Xenophon *Symposium* 4, 6–8

E6 The Poet as Educator

Aristophanes in The Frogs *puts into the mouth of Aeschylus a justification of poetry in education. The thought is not one which immediately 'clicks' with us, but the poets, Homer and Hesiod especially, were regarded as the transmitters of 'the inherited conglomerate', of the accumulated tribal wisdom. There is an exceptionally interesting treatment of the whole theme in Eric Havelock's controversial* Preface to Plato *(Blackwell 1963). Plato* Republic *10, 598d–e criticizes the claim that Homer and the tragedians know all human skills and ethics. See also Isocrates 1, 51; 2, 3; 2, 13.*

(a)

AESCHYLUS: This is the poet's appropriate task. Think from the beginning
the blessings the masters of verse are bringing.
Orpheus taught us religion, and that murder is wrong,
Musaeus taught medicine and oracles, Hesiod's song
taught farming, the season to harvest and plough, and Homer
won glorious renown – 'divine' was no misnomer –
by teaching strategy, tactics and military valour.

Aristophanes *Frogs* 1030–36

(b) *Aeschylus is chosen to be resurrected from the dead by reason of his wise guidance.*

PLUTO: Goodbye, Aeschylus, go
and keep our state safe
with good advice, and educate
the fools; there are plenty of them.

Aristophanes *Frogs* 1500–3

E7 Athletics Training

Group coaching is nothing new.

STRANGER: You, like other countries, have group training with an eye to victory in running and other sports.

YOUNG SOCRATES: Yes, and plenty of it.

STRANGER: It's useful to remember the instructions given by professional athletics trainers in these systems of instruction.

YOUNG SOCRATES: What sort of instructions?

STRANGER: They take the view that it is not possible to work in minute particulars, giving individual instruction. They regard it as necessary to give mass instruction, offering a training appropriate to the majority of people for the majority of the time.

YOUNG SOCRATES: Yes, that's right.

STRANGER: That is why they give the same exercises to a massed group, whether in running, wrestling or any other physical training, with a single word of command to all to start or finish.

Plato *Politicus* 294d–e

E8 The Control of the Teacher

Look at the legislation covering teachers. We have to place our children in their charge. Their livelihood depends on their good character; anything else would mean their ruin. Yet the legislation puts no trust in them. It prescribes the exact time at which the son of free parents is to go to the schoolroom, how many boys are to accompany him, and when he is to return home. The teachers are not allowed to open the school before sunrise and are bound to close it before sunset; the same applies to PE instructors at the sports ground. The law is extremely suspicious of allowing a teacher alone with a boy, especially in the dark. The law lays down what boys are to be admitted to school at what age; it provides an official superintendent of schools; it legislates about the boys' slave-attendants, about school festivals and athletic festivals, and, finally, about the boys' own associations and their dancing in the round.

Aeschines *Against Timarchus* 9–10

E9 The Tutor

The tutor (paedagogus) *was a slave-attendant who accompanied the boy through the streets, as to and from school, and was responsible for his behaviour. Socrates is talking to a boy named Lysis.*

'Tell me one more thing. Do your parents let you control your own life, or is that another thing they don't let you do?'

'Of course they don't.'

'So someone is in charge of you.'

'Yes, my tutor here.'

'A slave?'

'Oh yes. He belongs to us.'

'How odd to put a free man under the control of a slave! How does your tutor exercise his authority over you?'

'By conducting me to school, I suppose.'

Plato *Lysis* 208c

E10 An Athenian View of Fifth-century Science

Plato puts these reflections into the mouth of Socrates on his last day. Socrates was apparently interested in science in the 420s (see Aristophanes's Clouds*), and Archelaus was said to have guided him. The questions raised fit the science of the mid-fifth century better than the science to which Plato would have been exposed later. See the notes in J. Burnet* Plato's Phaedo *(Oxford 1911). Archelaus held that growth was due to decay brought about by the Hot and the Cold. That thinking was due to blood was the view of Empedocles, to air that of Anaximenes and, more recently, Diogenes of Apollonia, to fire that of Heraclitus and his followers, to the brain that of Alcmaeon and the Hippocratic doctors, and it was Alcmaeon who said that scientific knowledge emerges from memory and belief.*

Then I will tell you, said Socrates. When I was young, Cebes, I had a prodigious desire to know that department of philosophy which is called the investigation of nature; to know the causes of things, and why a thing is and is created or destroyed appeared to me to be a lofty profession; and I was always agitating myself with the consideration of questions such as these: – Is the growth of animals the result of some decay which the hot and cold principle contracts, as some have said? Is the blood the element with which we think, or the air, or the fire? or perhaps nothing of the kind – but the brain may be the originating power of the perceptions of hearing and sight and smell, and memory and opinion may come from them, and science may be based on memory and opinion when they have attained fixity. And then I went on to examine the corruption of them, and then to the things of heaven and earth, and at last I concluded myself to be utterly and absolutely incapable of these enquiries, as I will satisfactorily prove to you.

Plato *Phaedo* 96a
tr. B. Jowett (Oxford 1953)

E11 One Sophist's Views on Higher Education

The word 'sophist' originally only meant 'expert'. The sophists were a group who tried to meet the demand for higher education by offering courses for fees on a variety of subjects.

'Hippocrates, by becoming a pupil of Protagoras, will, on the very day he joins him, go home a better man, and on each successive day will make similar progress – towards what, Protagoras, and better at what?'

Protagoras heard me out and said: 'You put your questions well, and I enjoy answering good questioners. When he comes to me, Hippocrates will not be put through the same things that another Sophist would inflict on him. The others treat their pupils badly: these young men, who have deliberately turned their backs on specialization, they take and plunge into special studies again, teaching them arithmetic and astronomy and geometry and music' – here he glanced at Hippias – 'but from me he will learn only what he has come to learn. What is that subject? The proper care of his personal affairs, so that he may best manage his own household, and also of the State's affairs, so as to become a real power in the city, both as speaker and man of action.'

'Do I follow you?' said I. 'I take you to be describing the art of politics, and promising to make men good citizens.'

'That,' said he, 'is exactly what I profess to do.'

Plato *Protagoras* 318d–9a
tr. W. K. C. Guthrie (Penguin 1956)

E12 A Defence of the Old Education

Aristophanes's Clouds *is an attack on the New Learning, personified by Socrates. Phrynis was a musician from Mytilene, who settled in Gela in the mid-fifth century.*

RIGHT THINKING: I'll tell you the state of education in the past
when modesty was honoured, and I flourished speaking right.
First rule: that children should be seen and not heard.
Second: in the streets they should walk in order to music-lesson,
all from one district together, lightly dressed, the snow no matter.
Third, they were taught to sing, standing legs apart,
Pallas Fierce Sacker of Cities or *A Shout from Afar,*
sticking to the traditional tune.
If anyone made nonsense of it with trilled ornaments
or the laborious contrivances of Phrynis and his school,
he received six of the best as dishonouring the Muses.
In PE the boys would sit with legs outstretched,
not offering any vulgar spectacle to Peeping Toms.
Then again when they stood up they would smooth the sand,
careful to leave no imprint to excite a lover.
No lad oiled his skin below the belt; their sex-organs
bloomed freshly and naturally like a peach.
They did not try to attract lovers by softly spoken words,
or walk exposing themselves to the gaze of lust.
At table they would not dare to take even a radish,
or grab anise or parsley in the presence of their elders,
or munch fish or gourmandize or cross their legs.

Aristophanes *Clouds* 961–83

E13 Xenophon on Sophistic and True Education

The word for virtue is arete *(nos. F1–F7).*

I am astonished at the so-called sophists. The majority of them profess to direct the young towards virtue and direct them in the opposite direction. We have never seen any man whose goodness was due to the present generation of sophists or to their writings. They write extensively on trivialities leading the young to idle pleasures not to virtue. It is a sheer waste of time to read them in the hope of learning anything from them – harmful instruction and a distraction from other useful activities. I blame them in proportion to their faults which are large. The style of their compositions is obscure, and the sort of beneficial maxims which might educate the young in virtue are nowhere to be found. I'm only an ordinary man, but I know that the best thing is to learn what is good from one's own nature, and the next best to learn from others who really know what is good – not from these persuasive frauds. Possibly I am not using academic language. I'm not trying to. I'd rather put forward true maxims which will help those who have had a decent education on towards virtue. It's decent maxims not language that provide real education. There are many others who criticize our contemporary sophists – philosophers they are not; their cleverness lies in words not in ideas.

Of course I know that one of that crowd will perhaps say that what is well and carefully thought out is not well and carefully presented. It would be easy for them to make quick criticisms – and unjustified. My object in writing is to be right – to produce really good men not men like sophists. I want my work to have the reality not just the semblance of usefulness, and to stand permanently solid. The sophists speak and write to lead astray, for personal profit not to help others. There is not and never has been a man of wisdom among them. Every one of them is content with the title of sophist, which is a term of reproach among men of sense. My advice is to avoid the injunctions of the sophists, but to respect the conclusions of the philosophers. The sophists hunt down rich young men. The philosophers are friends to everyone and share with all. They are no respecters of men's fortunes.

Xenophon *On Hunting* 13, 1–9

E14 False Education

A passage from a fragmentary work criticizing other systems of education and no doubt going on to defend the author's own system. The date is perhaps 389. Isocrates claimed to be a sophist, that is, roughly, a professor, but claimed to be different from the rest.

Take the sophists who have suddenly sprung up and dropped into these magniloquent claims. They are prominent enough at present. But I am quite sure they will all be brought round to this position. What of our predecessors who had the courage to write on the science of oratory? They are not to be dismissed without criticism. Some of them claimed to teach forensic advocacy – a thoroughly discredited term, which you would expect to hear from the opponents not from the practitioners of that form of education. The skill itself, in so far as it can be taught, is of no greater value to legal pleading than to any other form of public speaking. These were even worse than those who dabble in eristic argument. The latter expound hair-splitting theories which would be disastrous to anyone practising them, but they did at least make some profession of ethical principle. The others advertise the study of politics, ignore the appropriate positive qualities, and offer an education in profiteering and interference.

Isocrates *Against the Sophists* 19–20

E15 A School for Oratory

For you must not lose sight of the fact that Athens is looked upon as having become a school for the education of all able orators and teachers of oratory. And naturally so; for people observe that she holds forth the greatest prizes for those who have this ability, that she offers the greatest number and variety of fields of exercise to those who have chosen to enter contests of this character and want to train for them, and that, furthermore, everyone obtains here that practical experience which more than any other thing imparts ability to speak; and, in addition to these advantages they consider that the catholicity and moderation of our speech as well as our flexibility of mind and love of letters, contribute in no small degree to the education of the orator. Therefore they suppose, and not without just reason, that all clever speakers are the disciples of Athens.

Isocrates *Antidosis* 295–6
tr. G. Norlin (Loeb 1928)

E16 Medical Science

Hippocrates lived on the island of Cos in the fifth century. Here medicine was developed on a scientific basis using clinical observation.

(a)
Life is short, science long, opportunity fleeting, experience ambiguous, the decision at the critical moment difficult. It is the physician's job to do his own duty and to secure the full cooperation of patients, attendants and external circumstances.

Hippocrates *Aphorisms* 1

(b)

We physicians base our diagnosis on our general knowledge of disease and of particular diseases, and on our special knowledge of the malady we are treating, of the patient, his previous history and his previous doctor. Factors include the prevailing climate, the patient's origin, his way of life, his work, his age, his conversation, his idiosyncrasies, his silences, his thoughts, his capacity for sleep, his dreams (their number and nature), any picking or scratching, hysteria, discharges, sneezing or sickness. We are meticulous in noting the progress of the illness to the critical point, checking such details as perspiration, chill, stiffness, coughs or sneezing, hiccoughing, heavy breathing, internal bleeding. It is our professional duty to observe all these factors and their consequences.

Hippocrates *Epidemics* 1, 23

E17 The Objects of Education

Isocrates's last manifesto, at the age of 97.

If I exclude from education practical skills, theoretical knowledge and specialized training, whom do I call educated? First, those who cope effectively with their daily experiences, with a sound judgment for the occasion and a clear enough view of the best course of action. Secondly, those who are upright and honourable in their dealings with their neighbours, putting up tolerantly with pinpricks and unpleasantnesses from others and showing themselves reasonably easy and sensible in company. Thirdly, those who are masters of their pleasures, and do not allow themselves to be crushed by misfortunes but face them with a courage worthy of a man. Fourthly and supremely, those who are not corrupted by prosperity, and do not get above themselves, but hold their place as men of reason, with more delight in the blessings which originate in their own intelligent nature than in those that come by chance. And I assert that those whose characters reflect all four of these qualities are men of wisdom, men in the full sense, endowed with every virtue.

Isocrates *Panathenaicus* 30–32

F SOCIAL VALUES

The traditional social values as exemplified by the Homeric heroes began to be questioned in fifth-century Athens. The scientific thinking in Ionia of the previous century and the demands of a democratic society created a need for new values; the man whose only virtues were bravery, strength and noble lineage would not achieve much in the Athenian assembly. There were those who defended the old values and some (e.g. Plato's Thrasymachus) denied any objective values at all, but this uncertainty stimulated searches along new and sometimes radical lines of reasoning.

Important books in this field are: E. A. Havelock *The Liberal Temper in Greek Politics* (Jonathan Cape 1957); A. W. H. Adkins *Merit and Responsibility* (Oxford University Press 1960) and *Moral Values and Political Behaviour in Ancient Greece from Homer to the Fifth Century* (Chatto and Windus 1972).

F1 'Arete' in the Homeric Poems

The Iliad *and* The Odyssey *were an inescapable integral part of the climate of thought in Classical Athens (see nos. E4, E5).* Agathos *(good) and* arete *(virtue) and similar words refer to social effectiveness, and involve wealth and social position, and, in war, skill and courage. To be* agathos *is to be a strong man, and it is possible to have* arete *without necessarily having prudence or justice. The culture is a 'shame-culture' not a 'guilt-culture'; that is to say that the standard of action is found in the opinion of others, not in the inward conscience. For the dichotomy see Ruth Benedict* The Chrysanthemum and the Sword *(London University Press 1967) p. 156 ff and also E. R. Dodds* The Greeks and the Irrational *(University of California Press 1951).*

(a) *Nestor warns Agamemnon.* Agathos *clearly means 'powerful'.*

Do not, *agathos* though you be, take the girl from him.

Homer *Iliad* 1, 275

(b)

Suppose all the best of us were now, by the ships,
to be picked for an ambush, where men's *arete* is most surely seen.

Homer *Iliad* 13, 276–7

(c)

A son, born of a father far worse, himself better
in all forms of *arete,* running and fighting.

Homer *Iliad* 15, 641–2

(d)

Zeus, who thunders afar, takes away half a man's
arete, when the day of slavery grips him.

Homer *Odyssey* 17, 322–3

F2 'Arete' in Pindar

Pindar was born in Thebes about 522. His surviving complete poems are songs in honour of victors in the Games at the great festivals at Olympia, Delphi, Nemea and the Isthmus. Arete *here has to do with success in the games, involving money and training and glorifying one's own city.*

(a)

Always hard work and expense strive for *aretai* towards an end,
dangerous, veiled. Those who succeed are reckoned wise by their fellow-citizens.

Pindar *Olympians* 5, 15–16

(b)

If a man pursues *arete* with all his spirit,
sparing no expense or work,
it is right when he succeeds
to offer ennobling praise
with ungrudging mind.

Pindar *Isthmians* 1, 41–5

1 Ostraka with blackballed names: Themistocles, Pericles, 5th century BC (Agora Museum)

2 Silver tetradrachm of Athens, c.440 – 430 BC. On the obverse is the head of Athene, patron deity of the city, and on the reverse her symbol, the owl, with the first three letters in Greek of the name of the state. (British Museum)

3 Trireme (relief, Athens, National Museum)

4 Athene and Hera (patron goddesses of Athens and Samos): treaty between Samos and Athens (Athens, National Museum)

5 Shoemaker: Attic black-figure pelike from Rhodes by the Eucharides Painter. Early 5th century BC (Ashmolean Museum, Oxford)

6 Vase painters: Attic red-figure krater, 5th century BC, by the Komaris painter (Ashmolean Museum, Oxford)

7 School scenes: Attic red-figure kylix of Douris, c.500 – 480 BC (Berlin)

8 Folding clothes: stamnos, early 5th century BC (place unknown)

9 Young women washing – Attic stamnos, c. 450 BC (Museum Antiken Kleinkunst, Munich)

10 Banqueting scene: Attic red-figure cup, 480 – 470 BC Douris painter (British Museum)

11 Eleusinian relief: the boy representing the Athenian people receives the gift of corn from Demeter and Kore

12 Below: sacrificial scene: Attic red-figure cup, c. 460 BC Pan Painter (Ashmolean Museum, Oxford)

13 Below: scene from the palaestra: Attic red-figure cup, c. 500 BC, signed both by the potter Hischylus and the painter Phidippus. The thin youth teases the fat one; another adjusts the finger thong on his javelin, while the fourth practises the discus. (British Museum)

14 Caryatid porch of the Erechtheum

15 Parthenon frieze – young men leading a heifer for the sacrifice (south frieze, slab XL) (British Museum)

16 Hermes with infant Dionysus. Praxiteles, c. 350 – 330 BC (Olympia Museum)

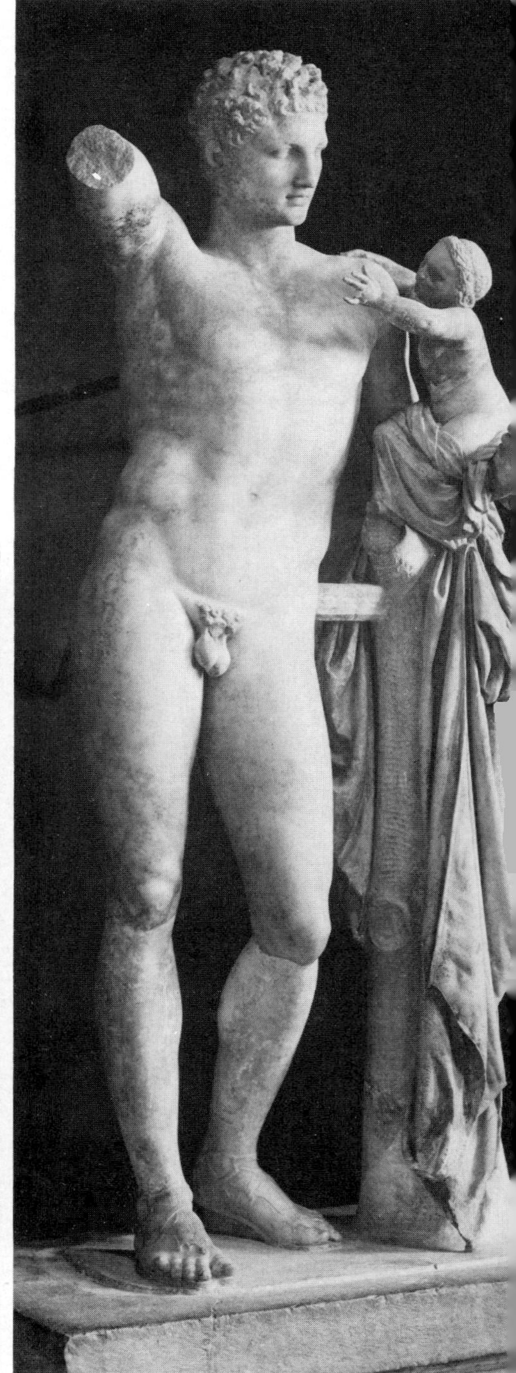

17 Demosthenes (Vatican Museum, Rome)

F3 A Proverb

Theognis was a sixth-century poet from nearby Megara. In the verses attributed to him arete *may refer to success and wealth, but it may refer to preserving the traditional values of one's social class, even if other classes have become more wealthy and more successful politically (865 ff). One couplet represents a startling change. Two centuries later Aristotle (*Ethics *1129b 29) cites it as a proverb: when it was first said it was new and revolutionary.*

The whole of *arete* is summed up in justice.
Every man, Cyrnus, if just, is *agathos*.

Theognis 147–8

F4 'Arete' in the Plague

The plague broke out in Athens in the second year of the Peloponnesian War (430). See Thucydides 2, 47–54 for his full account.

If they were not prepared out of fear to visit one another, they died in solitude. Whole households vanished for want of help. If they called on their neighbours, death followed, particularly for those with a sense of *arete,* whose sense of honour meant that they did not spare themselves to visit their friends.

Thucydides 2, 51, 5

F5 'Arete' in Plato's 'Meno'

Plato's Meno *is a discussion of the question 'Can* arete *be taught?' The dramatic date is 402; the date of writing perhaps fifteen years later.*

(a)

MENO: Socrates, can you tell me this? Can *arete* be taught? Or is it acquired by practice rather than teaching? Or is it neither of these, but implanted naturally in human beings, or by some other means?

Plato *Meno* 70a

(b) *Meno's first definition*

MENO: It's quite easy to explain, Socrates. In the first place, take the *arete* of a man. It's easy to see that the *arete* of a man is to be capable of sharing in political life in such a way as to benefit his friends and damage his enemies while taking care to avoid harm to himself. Take a woman's *arete*. That's easy to define. It's the need to look after the house properly, checking the contents and obeying her husband. Children have a different *arete*, different again for girls and boys. So do older men, different, if you like, for slave and free. And there are plenty of other *aretai*. There's no lack of material to give an account of *arete*. Every activity, every age-group, every individual with his particular work has his *arete* . . .

SOCRATES: Meno, what a stroke of luck. I ask for one *arete*, and find that you possess a whole swarm of them.

Plato *Meno* 71e–72a

(c) *Socrates leads Meno to the idea of one single* arete. *Gorgias was a rhetorician from Magna Graecia who made a great impact on Athens.*

SOCRATES: Then, since *arete* is the same in all instances, try and remember what Gorgias – with your agreement – said about it.

MENO: Just that it is the capacity to govern human beings.

Plato *Meno* 73c

(d) *Socrates moralizes the concept.*

MENO: Yes, Socrates, justice is *arete*.

SOCRATES: *Arete*, Meno, or an *arete*?

MENO: What does that mean?

SOCRATES: These are similar examples. Take roundness. I should call it a shape, not just shape, since there are other shapes.

MENO: Quite right too – and I say that there are other *aretai* as well as justice.

SOCRATES: What? Tell me. I could name you other shapes if you asked. You name me other *aretai*.

MENO: Well, I would think courage an *arete*, and good sense, and wisdom, and magnificence and plenty of others.

Plato *Meno* 73d–74a

(e) *A new definition. The quotation is perhaps from Simonides.*

MENO: Well, Socrates, I think *arete* is, in the words of the poet
enjoying glory, with power.
That's what I call *arete*, having one's heart set on glory and being able to attain it.

Plato *Meno* 77b

(f) *Another definition*

SOCRATES: Then according to your account, *arete* is the ability to secure good things *(agatha)*.
MENO: Absolutely, Socrates.

Plato *Meno* 78b–c

(g) *The conclusion is that* arete *cannot be taught if it cannot be defined. Those who claim to teach it make false claims. Statesmen do not operate by wisdom. The conclusion is, of course, ironical.*

SOCRATES: So, Meno, the conclusion of our discussion is that *arete* comes to those of us who enjoy it by a divine dispensation. But we shall understand this clearly only when, before asking how men possess *arete*, we first try to investigate what *arete* in itself is.

Plato *Meno* 100b

F6 'Arete' as Relative

A dialogue between Socrates and Thrasymachus, a sophist well known in Athens by 428–7.

'Good,' I said. 'Do you also think that everything which has attached to it a specific function has also a specific *arete*? Let's go back to the same examples. The eyes have a specific function?' 'Yes.' 'Then have they a specific *arete*?' 'Yes.' 'The ears have their own function?' 'Yes.' 'And their own *arete*?' 'Yes.' 'And the same with everything else?' 'Yes.' 'All right. Now suppose the eyes did not have their peculiar *arete* but its opposite instead, could they properly fulfil their function?' 'Of course not,' he said, 'if you mean blindness in place of sight.' 'Whatever their *arete* is,' I replied. 'I haven't yet reached that question. I'm asking whether anything with a function will fulfil that function well through its peculiar *arete* and badly without it.' 'True enough,' he answered. 'Then ears deprived of their special *arete* will fulfil their function poorly.' 'Yes.' 'And so with everything else.' 'I think so.' 'Next consider this. Has the soul a specific function which you couldn't fulfil in any other way – say, management, authority, deliberation and so on? Could we properly assign these functions to anything but soul?' 'No.' 'And life? Are we to call that a function of soul?' 'Surely.' 'Then we say that soul has its peculiar *arete*?' 'Yes.' 'Then, Thrasymachus, will the soul perform its peculiar function properly if deprived of its special *arete*?' 'Impossible.' 'Then a bad soul will exercise authority and management badly and a good soul well?' 'Yes.' 'And we agreed that the *arete* of the soul is justice and its absence injustice?' 'We did.' 'Then the just soul and the just man will enjoy a good life, the unjust man will not.' 'Apparently by your argument,' he said.

Plato *Republic* 1, 353b–e

F7 Aristotle and 'Arete'

The Nicomachean Ethics *is a treatise on happiness:* arete *is a means to that end.*

(a) *The good for man. The* psyche *('soul') embraces life, intelligence, self.*

In that case the good for man is the active exercise of his *psyche* in accordance with *arete,* and if there is more than one *arete,* in accordance with the highest and most complete.

Aristotle *Ethics* 1, 7, 15, 1048a16

(b)

Arete is similarly divided. We call some *aretai* intellectual and some moral. Wisdom (or intelligence) and sound judgment are intellectual *aretai,* liberality and self-discipline are moral *aretai.*

Aristotle *Ethics* 1, 13, 2, 1103a4

(c) *The definition of* arete. *The mean is at first sight a surprising concept, but an example may help. Thus courage is a mean between cowardice and rashness. Aristotle says that* arete *is a mean in definition but a peak in value.*

Arete is a disposition arising from choice, located in a relative mean, the mean being determined by reason, as it would be determined by a man of sound judgment.

Aristotle *Ethics* 2, 6, 15, 1106b36

(d) *Happiness*

If happiness is activity in accordance with *arete,* it is reasonable that it should be in accordance with the highest *arete,* i.e. the *arete* of the best part of us. Whether this is intelligence or some other element with a natural capacity to rule and lead and have understanding of nobility and divinity (whether itself divine or the nearest thing to the divine possible to humans), complete happiness will be the activity of that part in accordance with its peculiar *arete.* As I have said, that is contemplation.

Aristotle *Ethics* 10, 7, 1, 1177a12

(e) *A passage from* Politics *shows that Aristotle has not lost the idea of* arete *as social effectiveness.*

The ownership of property must be vested in the upper classes. These are the citizens and the citizens have to be well off. Manual workers have no share in the state; the same applies to any other group which does not produce *arete.* This is clear from our presupposition. Happiness must be associated with *arete.* A state cannot achieve happiness in regard to a portion of its citizens but the whole citizen body.

Aristotle *Politics* 7, 8, 5, 1329a19

F8 Justice in 'The Republic'

Plato's Republic *purports to be an investigation into the nature of justice.*

(a) *The first definition of justice, from Cephalus, represents the gathered wisdom of an older generation.*

To tell the truth and return what you have received.

Plato *Republic* 1, 331d

(b) *A refinement of this, later accepted in Roman law*

To give each man his due.

Plato *Republic* 1, 332d

(c) *A closer definition*

To do good to friends and harm to enemies.

Plato *Republic* 1, 332d

(d) *Thrasymachus rejects popular definitions.*

Just you answer and tell me what you say justice is. And don't go telling me that it means morally obligatory or useful or beneficial or profitable or advantageous. Just tell me clearly what you mean. I won't put up with rubbish of that sort.

Plato *Republic* 1, 336c–d

(e) *Thrasymachus's definition*

Justice is the advantage of the stronger.

Plato *Republic* 1, 338d

(f) *The social contract:* nomos *and* physis

They say that by nature to commit injustice is good, to suffer it is evil, but the evil of the latter outweighs the good of the former. The result is that in a situation of mutual injustice when people experience both, those who are not in a position to choose injustice for themselves while evading it from others decide that it is to their advantage to make a compact to avoid committing or suffering injustice. This is the beginning of legislation and social contracts. They call the ordinance of the law 'lawful' and 'just'. This is the origin and essential nature of justice, a midway point between the best, to commit injustice without penalty, and the worst, to suffer injustice without retribution. Justice is a compromise between the two, tolerated not as a real good, but receiving respect out of weakness in injustice.

Plato *Republic* 2, 359a

(g) *Socrates's definition*

Then in some sense justice is the principle of attending to one's own business. . . .

Let us put it this way. If the three classes, one making money, one providing auxiliary services for government and one ruling, each fulfils its proper function in the state . . . that would constitute justice and would make the state just. . . . And a just man will not be different from a just state so far as the essence of justice is concerned; he will be the same. . . . There are two faculties in the soul, Reason and Desire . . . and a third as well, Temper. . . . Each of us in whom each part of himself performs its proper function is attending to his own business, and is just.

Plato *Republic* 4, 434a–441c

F9 The Authentic Thrasymachus

The gods are not interested in human affairs, or they would not have overlooked the supreme blessing for men – justice. We can see that men do not practise this.

Thrasymachus fr. 8

F10 'Nomos' and 'Physis'

There was much fifth-century debate about the relations between nomos *(law, custom, convention) and* physis *(nature). Once it was seen that different peoples conceived right in different ways, questions were bound to be raised about the validity of any one of these, or indeed all of them. Two extreme answers were that* nomos *was an unjustified shackle on* physis, *or that* physis *was violent and uncontrolled, and* nomos *was the means to civilization. F. Heinemann* Nomos and Physis *(Verlag Friedrich Reinhardt AG, Basel 1945) is an important study.*

(a) *Antiphon was an Athenian, probably of the last part of the fifth century, who wrote a book on* Truth, *fragments of which have survived in two papyri from Oxyrhynchus. There is an interesting chapter on Antiphon in Eric Havelock* The Liberal Temper in Greek Politics *(London University Press 1957). See also W. C. Greene* Moira *(Harvard University Press 1944) pp. 232–40.*

Justice, then, is not to transgress that which is the law of the city in which one is a citizen. A man therefore can best conduct himself in harmony with justice, if when in the company of witnesses he upholds the laws, and when alone without witnesses he upholds the edicts of nature. For the edicts of the laws are imposed artificially, but those of nature are compulsory. And the edicts of the laws are arrived at by consent, not by natural growth, whereas those of nature are not a matter of consent.

So, if the man who transgresses the legal code evades those who have agreed to these edicts, he avoids both disgrace and penalty; otherwise not. But if a man violates against possibility any of the laws which are implanted in nature, even if he evades all men's detection, the ill is no less, and even if all see, it is not greater. For he is not hurt on account of an opinion, but because of truth. The examination of these things is in general for this reason, that the majority of just acts according to law are prescribed contrary to nature. For there is legislation about the eyes, what they must see and what not; and about the ears, what they must hear and what not; and about the tongue, what it must speak and what not; and about the hands, what they must do and what not; and about the feet, where they must go and where not. Now the law's prohibitions are in no way more agreeable to nature and more akin than the law's injunctions. But life belongs to nature, and death too, and life for them is derived from advantages, and death from disadvantages. And the advantages laid down by the laws are chains upon nature, but those laid down by nature are free. So that the things which hurt, according to true reasoning, do not benefit nature more than those which delight; and things which grieve are not more advantageous than those which please; for things truly advantageous must not really harm, but must benefit. The naturally advantageous things from among these . . .

We revere and honour those born of noble fathers, but those who are not born of noble houses we neither revere nor honour. In this we are, in our relations with one another, like barbarians, since we are all by nature born the same in every way, both barbarians and Hellenes. And it is open to all men to observe the laws of nature, which are compulsory. Similarly all of these things can be acquired by all, and in none of these things is any of us distinguished as barbarian or Hellene. We all breathe into the air through mouth and nostrils, and we all eat with hands. . . .

(From another book of 'Truth')

If justice were taken seriously, then witnessing the truth among one another is considered just, and useful no less for men's business affairs. But he who does this is not just, since not to wrong anyone unless wronged oneself is just; for it is inevitable for the witness, even if he witnesses to the truth, nevertheless to wrong another in some way, and at the same time himself be wronged later, because of what he said; in that because of the evidence given by him, the person witnessed against is condemned, and loses either money or his life, through someone to whom he does no wrong. Therein therefore he wrongs the man against whom he gives evidence, in that he wrongs someone who did him no wrong; and he himself is wronged by the man against whom he gave evidence, because he is hated by him for having given truthful evidence. And (*he is wronged*) not only by this hatred, but also because he must for the whole of his life be on his guard against the man against whom he gave evidence; for he has an enemy such that he will say or do him any harm in his power. Indeed, these are clearly no small wrongs which he himself suffers and which he inflicts; for these cannot be just, nor can the demand to do no wrong (*if one is not wronged?*). But it is inevitable that either both are just or both unjust. It is clear, also, that to judge, give judgment, and arbitrate for a settlement are not just; for that which helps some, hurts others; and in this case, those who are benefited are not wronged, but those who are injured are wronged. . . .

Antiphon
tr. K. Freeman *Ancilla to the Pre-Socratic Philosophers* (Blackwell 1948)

(b) *Archelaus was an Athenian, responsible for introducing Ionian natural philosophy into Athens. He was reputed to have influenced Socrates. Diogenes Laertius wrote his lives of the philosophers some time before the third century AD.*

Archelaus said that the concepts 'just' and 'shameful' depend on convention (*nomos*) not nature (*physis*).

Diogenes Laertius 2, 16

(c) *Herodotus illustrates different conventions* (nomoi).

If you were to invite all mankind to choose the best customs (*nomous*) out of all the customs in the world, after careful consideration they would all choose their own. Everyone thinks their own customs much the best. . . . Here, among many others, is an excellent piece of evidence that all people take this view of their own customs. Darius sent for the Greeks in attendance at his court, and asked them how much they would take to eat the dead bodies of their fathers. They said they would not do so at any price. Darius then called a tribe of Indians called the Callatiae, who do eat their parents, and in the presence of the Greeks (who could understand what was being said through an interpreter) asked how much they would take to burn their fathers' bodies. They shrieked aloud, telling him not to utter such accursed words. This shows the power of custom. I think Pindar was right to call it king of all.

Herodotus 3, 38

(d) *Antigone in Sophocles's play affirms divine laws. Compare* Oedipus *863–73.*

ANTIGONE: I did not think your edicts had the power
to override the unwritten, unchangeable laws
of the gods – you are a mortal.
Those laws are not of today or yesterday; they live
forever, and no one knows their origin.

I do not intend, from fear of any man's
authority, to offend against the gods in this.

Sophocles *Antigone* 453–60

F11 Arguments for the Rule of 'Nomos' (Law)

Crito is trying to persuade Socrates, under sentence of death, to escape from prison. Socrates answers that if he accepts the laws' protection he must accept their adverse verdict.

SOCRATES: Look at it in this way. Suppose that while we were preparing to run away from here (or however one should describe it) the Laws and Constitution of Athens were to come and confront us and ask this question: 'Now, Socrates, what are you proposing to do? Can you deny that by this act which you are b contemplating you intend, so far as you have the power, to destroy us, the Laws, and the whole State as well? Do you imagine that a city can continue to exist and not be turned upside down, if the legal judgments which are pronounced in it have no force but are nullified and destroyed by private persons?' – how shall we answer this question, Crito, and others of the same kind? There is much that could be said, especially by a professional advocate, to protest against the invalidation of this law which enacts that judgments once pronounced shall be binding. Shall we say 'Yes, I do intend to destroy the laws, c because the State wronged me by passing a faulty judgment at my trial'? Is this to be our answer, or what?

CRITO: What you have just said, by all means, Socrates.

SOCRATES: Then what supposing the Laws say: 'Was there provision for this in the agreement between you and us, Socrates? Or did you undertake to abide by whatever judgments the State pronounced?' If we expressed surprise at such language, they would probably say: 'Never mind our language, Socrates, but d answer our questions; after all, you are accustomed to the method of question and answer. Come now, what charge do you bring against us and the State, that you are trying to destroy us? Did we not give you life in the first place? was it not through us that your father married your mother and begot you? Tell us, have you any complaint against those of us Laws that deal with marriage?' 'No, none,' I should say. 'Well, have you any against the laws which deal with children's upbringing and education, such as you had yourself? Are you not grateful to those of us Laws which were instituted for this end, for requiring e your father to give you a cultural and physical education?' 'Yes,' I should say. 'Very good. Then since you have been born and brought up and educated, can you deny, in the first place, that you were our child and servant, both you and your ancestors? And if this is so, do you imagine that what is right for us is equally right for you, and that whatever we try to do to you, you are justified in

retaliating? You did not have equality of rights with your father, or your employer (supposing that you had had one), to enable you to retaliate; you were
51 not allowed to answer back when you were scolded or to hit back when you were beaten, or to do a great many other things of the same kind. Do you expect to have such licence against your country and its laws that if we try to put you to death in the belief that it is right to do so, you on your part will try your hardest to destroy your country and us its Laws in return? and will you, the true devotee of goodness, claim that you are justified in doing so? Are you so wise as to have forgotten that compared with your mother and father and all the rest of your ancestors your country is something far more precious, more
b venerable, more sacred, and held in greater honour both among gods and among all reasonable men? Do you not realize that you are even more bound to respect and placate the anger of your country than your father's anger? that if you cannot persuade your country you must do whatever it orders, and patiently submit to any punishment that it imposes, whether it be flogging or imprisonment? And if it leads you out to war, to be wounded or killed, you must comply, and it is right that you should do so; you must not give way or retreat or abandon your position. Both in war and in the law-courts and everywhere
c else you must do whatever your city and your country commands, or else persuade it in accordance with universal justice; but violence is a sin even against your parents, and it is a far greater sin against your country.' – What shall we say to this, Crito? – that what the Laws say is true, or not?

CRITO: Yes, I think so.

SOCRATES: 'Consider, then, Socrates,' the Laws would probably continue, 'whether it is also true for us to say that what you are now trying to do to us is not right. Although we have brought you into the world and reared you and
d educated you, and given you and all your fellow-citizens a share in all the good things at your disposal, nevertheless by the very fact of granting our permission we openly proclaim this principle: that any Athenian, on attaining to manhood and seeing for himself the political organization of the state and us its Laws, is permitted, if he is not satisfied with us, to take his property and go away wherever he likes. If any of you chooses to go to one of our colonies, supposing that he should not be satisfied with us and the State, or to emigrate to any other country, not one of us Laws hinders or prevents him from going away wherever
e he likes, without any loss of property. On the other hand, if any one of you stands his ground when he can see how we administer justice and the rest of our public organization, we hold that by so doing he has in fact undertaken to do anything that we tell him; and we maintain that anyone who disobeys is guilty of doing wrong on three separate counts: first because we are his parents, and secondly because we are his guardians; and thirdly because, after promising obedience, he is neither obeying us nor persuading us to change our decision if we are at fault in any way; and although all our orders are in the
52 form of proposals, not of savage commands, and we give him the choice of either persuading us or doing what we say, he is actually doing neither. These

are the charges, Socrates, to which we say that you will be liable if you do what you are contemplating; and you will not be the least culpable of your fellow-countrymen, but one of the most guilty.' If I said 'Why do you say that?' they would no doubt pounce upon me with perfect justice and point out that there are very few people in Athens who have entered into this agreement with them
b as explicitly as I have. They would say: 'Socrates, we have substantial evidence that you are satisfied with us and with the State. You would not have been so exceptionally reluctant to cross the borders of your country if you had not been exceptionally attached to it. You have never left the city to attend a festival or for any other purpose, except on some military expedition; you have never travelled abroad as other people do, and you have never felt the impulse to acquaint yourself with another country or constitution; you have been content
c with us and with our city. You have definitely chosen us, and undertaken to observe us in all your activities as a citizen; and as the crowning proof that you are satisfied with our city, you have begotten children in it. Furthermore, even at the time of your trial you could have proposed the penalty of banishment, if you had chosen to do so; that is, you could have done then with the sanction of the State what you are now trying to do without it. But whereas at that time you made a noble show of indifference if you had to die, and in fact preferred death, as you said, to banishment, now you show no respect for your earlier professions, and no regard for us, the Laws, whom you are trying to destroy;
d you are behaving like the lowest type of menial, trying to run away in spite of the contracts and undertakings by which you agreed to live as a member of our State. Now first answer this question: Are we or are we not speaking the truth when we say that you have undertaken, in deed if not in word, to live your life as a citizen in obedience to us?' What are we to say to that, Crito? Are we not bound to admit it?

CRITO: We cannot help it, Socrates.

SOCRATES: 'It is a fact, then,' they would say, 'that you are breaking covenants
e and undertakings made with us, although you made them under no compulsion or misunderstanding, and were not compelled to decide in a limited time; you had seventy years in which you could have left the country, if you were not satisfied with us or felt that the agreements were unfair. You did not choose Sparta or Crete – your favourite models of good government – or any other
53 Greek or foreign state; you could not have absented yourself from the city less if you had been lame or blind or decrepit in some other way. It is quite obvious that you stand by yourself above all other Athenians in your affection for this city and for us its Laws; – who would care for a city without laws? And now, after all this, are you not going to stand by your agreement? Yes, you are, Socrates, if you will take our advice; and then you will at least escape being laughed at for leaving the city.'

Plato *Crito* 50a6–53a7
tr. H. Tredennick (Penguin 1959)

G WOMEN

Women had less freedom in Athens than in the Dorian states. On the whole it is fair to say that the woman's place was in the home. Home management involved turning raw materials into usable goods; preparing and preserving food as well as spinning and weaving (see no. G2). Another important facet of their social role was the bearing of legitimate heirs. Yet the end of the Funeral Speech, where Pericles asserts that a woman's greatest glory is not to be talked about by men for *good or ill,* is justly cited as a characteristic Athenian ideal. They married young, immediately on puberty, at twelve to fifteen, being much younger than their husbands. If 'Oriental seclusion' is an overstatement, Victorianism is not far out. A different view is taken by A. W. Gomme *Essays in History and Literature* (Oxford University Press 1937) pp. 89–115; H. D. F. Kitto *The Greeks* (Penguin 1951); C. T. Seltman 'Atalanta' *Cornhill Magazine* 983 (1950) 296–305. For a careful disagreement see W. K. Lacey *The Family in Classical Greece* (London University Press 1968). The *hetairai, femmes de société,* of whom Aspasia was the most celebrated, had more social freedom.

G1 The Woman's Place

A close parallel with Pericles's words in Thucydides 2, 45 (Introduction).

ANDROMACHE: Fault them or not, there is
one prime source of scandal
for a woman, when she won't stay indoors.
I longed to go out, but no! I stayed at home
And indoors I didn't practise saucy speech,
like some women. My mind, sound by nature,
was my teacher. I needed no more.
I offered my husband a silent tongue
and gentle looks. I knew when to have my way and
when to let him have his.

Euripides *The Women of Troy* 642–51

G2 How to Bring up a Wife

This is the fundamental primary source for an upper-class Athenian home, and the relations between husband and wife.

– 'But pray tell me,' said Socrates, 'did you instruct your wife how to manage your house, or was it her father and mother that gave her sufficient instructions to order a house before she came to you?' – 'My wife,' answered Ischomachus, 'was but fifteen years old when I married her; and till then she had been so negligently brought up, that she hardly knew anything of worldly affairs.' – 'I suppose,' said Socrates, 'she could spin, and card, or set her servants to work.' – 'As for such things, good Socrates,' replied Ischomachus, 'she had her share of knowledge.' – 'And did you teach her all the rest,' said Socrates, 'which relates to the management of a house?' – 'I did,' replied Ischomachus, 'but not before I had implored the assistance of the gods, to show me what instructions were necessary for her; and that she might have a heart to learn and practise those instructions to the advantage and profit of us both.' – 'But, good Ischomachus, tell me,' said Socrates, 'did your wife join with you in your petition to the gods?' – 'Yes,' replied Ischomachus, 'and I looked upon that to be no bad omen of her disposition to receive such instructions as I should give her.' – 'I pray you, good Ischomachus, tell me,' said Socrates, 'what was the first thing you began to show her? for to hear that, will be a greater pleasure to me, than if you were to describe the most triumphant feast that had ever been celebrated.' – 'To begin then, good Socrates, when we were well enough acquainted, and were so familiar that we began to converse freely with one another, I asked her for what reason she thought I had taken her to be my wife, that it was not purely to make her a partner of my bed, for that she knew I had women enough already at my command; but the reason why her father and mother had consented she should be mine, was because we concluded her a proper person to be a partner in my house and children: for this end I informed her it was, that I chose her before all other women; and with the same regard her father and mother chose me for her husband: and if we should be so much favoured by the gods that she should bring me children, it would be our business jointly to consult about their education, and how to bring them up in the virtues becoming mankind; for then we may expect them to be profitable to us, to defend us, and comfort us in our old age. I further added, that our house was now common to us both, as well as our estates; for all that I had I delivered into her care, and the same she did likewise on her part to me; and likewise that all these goods were to be employed to the advantage of us both, without upbraiding one or the other, which of the two had brought the greatest fortune; but let our study be, who shall contribute most to the improvement of the fortunes we have brought together; and accordingly wear the honour they may gain by their good management.

'To this, good Socrates, my wife replied, "How can I help you in this?" . . .

. . . "Use your endeavour, good wife," said Ischomachus, "to do those things which are acceptable to the gods, and are appointed by the law for you to do." – "And what things are those, dear husband?" said the wife of Ischomachus. "They are things," replied he, "which are of no small concern, unless you think that the bee which remains always in the hive, is unemployed: it is her part to oversee the bees that work in the hive, while the others are abroad to gather wax and honey; and it is, in my opinion, a great favour of the gods to give us such lively examples, by such little creatures, of our duty to assist one another in the good ordering of things; for, by the example of the bees, a husband and wife may see the necessity of being concerned together towards the promoting and advancing of their stock: and this union between the man and woman is no less necessary to prevent the decay and loss of mankind, by producing children which may help to comfort and nourish their parents in their old age. . . .

. . . Little children must be brought up in the house, bread must be made in the house, and all kinds of meats must be dressed in the house; likewise spinning, carding and weaving, are all works to be done within doors; so that both the things abroad, and those within the house, require the utmost care and diligence; and it appears plainly, by many natural instances, that the woman was born to look after such things as are to be done within the house: for a man naturally is strong of body, and capable of enduring the fatigue of heat and cold, of travelling and undergoing the harsher exercise; so that it seems as if nature had appointed him to look after the affairs without doors: the woman being also to nurse and bring up children, she is naturally of a more soft and tender nature than the man; and it seems likewise that nature has given the woman a greater share of jealousy and fear than to the man, that she may be more careful and watchful over those things which are intrusted to her care; and it seems likely, that the man is naturally made more hardy and bold than the woman, because his business is abroad in all seasons, and that he may defend himself against all assaults and accidents. But because both the man and the woman are to be together for both their advantages, the man to gather his substance from abroad, and the woman to manage and improve it at home, they are indifferently endowed with memory and diligence. It is natural also to both to refrain from such things as may do them harm, and likewise they are naturally given to improve in every thing they study, by practice and experience; but as they are not equally perfect in all things, they have the more occasion of one another's assistance: for when the man and woman are thus united, what the one has occasion for is supplied by the other: therefore, good wife, seeing this is what the gods have ordained for us, let us endeavour, to the utmost of our powers, to behave ourselves in our several stations to the improvement of our fortune: and the law, which brought us together, exhorts us to the same purpose. And also, as it is natural, when we are thus settled, to expect children, the law exhorts us to live together in unity, and to be partakers of one another's benefits: so nature, and the law which is directed by it, ordains that each severally should regard the business that is appointed for them. From whence it appears, that it is more convenient for a woman to be at home and mind her domestic affairs, than to gad abroad; and it is as shameful for a man to be at home idling, when his business requires him to be abroad: if any man acts in a different capacity from that he is born to, he breaks through the decrees of nature, and will certainly meet his punishment, either because he neglects the business which is appointed for him, or because he invades the property of another. I think that the mistress bee is an excellent example for the wife." – "And what is the business of the mistress bee," said the wife of Ischomachus, "that I may follow the example of that which you so much recommend to me, for it seems you have not yet fully explained it?" – "The mistress bee," replied Ischomachus, "keeps always in the hive, taking care that all the bees, which are in the hive with her, are duly employed in their several occupations; and those whose business lies abroad, she sends out to their several works. These bees, when they bring home their burthen, she receives, and appoints them to lay up their harvest, till there is occasion to use it, and in a proper season dispenses it among those of her colony, according to their several offices. The bees who stay at home, she employs in disposing and ordering the combs, with a neatness and regularity becoming the nicest observation and greatest prudence. She takes care likewise of the young bees, that they are well nourished, and educated to the business that belongs to them; and when they are come to such perfection that they are able to go abroad and work for their living, she sends them forth under the direction of a proper leader." – "And is this my business, dear Ischomachus?" said his wife. – "This example, good wife," replied Ischomachus, "is what I give you as a lesson worthy your practice: your case requires your presence at home, to send abroad the servants whose business lies abroad, and to direct those whose business is in the house. You must receive the goods that are brought into the house, and distribute such a part of them as you think necessary for the use of the family, and see that the rest be laid up till there be occasion for it; and especially avoid the extravagance of using that in a month which is appointed for twelve months' service. When the wool is brought home, observe that it be carded and spun for weaving into cloth; and particularly take care that the corn, which is brought in, be not laid up in such a manner that it grow musty and unfit for use. But, above all, that which will gain you the greatest love and affection from your servants, is to help them when they are visited with sickness, and that to the utmost of your power." Upon which his wife readily answered, "That is surely an act of charity, and becoming every mistress of good nature; for, I suppose, we cannot oblige people more than to help them when they are sick: this will surely engage the love of our servants to us, and make them doubly diligent upon every occasion." . . .

. . . "Suppose, dear wife," replied Ischomachus, "you take into your service one who can neither card nor spin, and you teach her to do those works, will it not be an honour to you? Or if you take a servant which is negligent, or does not understand how to do her business, or has been subject to pilfering, and you make her diligent, and instruct her in the manners of a good servant, and teach her honesty, will not you rejoice in your success? and will you not be pleased with your action?

So again, when you see your servants sober and discreet, you should encourage them and show them favour; but as for those who are incorrigible and will not follow your directions, or prove larcenaries, you must punish them. Consider, how laudable it will be for you to excel others in the well-ordering your house; be therefore diligent, virtuous, and modest, and give your necessary attendance on me, your children, and your house, and your name shall be honourably esteemed, even after your death; for it is not the beauty of your face and shape, but your virtue and goodness, which will bring you honour and esteem, which will last for ever." – 'After this manner, good Socrates,' cried Ischomachus, 'I first discoursed with my wife concerning her duty and care of my house.' . . .

. . . 'But tell me, good Ischomachus,' said Socrates, 'did your wife understand and practise what you taught her? – 'She promised me,' answered Ischomachus, 'both by words and by her countenance, that she agreed to what I said, and was delighted that method and good order would take off so great a share of her trouble; she rejoiced to think she should be delivered from the perplexed state she was in before, and desired that I would not delay putting my promise in practice as soon as possible, that she might reap the fruits of it.' – 'And how did you proceed, good Ischomachus?' said Socrates. 'I answered her,' said Ischomachus, 'in such a manner, that she might learn first what a house was properly designed for; that it was not ordained to be filled with curious paintings or carvings, or such unnecessary decorations; but that the house should be built with due consideration, and for the conveniency of the inhabitants; and as a proper repository for those necessaries which properly belong to a family, and, in some measure, directs us to the proper places wherein every particular ought to be placed: the most private and strongest room in the house seems to demand the money, jewels, and those other things that are rich and valuable; the dry places expect the corn; the cooler parts are the most convenient for the wine; and the more lightsome and airy part of the house for such things as require such a situation. I showed her likewise,' continued Ischomachus, 'which were the most convenient places for parlours and dining-rooms, that they might be cool in summer and warm in winter; and also, that as the front of the house stood to the south, it had the advantage of the winter's sun; and in the summer it rejoiced more in the shade, than it could do in any other situation. Then,' said Ischomachus, 'I appointed the bedchambers, and the nursery, and apartments for the women, divided from the men's lodging, that no inconveniency might happen by their meeting without our consent or approbation; for those who behave themselves well, and we allow to come together to have children, they will love us the better for it; but those, who through subtlety will endeavour to gain their ends with any of the women without consent, will be always contriving and practising ways to our disadvantage, to compass or carry on their lewd designs. When we were come thus far,' proceeded Ischomachus, 'we began to set our goods in order. In the first place, we assorted all the materials belonging to sacrifices: after that, my wife's apparel was assigned to their proper places; her richest habits by themselves, and those which were in more common use by themselves. Next to these, we appointed a wardrobe for the master's clothes; one part for his armour and such accoutrements as he used in war, and another for his wearing apparel, to be used upon common occasions: after these, we directed places for the instruments which belong to spinning, and for the bakehouse, the kitchen, and the baths; and took care, in the appointment of all these things, to make a division between those things which are most commonly required to be in use, and such as are only in use now and then: we likewise separated those things which were for a month's service from those which were to serve twelve months; for by this means we might know the better how our stock is employed. When we had done this, we instructed every servant respectively where every thing belonging to his office might be found, and directed them carefully to observe, that every implement under their care should be put into the same place where they took it from, when they had done using it; and as for such things as are but seldom required to be used, either upon festivals, or upon the reception of strangers; those we delivered into the care of a discreet woman, whom we instructed in her province; and when we had made an account with her of the goods delivered into her care, and taken it in writing, we directed her to deliver them out to those under her, as she saw proper occasions, and be careful to remember who were the persons to which she delivered every particular; and that upon receiving again the things which she had delivered out, they should be every one laid up in their proper place. In the next place, we chose a discreet, sober, and judicious woman to be our storekeeper or housekeeper, one who had a good memory, and was diligent enough to avoid faults, studying our pleasure and satisfaction in all her business, and endeavouring to gain our esteem, which we always signified by presents, by which means we gained her love and friendship for us; so that, whenever we had occasion to rejoice, we made her partaker of our mirth; or if any accident happened which brought sorrow with it, we made her acquainted with that likewise, and consulted her in it: this made her bend her mind to the advancement of our fortunes. We instructed her to show more esteem for those servants in the house whom she found were deserving of favour, than the others who neglected their duty; for we took care to observe to her, that those who did well were worthy reward in the world; while those who were deceitful and evil-minded, were rejected of the people. And then, good Socrates,' said Ischomachus, 'I let my wife know that all this would be of little effect, unless she was careful to observe that every thing was preserved in the good order we had placed it: for in cities, and in other governments that are well ordered, it is not enough to make good laws for their conduct, unless there are proper officers appointed to see them put in execution, either to reward those who deserve well, or punish the malefactors. "This, dear wife, I chiefly recommend to you," continued Ischomachus, "that you may look upon yourself as the principal overseer of the laws within our house." And I informed her also, that it was within her jurisdiction to overlook, at her own pleasure, every thing belonging to the house, as a governor of a garrison inspects into the condition of his soldiers, or as the senate of Athens review the men of arms, and the condition of their horses; that she had as great power as a queen in her own house, to distribute rewards to the virtuous and diligent, and punish those servants who deserved it. But I further desired her, not to be displeased, if I intrusted her with more things, and more business, than I had done any of our servants;' . . .

. . . 'Then,' continued Ischomachus, 'I remember, on a particular day, she had painted her face with a certain cosmetic, attempting to make her skin look fairer than it was; and with another mixture had endeavoured to increase the natural bloom of her cheeks; and also had put on higher shoes than ordinary, to make her look taller than she naturally was. When I perceived this,' said Ischomachus, 'I saluted her in the following manner: "Tell me, good wife, which would make me the most acceptable in your eyes, to deal sincerely by you, in delivering into your possession those things which are really my own, without making more of my estate than it is; or for me to deceive you, by producing a thousand falsities which have nothing in them: giving you chains of brass instead of gold, false jewels, false money, and false purple, instead of that which is true and genuine?" To which she presently replied: "May the gods forbid that you should be such a man! for, should you harbour such deceit in your heart, I should never love you." – "I tell you then, dear wife," replied Ischomachus, "we are come together, to love one another, and to delight in each other's perfections: do you think I should be the more agreeable to you in my person, or should you love me the better, if I was to put a false lustre upon myself, that I might appear better complexioned, more fair in body, or more manly than what nature has made me; or that I should paint and anoint my face, when you receive me to your arms, and give you this deceit instead of my natural person?" – "Surely, dear Ischomachus," replied his wife, "your own person, in its natural perfections, is preferable to all the paints and ointments you can use to set it off; nor can all the art you might use be comparable to your natural appearance." – "Believe then, good wife," said Ischomachus, "that I have the same abhorrence of false lustre that you have: can there be any thing more complete in nature than yourself? or would there be any thing less engaging to me than that you should use any means to hide or destroy those perfections in you which I so much admire? The God of nature has appointed beauties in all creatures, as well in the field as among the human race; the magnificence of the male to be admired by the female, and the tender and curious texture of the female to be admired by the male. It is natural for the creatures in the field to distinguish one another by the purity of their beauties; there is no deceit, there is no corruption: so the men always admire that body which is most pure, or the least deformed by art. Such wiles and deceits may, perhaps, deceive strangers, because they will not have opportunities of discovering and laughing at them; but if such things should be practised between those who are daily conversant with one another, how soon will the imposition be discovered! how soon will they be ridiculed! For these deceits appear at the rising out of bed, and from that time till the persons have had opportunity of renewing them; as well as when they sweat, when they shed tears, when they wash, and when they bathe themselves." . . .

. . . I then directed her that she should not sit too much, but exercise herself about the house as a mistress, to examine how her several works went forward;

sometimes to go among the spinners or weavers, to see that they did their duty, and to instruct those who were ignorant, and encourage the most deserving among them; sometimes to look into the bake-house, to see the neatness and order of the woman that looks after it; and sometimes visit her housekeeper, to account with her for the yarn, or other commodities, that are brought into her charge: and now and then to take a turn about her house, to see that every thing is disposed in its proper place. This method, I suppose,' said Ischomachus, 'would be a means of giving her a healthful exercise, and at the same time of leading her to that business which would be for her advantage, in benefiting our fortune. I also told her, the exercise of bolting, baking, and looking after the furniture of her house, to brush it and keep it clean, when she wanted something to do, would be commendable, and help to employ her; for I recommended exercise to her as a great benefit: "for exercise," said Ischomachus, "will create you an appetite to your meat, and by that means you will be more healthful, and add, if possible, to the bloom of your beauty: and also the clean appearance of the mistress among the servants, and her readiness to set her hand to work, will encourage them to follow her example; for a good example does more than all the compulsion that can be used. Those who study nothing but their dress, may indeed be esteemed by those who understand nothing else; but the outside appearance is deceitful. And now, good Socrates, I have a wife who lives up to the rules given her.'

Xenophon *Oeconomicus* 7–10
tr. R. Bradley (London 1727)

G3 Eugenics in Plato's Ideal State

The law, I said, which is the sequel of this and of all that has preceded, is to the
457 d following effect, – 'that all these women are to be common to all the men of the same class, none living privately together; and, moreover, that their children are to be common, and no parent is to know his own child, nor any child his parent.'

Yes, he said, you will find it much harder to convince anyone either of the possibility or of the usefulness of such a law.

I do not think, I said, that there can be any dispute about the very great utility of having both women and children in common; the possibility is quite another matter, and will, no doubt, be very much disputed. . . .

First, I think that if our rulers and their auxiliaries are to be worthy of the name which they bear, there must be the power of command in the one and willingness to
458 c obey in the other; the guardians must themselves obey the laws, and they must also imitate the spirit of them in any details which are entrusted to their care.

That is right, he said.

You, I said, who are their legislator, having selected the men, will now select the women and give them to them; – they must be as far as possible of like natures with them; and they must live in common houses and meet at common meals. None of them will have anything specially his or her own; they will be together, and will be brought up together, and will associate at gymnastic exercises. And so they will be drawn by a necessity of their natures to have intercourse with each other – necessity is not too strong a word, I think? d

Yes, he said; – necessity, not geometrical, but another sort of necessity which lovers know, and which is far more convincing and constraining to the mass of mankind.

True, Glaucon, I said; but now we can hardly allow promiscuous unions, or any other kind of disorder; in a city of the blessed, licentiousness is an unholy thing which the rulers will forbid. e

Yes, he said, and it ought not to be permitted.

Then clearly the next thing will be to arrange marriages that are sacred in the highest degree; and what is most beneficial will be deemed sacred?

Exactly.

And how can marriages be made most beneficial? – that is a question which I put to you, because I see in your house dogs for hunting, and of the nobler sort of birds not a few. Now, I beseech you, do tell me, have you ever attended to their pairing and breeding? 459

In what particulars?

Why, in the first place, although they are all of good pedigree, do not some prove to be better than others?

True.

And do you breed from them all indifferently, or do you take care to breed from the best only?

From the best.

From the oldest or the youngest, or only those of ripe age? b

From those of ripe age.

And if care was not taken in the breeding, your dogs and birds would greatly deteriorate?

Certainly.

What of horses and of animals in general? Is there any difference?

No, it would be strange if there were.

Good heavens! my dear friend, I said, what consummate skill will our rulers need if the same principle holds of the human species!

Certainly, the same principle holds; but why does this involve any particular skill? c

Because, I said, our rulers will often have to practise upon the body corporate with medicines. Now you know that when patients do not require medicines but have only to be put under a regimen, the inferior sort of practitioner is deemed to be good enough; but when medicine has to be given, then the doctor should be more of a man.

That is quite true, he said; but to what are you alluding?

I mean, I replied, that our rulers will find a considerable dose of falsehood and deceit necessary for the good of their subjects: we said before that the use of all
d these things regarded as medicines might be of advantage.

And we were very right.

And this lawful use of them seems likely to be often needed in the regulations of marriages and births.

How so?

Why, I said, the principle has been already laid down that the best of either sex should be united with the best as often, and the inferior with the inferior as seldom, as possible; and that they should rear the offspring of the one sort of un-
e ion but not of the other, if the flock is to be maintained in first-rate condition. Now these goings-on must be a secret which the rulers only know, in order to keep our herd, as the guardians may be termed, as free as possible from dissension.

Very true.

Had we not better appoint certain festivals at which we will bring together the brides and bridegrooms, and sacrifices will be offered, and suitable hymeneal
460 songs composed by our poets: the number of weddings is a matter which must be left to the discretion of the rulers, whose aim will be to preserve the same total number of guardians, having regard to wars, plagues, and any similar agencies, in order as far as this is possible to prevent the State from becoming either too large or too small.

Certainly, he replied.

We shall have to invent some ingenious kind of lottery, so that the less worthy may, on each occasion of our bringing them together, accuse their own ill luck and not the rulers.

To be sure, he said.

b And I think that our braver and better youth, besides their other honours and rewards, might have greater facilities of intercourse with women given them; their bravery will be a reason, and such fathers ought to have as many sons as possible.

True. . . .

We were saying that the parents should be in the prime of life?

Very true.

e And what is the prime of life? May it not be defined as a period of about twenty years in a woman's life, and thirty in a man's?

Which years do you mean to include?

A woman, I said, at twenty years of age may begin to bear children to the State, and continue to bear them until forty; a man may begin at five-and-twenty, when he has passed the point at which the pulse of life beats quickest, and continue to beget children until he be fifty-five.

461 Certainly, he said, both in men and women those years are the prime of physical as well as of intellectual vigour.

Anyone above or below the prescribed ages who presumes to beget children for the commonwealth shall be said to have done an unholy and unrighteous thing; the child of which he is the father, if it steals into life, will have been conceived under auspices very unlike the sacrifices and prayers which at each hymeneal priestesses and priests and the whole city will offer, that the new generation may be better and more useful than their good and useful parents; whereas his child will be the offspring of darkness and strange lust. b

Very true, he replied.

And the same law will apply to any one of those within the prescribed age who forms a connection with any woman in the prime of life without the sanction of the rulers; for we shall say that he is raising up a bastard to the State, unsponsored and unconsecrated.

Very true, he replied.

This applies, however, only to men and women within the specified age: after that we shall probably allow them to range at will, except that a man may not marry his daughter or his daughter's daughter, or his mother or his mother's c mother; and women, on the other hand, are prohibited from marrying their sons or fathers, or son's son or father's father, and so on in either direction. And we grant all this, accompanying the permission with strict orders to prevent any embryo which may come into being from seeing the light; and if any force a way to the birth, the parents must understand that the offspring of such a union cannot be maintained, and arrange accordingly.

That also, he said, is a reasonable proposition. But how will they know who are fathers and daughters, and so on? d

They will never know. The way will be this: – dating from the day of the hymeneal, the bridegroom who was then married will call all the male children who are born in the tenth month afterwards, and indeed in the seventh, his sons, and the female children his daughters, and they will call him father, and he will call their children his grandchildren, and they will call the elder generation grandfathers and grandmothers. All who were begotten at the time when their fathers and mothers came together will be called brothers and sisters, and these, as I was saying, will be forbidden to intermarry. This, however, is not an absolute prohibition of the marriage of brothers and sisters; if the lot favours them, and they e receive the sanction of the Pythian oracle, the law will allow them.

Quite right, he replied.

Such is the scheme, Glaucon, according to which the guardians of our State are to have their wives and families in common. And now you would have it established by argument that this community is consistent with the rest of our polity, and also that nothing can be better – would you not?

Plato *Republic* 5, 457c–e; 458b–460b; 460d–461e
tr. B. Jowett (Oxford 1953)

G4 Home Life

A husband who killed his wife's seducer gives a picture of their domestic arrangements.

Athenians, when I decided to marry, and brought a wife to my house, for a while I was inclined not to bother her, but neither was she to be too free to do as she wished. I watched her as much as was possible, and took my duty as a husband seriously. But when my son was born, I began to trust her, and put all my possessions in her hands, presuming that this was the greatest proof of intimacy.

In the beginning, Athenians, she was the best of all wives. She was clever, economical, and kept everything neat in the house. But then my mother died; and her death was the cause of all my troubles. For when my wife attended her funeral, she was seen by this man, and, as time passed, he seduced her. He looked out for our slave who goes to market and, making propositions, he corrupted her.

Now first, gentlemen, I must tell you that I have a small two-storey house, with the women's quarters upstairs, the men's downstairs, each having equal space.

When our son was born, his mother nursed him; but in order that she might avoid the risk of climbing downstairs each time she had to clean the baby, I used to live upstairs and the women below. And so it became quite customary for my wife to go downstairs often and sleep with the child, so that she could give him the breast and keep him from crying.

This was the situation for a long time, and I never became suspicious, but I was so simple-minded that I believed my own was the chastest wife in the city.

Time passed, gentlemen; I came home unexpectedly from the country, and after dinner my son began crying and fretting. Actually, the slave was annoying him on purpose to make him do this, for the man was in the house – as I found out later.

I told my wife to go and give the baby the breast, to stop his crying. At first she refused, as though glad to see me home again after my long absence. Then I became angry and told her to go.

'Oh, yes,' she said, 'so that you can have a try at the little slave girl here. You dragged her about before, when you were drunk!'

I laughed. She got up, went out of the room, closed the door, pretending it was a joke, and turned the key in the lock. I, thinking nothing about it, nor having the slightest suspicion, was glad to go to sleep after my journey from the country.

Toward dawn she returned and unlocked the door. I asked her why the doors had been creaking during the night. She said that the lamp beside the baby had gone out and she had gone to get a light at the neighbour's.

I was silent, and thought it really was so. But it did seem to me, gentlemen, that she had put make-up on her face, despite her brother's death less than thirty days before. Even so, I said nothing about what she did. I just left, without a word.

Lysias 1, 6–14
tr. Sarah P. Pomeroy *Goddesses, Whores, Wives and Slaves*
(Schocken Books 1975)

G5 The Object of Marriage

Socrates is speaking to his son. See also Demosthenes Against Neaera *122.*

Plainly we look for wives who will produce the best children for us, and marry them to raise a family. The husband supports the wife who is to share in the production of his family, and provides in advance whatever he thinks the expected children will find useful for life, on as generous a scale as possible. The wife conceives and bears her burden. She suffers pains and endangers her life; she gives away the food that sustains her. She goes through a period of labour, gives birth and brings up the child with care. She has had no blessing in advance. The baby does not know its helper, and cannot convey its needs. She has to guess what is good for it and will satisfy it, and tries to provide these to the full. She cares for the baby night and day laboriously for a long period, with no expectation of reward.

Xenophon *Memorabilia* 2, 2, 4–5

G6 A Wife's Financial Position

This passage shows that some women were concerned with more than housework, and could initiate steps to protect themselves. (The expedition referred to was that of 409.)

Diodotus and Diogeiton, gentlemen of the jury, were brothers. . . . When Diodotus had made a large fortune in shipping business, Diogeiton induced him to marry the one daughter that he had, and two sons and a daughter were born to him. Some time later, when Diodotus was enrolled for infantry service, he summoned his wife who was his niece, and her father, who was also his father-in-law and his brother . . . he then gave him a will and five talents of silver in deposit; and he also produced an account of his loans on bottomry, amounting to seven talents and forty minae. . . . He charged him, in case anything should happen to himself, to dower his wife and his daughter with a talent each, and to give his wife the contents of the room; he also bequeathed to his wife twenty minae and thirty staters of Cyzicus. Having made these arrangements and left duplicate deeds in his house, he went to serve abroad with Thrasyllus. He was killed at Ephesus: for a time Diogeiton concealed from his daughter the death of her husband, and took possession of the deeds . . .

(The wife is remarried and seven years later when the oldest son came of age the boys were thrown out of their uncle's house, their patrimony unaccounted for. The wife goes to her son-in-law for help.)

. . . In the end, their mother implored and entreated me to assemble her father and friends together, saying that even though she had not before been accustomed to speak in the presence of men, the severity of their misfortunes would compel her to give us a full account of their hardships. . . . When we held our meeting, the mother asked him what heart he could have, that he thought fit to take such measures with the children. . . . 'For you received from him, when he went on the expedition, five talents in deposit . . .' And she convicted him further of having recovered seven talents and four thousand drachmae of bottomry loans, and she produced the record of these; for she showed that in the course of his removal from Collytus to the house of Phaedrus the children had happened upon the register, which had been mislaid, and had brought it to her. She also proved that he had recovered a hundred minae which had been lent at interest on land mortgages, besides two thousand drachmas and some furniture of great value: and that corn came in to them every year from the Chersonese.

Lysias 32, 4–7, 11–15
tr. W. R. Lamb (Loeb 1930)

G7 Women

In Aristophanes's The Women in Parliament *Praxagora is rehearsing a speech which she will give in the assembly disguised as a man. Of course for comic purposes it includes some of the stock jokes against women, themselves indicative of social attitudes.*

PRAXAGORA: I will demonstrate that they are our
superiors. First one and all, they colour
their wool in boiling dyes, in the traditional
way; you'd never find them
changing. If we'd stuck loyally to this,

instead of chasing after novelties,
wouldn't our country have been saved?
They sit down to cook, as in days gone by;
they carry bundles on their heads, as in days gone by;
they celebrate Demeter's Mysteries, as in days gone by;
they bake their cakes, as in days gone by;
they nag their husbands, as in days gone by;
they receive their lovers, as in days gone by;
they buy goodies on the sly, as in days gone by;
they adore pure wine, as in days gone by;
they enjoy sex, as in days gone by.

Aristophanes *Ecclesiazusae* 214–28

G8 Domestic Duties

The women find it difficult to get to a meeting.

CALONICE: Oh my dear,
they'll come. It's not easy for women to get away.
We're always dancing attendance on our husbands,
or getting the maid moving, or putting
the baby to bed, bathing it, feeding it.

Aristophanes *Lysistrata* 15–19

G9 Putting the Ladies to Work

One day he saw Aristarchus looking grim, and said, 'My dear Aristarchus, you seem to have something on your mind. You should share it with your friends; we might perhaps relieve you.'

'Well, Socrates,' said Aristarchus, 'I don't really know what to do. Since the revolution there's been a general exodus to Piraeus. My sisters and cousins and nieces were left behind, and have come *en masse* to me. That makes fourteen in the house, not counting the slaves . . . It's hard to see one's own family die, but I can't support that number in times like this.'

Socrates listened and replied, ' I wonder why Ceramon with a large household to feed provides for himself and his family and makes a handsome profit, while you're scared that you'll all starve to death.'

'That's easy,' he said. 'His are slaves, mine free.'

'Which are better, your free women or Ceramon's slaves?'

'My free women, of course.'

'Isn't it a disgrace for you to be brought to penury by higher-class people, when he prospers through lower-class people?'

'Ah, but his are workers, mine have had a liberal education.'

'What's a worker? Someone who knows how to produce something useful?'

'Yes' . . .

'Are clothes for men and women useful?'

'Very much so.'

'Don't your household know how to make that sort of thing?'

'I fancy they could' . . .

'And just because they are freeborn and relatives of yours, do you think they should do nothing but eat and sleep? . . . They understand the work and it is totally appropriate for women. Understanding brings ease, speed, satisfaction and pleasure. Don't hesitate to propose it to them. It'll help you all and I fancy they'll welcome it.'

'By the gods,' said Aristarchus, 'a good idea, Socrates. I was reluctant to borrow money which I wouldn't be able to repay, but I believe I'll borrow capital to make a start.'

He did so, and purchased wool with it. The women lunched while working and only broke off for dinner. Frowns gave way to smiles, grumbles to contentment. They loved him as a protector, he was satisfied with them as being of practical use. Finally he went to Socrates and told him with a laugh that their only grouse against him was that he was the only person in the house who didn't work for his food.

Xenophon *Memorabilia* 2, 7, 1–12

G10 Honest Poverty

The wives of poor men might well be at work, in petty trading (like Euripides's mother, if we may believe Aristophanes) as mid-wives (like Socrates's mother) or as wet-nurses. In this speech Euxitheus is appealing against a decision to strike him off the register of citizens. The fact that his mother was a petty trader and a nurse is no evidence that she was an alien; on the contrary. The crisis was the end of the Peloponnesian War.

He has also charged my mother with acting as a wet-nurse. During the crisis, a period of widespread difficulties, this happened; we do not deny it. I will give you a complete picture of the occasion and reasons. Do not let this prejudice you, gentlemen. You will find many Athenian citizens acting as wet-nurses today; I will name them, if you like. Of course if we were rich we should not now be selling ribbons; we should not need to. But what has this to do with my family standing as a free-born Athenian? Nothing, I submit.

Demosthenes *Against Eubulides* 35

G11 The Family Hierarchy

Themistocles used to say of his son (who bullied his mother and, through her, himself) that he was the most powerful person in Greece. The Athenians controlled the rest of Greece, he himself controlled the Athenians, the boy's mother controlled him, and the boy controlled his mother.

Plutarch *Themistocles* 18

G12 Socrates's Wife

Many stories were later told of Socrates and Xanthippe, but they are typical anecdotes of the patient, or impractical, philosopher. Plato's story of his dismissal of her on the morning of his execution is a more reliable picture, though it is hard to know whether it is curt or kindly.

We went in and found Socrates just released from his chains, and Xanthippe – you know her – sitting by him with their child in her arms. When Xanthippe saw us she burst out with the sort of sentiments women will produce: 'Socrates, this is the last time you and your friends will talk together.' Socrates looked towards Crito and said, 'Crito, someone had better take her home.'

Plato *Phaedo* 60a

G13 Aspasia

In an Athens where the woman's place was in the home, a woman like Aspasia, daughter of Axiochus of Miletus, a woman of high culture and political acumen, created something of a sensation.

It has been suggested that Aspasia's influence on Pericles was due to her political acumen. Socrates used to bring his circle to visit her, and his associates brought their wives along to listen to her talk, ignoring the disreputable business she managed, the training of young prostitutes. Aeschines tells us that a sheep-dealer named Lysicles, a man of humble origin, attained a leading place in Athens through his association with Aspasia after Pericles's death. In Plato's *Menexenus*, recognizing that the initial passages were written for their entertainment value, there is the factual statement that the woman had a high reputation in Athens for her crowded seminars on public speaking. However, Pericles's attachment to Aspasia was clearly sexual. His own wife was a relative, previously married to Hipponicus. Their son was the millionaire Callias; she and Pericles produced Xanthippus and Paralus. Later, he became disenchanted with their married life and by mutual agreement arranged for her remarriage. He took Aspasia and loved her dearly. Every day on leaving for his public business and on returning he would kiss her.

Plutarch *Pericles* 24

G14 Prostitutes

A description from Middle Comedy, from Alexis's Fair Measure.

In the first place, they are aiming at profit and robbing their
neighbour,
all else goes for nothing, they're busily stitching
plots against all. And when they get rich,
they take in fresh prostitutes, new to the profession.
They are quick to remodel them; their ways,
their looks are no longer as before.
One is rather short. A cork sole is stitched
into her shoes. One is too tall. She wears thin slippers,
and carries her head on one side while walking,
to take away from her height. One has no hips.
She sews on a bustle under her dress, and those who see it

shout, 'What a lovely bottom!' One has a thick waist.
They have bosoms of the stuff actors in comedy use
padding themselves straight, and pulling and hauling
the corsets forward; they need punt-poles to do it.
One has blonde eyebrows. They paint them with lampblack.
One is too dark-complexioned; she is smeared with white-lead.
One is too pale; she applies rouge.
One is beautiful – in part. That part is revealed bare.
One has attractive teeth. She must always be laughing
so that those present can see what a nice mouth she has.
If she doesn't want to laugh, she has to spend the whole day
indoors, and like the stuff on the butcher's counter,
when they are selling goat's head, she has to keep
a slim stick of myrtle vertically beween her lips,
till as time passes, she's grinning whether she wants to or not.

Alexis in Athenaeus 13, 568a–d

G15 Women's Ornaments

Aristophanes, in a fragment of his Thesmophoriazusae, *jokes about women's ornaments. Hellebore is an antidote to madness. Bubbles are a kind of cap. 'Sudden death' and 'death-pit' presumably refer to the sex-organs.*

A: Here's razor, mirror, scissors, wax-salve, soda,
A false front, trimmings, hair-ribbons, bandeaux,
Alkanet, 'sudden death', some face powder,
Some scent, a pumice-stone, breastbands, a hair-bag,
A veil, some rouge, two necklaces, some eye paint,
Peignoir, some hellebore, a hair-net, girdle,
Shawl, woollie, bordered wrapper, velvet gown,
Camisole, 'death-pit', tippet, curling-tongs –
The best is yet to come.

B: Well, tell me what.

A: Earrings, a pendant, *more* earrings – a lot,
Pins, necklet, armlet, bangles, carcanets,
Anklets, seals, chains, rings, plasters, bandelettes,
'Bubbles', carnelians, baubons, *more* earrings –
It's past man's power to tell you all the things.

Aristophanes fr. 320K
tr. J. M. Edmonds *The Fragments of Attic Comedy* I
(Leiden 1957) p. 663

G16 Male Chauvinism

A similar story is told of a number of people, including Socrates.

So Plato gave thanks to nature, first that he was born a human being rather than a dumb animal; second that he was a man rather than a woman; then that he was a Greek not a foreigner; finally that he was Athenian born in the time of Socrates.

Lactantius *Divine Institutions* 3, 19

H ARCHITECTURE AND SCULPTURE

There are few surviving descriptions of classical works of art that are even nearly contemporary, and the Greeks were surprisingly reticent in art criticism. Many of our sources, therefore, were written several centuries after the classical period. The material presented here consists partly of later descriptive and analytical works but also gives considerable weight to the contemporary epigraphical records which provide a fascinating insight into means of financing and methods of working.

For sculpture see the standard G. M. A. Richter *The Sculpture and Sculptors of the Greeks* (Yale University Press, New Haven 1970) and A. W. Lawrence *Greek and Roman Sculpture* (Jonathan Cape 1972). Technically important are C. Bluemel *Greek Sculptors at Work* (English translation, Phaidon 1969) and S. Adam *The Technique of Greek Sculpture in the Archaic and Classical Periods* (Proceedings of the British School at Athens Supp. 3 1966). For architecture there are three standard works: W. B. Dinsmoor *The Architecture of Ancient Greece* (B. T. Batsford 1950); D. S. Robertson *A Handbook of Greek and Roman Architecture* (Cambridge University Press 1959); A. W. Lawrence *Greek Architecture* (Penguin 1969). On the Parthenon see G. T. W. Hooker (ed) *Parthenos and Parthenon* (Greece and Rome Supplement 1963). J. J. Pollitt *Art and Experience in Classical Greece* (Cambridge University Press 1972) is a suggestive social commentary. Rhys Carpenter *Greek Art* (University of Pennsylvania Press 1962) tackles the central aesthetic questions. C. M. Robertson *Greek Art* (Cambridge University Press 1975, 2 vols) is an outstanding general study.

H1 The Importance of Environment

Plato in this very brief passage acknowledges the important effect of works of art on the spectator.

Thus, then, excellence of form and content in discourse and of musical expression and rhythm, and grace of form and movement, all depend on goodness of nature, by which I mean, not the foolish simplicity sometimes called by courtesy 'good nature', but a nature in which goodness of character has been well and truly established.

Yes, certainly.

So, if our young men are to do their proper work in life, they must follow after
401 these qualities wherever they may be found. And they are to be found in every sort of workmanship, such as painting, weaving, embroidery, architecture, the making of furniture; and also in the human frame and in all the works of nature: in all these grace and seemliness may be present or absent. And the absence of grace, rhythm, harmony is nearly allied to baseness of thought and expression and baseness of character; whereas their presence goes with that moral excellence and self-mastery of which they are the embodiment.

That is perfectly true.

b Then we must not only compel our poets, on pain of expulsion, to make their poetry the express image of noble character; we must also supervise craftsmen of every kind and forbid them to leave the stamp of baseness, licence, meanness, unseemliness, on painting and sculpture, or building, or any other work of their hands; and anyone who cannot obey shall not practise his art in our commonwealth. We would not have our Guardians grow up among representations of
c moral deformity, as in some foul pasture where, day after day, feeding on every poisonous weed they would, little by little, gather insensibly a mass of corruption in their very souls. Rather we must seek out those craftsmen whose instinct guides them to whatsoever is lovely and gracious; so that our young men, dwelling in a wholesome climate, may drink in good from every quarter, whence, like a breeze bearing health from happy regions, some influence from noble works constantly
d falls upon eye and ear from childhood upward, and imperceptibly draws them into sympathy and harmony with the beauty of reason, whose impress they take.

Plato *Republic* 3, 400e–401d
tr. F. M. Cornford *The Republic of Plato* (Oxford 1942)

H2 Vitruvius on Greek Architecture

Vitruvius Pollio was a Roman military engineer and architect who lived at the time of Augustus in the second half of the first century BC. His writing, while it draws on his own experience, is also indebted to the Hellenistic sources. His ten books on architecture are the only surviving treatise on architecture from the ancient world.

(a)

(1) The planning of temples depends upon symmetry: and the method of this architects must diligently apprehend. It arises from proportion (which in Greek is called *analogia*). Proportion consists in taking a fixed module, in each case, both for the parts of a building and for the whole, by which the method of symmetry is

put into practice. For without symmetry and proportion no temple can have a regular plan; that is, it must have an exact proportion worked out after the fashion of the members of a finely-shaped human body . . .

Vitruvius 3, 1, 1
tr. F. Granger (Loeb 1934)

(b)

Therefore we must follow the symmetries required by the style of the work. The angle columns also must be made thicker by the fiftieth part of their diameter, because they are cut into by the air and appear more slender to the spectators. Therefore what the eye cheats us of, must be made up by calculation. (12) The contractions, however, in the topmost necking of the columns, it seems, should be so made that from the smallest dimension up to fifteen feet, the lowest diameter should be divided into six parts and the top should be of five of those parts. Also in those which shall be from fifteen feet to twenty feet, the lowest part of the shaft is to be divided into six and a half parts; and of those parts five and a half are to be the upper diameter of the column. Also in those which shall be from twenty feet to thirty feet, let the lowest part of the shaft be divided into seven parts, and let the top contraction be made six of them. In the column which shall be from thirty to forty feet, let the lowest diameter be divided into seven and a half parts; of these let the column have six and a half at the top as the amount of contraction. Those which shall be from forty to fifty feet are also to be divided into eight parts, and these are to be contracted to seven at the top of the shaft under the capital. Further, if any are higher, let the contractions be determined proportionately in the same way. (13) It is on account of the variation in height that these adjustments are added to the diameters to meet the glance of the eye as it rises. For the sight follows gracious contours; and unless we flatter its pleasure, by proportionate alterations of the modules (so that by adjustment there is added the amount to which it suffers illusion), an uncouth and ungracious aspect will be presented to the spectators. As to the swelling which is made in the middle of the columns (this among the Greeks is called *entasis*), an illustrated formula will be furnished at the end of the book to show how the entasis may be done in a graceful and appropriate manner.

Vitruvius 3, 3, 11–13
tr. F. Granger (Loeb 1934)

H3 Politics and Art

(2) Now we can best observe this in the case of ancient statuaries and painters; for of these, those who have a recognized dignity and the influence based on commendation abide to after times in an everlasting remembrance: Myron, Polyclitus, Phidias, Lysippus and others who from their art have attained renown. For they got it by working for great states or kings or famous citizens. But those who had not less eagerness, and were distinguished by talent and skill, but being of humble fortune executed for their fellow-citizens works not less perfect, gained no reputation. For they were left behind not in perseverance or in skill but by Good Fortune: for example, Hegias of Athens, Chion of Corinth, Myagrus the Phocean, Pharax of Ephesus, Boedas of Byzantium and many others also; painters also not less, such as Aristomenes the Thasian, Polycles and Androcydes of Cyzicus, Theo the Magnesian, and others to whom neither industry nor craftsman's zeal nor skill was lacking: but their reputation was hindered, either by scanty possessions, or poor fortune, or the victory of rivals in competitions. (3) Yet we must not be surprised if excellence is in obscurity through the public ignorance of craftsmanship. But we ought to be specially indignant when also, as often happens, social influence beguiles men from exact judgments to a feigned approval.

Vitruvius 3, preface 2–3
tr. F. Granger (Loeb 1934)

H4 The Acropolis

Pausanias was a traveller and geographer who lived in the second century AD and gave an accurate record of the antiquarian, historical and religious remains which he saw on his travels. Unlike Vitruvius he was interested not in the principles of design, but in the details of the temples and statues and the myths and stories they commemorated.

22 (4) There is but one entrance to the Acropolis: it admits of no other, being everywhere precipitous and fortified with a strong wall. The portal (Propylaea) has a roof of white marble, and for the beauty and size of the blocks it has never yet been matched. Whether the statues of the horsemen represent the sons of Xenophon, or are merely decorative, I cannot say for certain. On the right of the portal is a temple of Wingless Victory. (5) From this point the sea is visible, and it was here, they say, that Aegeus cast himself down and perished.

(6) On the left of the portal is a chamber containing pictures. Among the pictures which time had not effaced, were Diomede and Ulysses, the one at Lemnos carrying off the bow of Philoctetes, the other carrying off the image of Athena from Ilium. Among the paintings here is also Orestes slaying Aegisthus, and Pylades slaying Nauplius' sons, who came to the rescue of Aegisthus, and Polyxena about to be slaughtered near the grave of Achilles. Homer did well to omit so savage a deed, and he did well, I think, to represent Scyros as captured by Achilles, therein differing from those who say that Achilles lived in the company of the maidens at Scyros: it is this latter version of the legend that Polygnotus has painted. Polygnotus also painted Ulysses at the river approaching the damsels who are washing clothes with Nausicaa, just as Homer described the scene. Amongst other paintings there is a picture of Alcibiades containing emblems of the victory won by his team at Nemea. Perseus is also depicted on his way back to Seriphos, carrying the head of Medusa to Polydectes. . . .

(8) Just at the entrance to the Acropolis are figures of Hermes and the Graces, which are said to have been made by Socrates, the son of Sophroniscus. The Hermes is named Hermes of the Portal. The Pythian priestess bore witness that Socrates was the wisest of men, a title which she did not give even to Anacharsis, though he was quite willing to receive it, and had indeed come to Delphi for the purpose.. . . **23** In regard to the statue (of Diitrephes) I was surprised that it was pierced with arrows, since the Cretans are the only Greek people who are accustomed to the use of the bow. . . . (5) Near the statue of Diitrephes (for I do not wish to mention the obscurer statues) are images of gods – one of Health, who is said to be a daughter of Aesculapius, and one of Athena, who is also surnamed Health. (6) There is also a stone of no great size, but big enough for a little man to sit on. They say that when Dionysus came into the country Silenus rested on this stone. Elderly Satyrs are named Silenuses. . . .

Among other things that I saw on the Acropolis at Athens were the bronze boy holding the sprinkler, and Perseus after he has done the deed on Medusa. The boy is a work of Lycius, son of Myron: the Perseus is a work of Myron. (9) There is also a sanctuary of Brauronian Artemis: the image is a work of Praxiteles. The goddess gets her surname from the township of Brauron; and at Brauron is the old wooden image which is, they say, the Tauric Artemis. (10) There is also set up a bronze figure of the so-called Wooden Horse. Every one who does not suppose that the Phrygians were the veriest ninnies, is aware that what Epeus made was an engine for breaking down the wall. But the story goes that the Wooden Horse had within it the bravest of the Greeks, and the bronze horse has been shaped accordingly. Menestheus and Teucer are peeping out of it, and so are the sons of Theseus. (11) Among the statues that stand after the horse, the one of Epicharinus, who practised running in armour, is by Critias. Oenobius was a man who did a good deed to Thucydides, son of Olorus; for he carried a decree recalling Thucydides from banishment. But on his way home Thucydides was murdered, and his tomb is not far from the Melitian gate. (12) The histories of Hermolycus, the pancratiast, and of Phormio, the son of Asopichus, have been told by other writers, so I pass them by. This much, however, I have to add as regards Phormio. He ranked among the Athenian worthies, and came of no obscure family, but he was in debt. So he retired to the township of Paeanieus, and lived there till the Athenians elected him admiral. But he said he could not go to sea, since he owed money, and could not look his men in the face until he had paid his debts. So the Athenians discharged all his debts, for they were determined that he should have the command.

24 (1) Here Athena is represented striking Marsyas the Silenus, because he picked up the flutes when the goddess had meant that they should be thrown away. (2) Over against the works I have mentioned is the legendary fight of Theseus with the bull, which was called the bull of Minos, whether this bull was a man or, as the prevalent tradition has it, a beast; for even in our time women have given birth to much more marvellous monsters than this. Here, too, is Phrixus, son of Athamas, represented as he appeared after being carried away by the ram to the land of the Colchians: he has sacrificed the ram to some god, apparently to him whom the Orchomenians call Laphystian; and having cut off the thighs according to the Greek custom, he is looking at them burning. Among the statues which stand next in order is one of Hercules strangling the serpents according to the story; and one of Athena rising from the head of Zeus. There is also a bull set up by the Council of the Areopagus for some reason or other: one might make many guesses on the subject if one chose to do so. (3) I observed before that the zeal of the Athenians in matters of religion exceeds that of all other peoples. Thus they were the first to give Athena the surname of the Worker, and [to make] images of Hermes without limbs; . . . and in the temple with them is a Spirit of the Zealous. He who prefers the products of art to mere antiquities should observe the following: – There is a man wearing a helmet, a work of Cleoetas, who has inwrought the man's nails of silver. There is also an image of Earth praying Zeus to rain on her, either because the Athenians themselves needed rain, or because there was a drought all over Greece. Here also is a statue of Timotheus, son of Conon, and a statue of Conon himself. A group representing Procne and Itys, at the time when Procne has taken her resolution against the boy, was dedicated by Alcamenes; and Athena is represented exhibiting the olive plant, and Poseidon exhibiting the wave. (4) There is also an image of Zeus made by Leochares, and another of Zeus surnamed Polieus ('urban'). . . .

(5) All the figures in the gable over the entrance to the temple called the Parthenon relate to the birth of Athena. The back gable contains the strife of Poseidon with Athena for the possession of the land. The image itself is made of ivory and gold. Its helmet is surmounted in the middle by a figure of a sphinx (I will tell the story of the sphinx when I come to treat of Boeotia), and on either side of the helmet are griffins wrought in relief. (6) Aristeas of Proconnesus says in his poem that these griffins fight for the gold with the Arimaspians who dwell beyond the Issedonians, and that the gold which the griffins guard is produced by the earth. He says, too, that the Arimaspians are all one-eyed men from birth, and that the griffins are beasts like lions, but with the wings and beak of an eagle. So

much for the griffins. (7) The image of Athena stands upright, clad in a garment that reaches to her feet: on her breast is the head of Medusa wrought in ivory. She holds a Victory about four cubits high, and in the other hand a spear. At her feet lies a shield, and near the spear is a serpent, which may be Erichthonius. On the pedestal of the image is wrought in relief the birth of Pandora. Hesiod and other poets have told how this Pandora was the first woman, and how before the birth of Pandora womankind as yet was not. The only statue I saw there was that of the Emperor Hadrian; and at the entrance there is a statue of Iphicrates, who did many marvellous deeds.

(8) Over against the temple is a bronze Apollo: they say the image was made by Phidias. They call it Locust Apollo, because, when locusts blasted the land, the god said he would drive them out of the country. And they know that he drove them out, but how he did it they do not say. . . .

25 (1) On the Acropolis at Athens is a statue of Pericles, the son of Xanthippus, and one of Xanthippus himself, who fought the sea-fight at Mycale against the Medes. The statue of Pericles stands in a different part of the Acropolis; but near the statue of Xanthippus is one of Anacreon the Teian, the first poet, after Sappho the Lesbian, to write mostly love poems. The attitude of the statue is like that of a man singing in his cups. The figures of women near it were made by Dinomenes: they represent Io, daughter of Inachus, and Callisto, daughter of Lycaon. The tales told of these two women are exactly alike – the love of Zeus, the wrath of Hera, and the transformation of Io into a cow, and of Callisto into a bear. (2) At the south wall are figures about two cubits high, dedicated by Attalus. They represent the legendary war of the giants who once dwelt about Thrace and the isthmus of Pallene, the fight of the Athenians with the Amazons, the battle with the Medes at Marathon, and the destruction of the Gauls in Mysia.

There is a statue also of Olympiodorus, who earned fame both by the greatness and the opportuneness of his exploits, for he infused courage into men whom a series of disasters had plunged in despair. . . .

26 Near the statue of Olympiodorus stands a bronze image of Artemis surnamed Leucophryenian. It was dedicated by the sons of Themistocles; for the Magnesians, whom the king gave to Themistocles to govern, hold Leucophryenian Artemis in honour. (5) But I must proceed, for I have to describe the whole of Greece. Endoeus was an Athenian by birth and a pupil of Daedalus. When Daedalus fled on account of the murder of Calus, Endoeus followed him to Crete. There is a seated image of Athena by Endoeus: the inscription states that it was dedicated by Callias and made by Endoeus.

(6) There is also a building called the Erechtheum. Before the entrance is an altar of Supreme Zeus, where they sacrifice no living thing; but they lay cakes on it, and having done so they are forbidden by custom to make use of wine. Inside of the building are altars: one of Poseidon, on which they sacrifice also to Erechtheus in obedience to an oracle; one of the hero Butes; and one of Hephaestus. On the walls are paintings of the family of the Butads. Within, for the building is double, there is sea-water in a well. This is not very surprising, for the same thing may be

seen in inland places, as at Aphrodisias in Caria. But what is remarkable about this well is that, when the south wind has been blowing, the well gives forth a sound of waves; and there is the shape of a trident in the rock. These things are said to have been the evidence produced by Poseidon in support of his claim to the country.

(7) The rest of the city and the whole land are equally sacred to Athena; for although the worship of other gods is established in the townships, the inhabitants none the less hold Athena in honour. But the object which was universally deemed the holy of holies many years before the union of the townships, is an image of Athena in what is now called the Acropolis, but what was then called the city. The legend is that the image fell from heaven, but whether this was so or not I will not inquire. Callimachus made a golden lamp for the goddess. They fill the lamp with oil, and wait till the same day next year, and the oil suffices for the lamp during all the intervening time, though it is burning day and night. The wick is made of Carpasian flax, which is the only kind of flax that does not take fire. A bronze palm-tree placed over the lamp and reaching to the roof draws off the smoke. Callimachus, who made the lamp, though inferior to the best artists in the actual practice of his art, so far surpassed them all in ingenuity, that he was the first to bore holes in stones, and assumed, or accepted at the hands of others, the title of the Refiner away of Art.

27 (1) In the temple of the Polias is a wooden Hermes, said to be an offering of Cecrops, but hidden under myrtle boughs. Amongst the ancient offerings which are worthy of mention is a folding-chair, made by Daedalus, and spoils taken from the Medes, including the corselet of Masistius, who commanded the cavalry at Plataea, and a sword said to be that of Mardonius. Masistius, I know, was killed by the Athenian cavalry; but as Mardonius fought against the Lacedaemonians, and fell by the hand of a Spartan, the Athenians could not have got the sword originally, nor is it likely that the Lacedaemonians would have allowed them to carry it off. (2) About the olive they have nothing to say except that it was produced by the goddess as evidence in the dispute about the country. They say, too, that the olive was burned down when the Medes fired Athens, but that after being burned down it sprouted the same day to a height of two cubits. (3) Contiguous to the temple of Athena is a temple of Pandrosus, who alone of the sisters was blameless in regard to the trust committed to them. (4) What surprised me very much, but is not generally known, I will describe as it takes place. Two maidens dwell not far from the temple of the Polias: the Athenians call them Arrephoroi. These are lodged for a time with the goddess; but when the festival comes round they perform the following ceremony by night. They put on their heads the things which the priestess of Athena gives them to carry, but what it is she gives is known neither to her who gives nor to them who carry. Now there is in the city an enclosure not far from the sanctuary of Aphrodite called Aphrodite in the Gardens, and there is a natural underground descent through it. Down this way the maidens go. Below they leave their burdens, and getting something else, which is wrapt up, they bring it back. These maidens are then discharged, and others are brought to the Acropolis in their stead.

(5) Near the temple of Athena is a well-wrought figure of an old woman, just about a cubit high, purporting to be the handmaid Lysimache. There are also large bronze figures of men confronting each other for a fight: they call one of them Erechtheus and the other Eumolpus. And yet Athenian antiquaries themselves are aware that it was Eumolpus' son Immaradus that was killed by Erechtheus. (6) On the pedestal there is a statue of . . ., who was soothsayer to Tolmides, and a statue of Tolmides himself. Tolmides, in command of an Athenian fleet, ravaged various places, particularly the coast of Peloponnese . . .

There are ancient images of Athena. No part of them has been melted off, though they are somewhat blackened and brittle; for the flames reached them at the time when the Athenians embarked on their ships, and the city, abandoned by its fighting men, was captured by the king. There is also the hunting of a boar, but whether it is the Calydonian boar I do not know for certain. There is also Cyenus fighting with Hercules. . . .

(8) Of the stories which they tell in Troezen about Theseus, there is one that . . . Aegeus deposited boots and a sword under a rock as tokens of the boy's identity, and then sailed away to Athens; but when Theseus was sixteen years old, he pushed up the rock and carried off what Aegeus had deposited there. There is a statue on the Acropolis illustrative of this story: it is all of bronze except the rock. (9) They have also dedicated a representation of another exploit of Theseus. . . . It is said that Theseus afterwards drove the bull of Marathon to the Acropolis and sacrificed it to the goddess. The offering was dedicated by the township of Marathon.

28 (1) Why they set up a bronze statue of Cylon, though he compassed the tyranny, I cannot say for certain. I surmise that it was because he was an extremely handsome man, and gained some reputation by winning a victory in the double race of Olympia. Moreover he had the honour to marry a daughter of Theagenes, tyrant of Megara. (2) Besides the things I have enumerated, there are two tithe-offerings from spoils taken by the Athenians in war. One is a bronze image of Athena made from the spoils of the Medes who landed at Marathon. It is a work of Phidias. The [battle] of the Lapiths with the Centaurs on her shield, and all the other figures in relief, are said to have been wrought by Mys, but designed, like all the other works of Mys, by Parrhasius, son of Evenor. The head of the spear and the crest of the helmet of this Athena are visible to mariners sailing from Sunium to Athens. There is also a bronze chariot made out of a tithe of spoils taken from the Boeotians and the Chalcidians of Euboea. There are two other offerings, a statue of Pericles, the son of Xanthippus, and an image of Athena, surnamed Lemnian, after the people of Lemnos who dedicated it. This image of Athena is the best worth seeing of the works of Phidias.

(3) The whole of the wall which runs round the Acropolis, except the part built by Cimon, son of Miltiades, is said to have been erected by the Pelasgians who once dwelt at the foot of the Acropolis.

Pausanias 1, 22, 4–1, 28, 3
tr. J. G. Frazer *Pausanias's Description of Greece* (London 1898)

H5 Pericles's Building Schemes

Also from the second century AD comes Plutarch's account of Pericles's building schemes, but though it is not contemporary there seems little reason to doubt its substantial accuracy.

Pericles' answer to the people was that the Athenians were not obliged to give the allies any account of how their money was spent, provided that they carried on the war for them and kept the Persians away. 'They do not give us a single horse, nor a soldier, nor a ship. All they supply is money,' he told the Athenians, 'and this belongs not to the people who give it, but to those who receive it, so long as they provide the services they are paid for. It is no more than fair that after Athens has been equipped with all she needs to carry on the war, she should apply the surplus to public works, which, once completed, will bring her glory for all time, and while they are being built will convert that surplus to immediate use. In this way all kinds of enterprises and demands will be created which will provide inspiration for every art, find employment for every hand, and transform the whole people into wage-earners, so that the city will decorate and maintain herself at the same time from her own resources.'

Certainly it was true that those who were of military age and physically in their prime could always earn their pay from the public funds by serving on Pericles' various campaigns. But he was also anxious that the unskilled masses, who had no military training, should not be debarred from benefiting from the national income, and yet should not be paid for sitting about and doing nothing. So he boldly laid before the people proposals for immense public works and plans for buildings, which would involve many different arts and industries and require long periods to complete, his object being that those who stayed at home, no less than those serving in the fleet or the army or on garrison duty, should be enabled to enjoy a share of the national wealth. The materials to be used were stone, bronze, ivory, gold, ebony, and cypress-wood, while the arts or trades which wrought or fashioned them were those of carpenter, modeller, coppersmith, stone-mason, dyer, worker in gold and ivory, painter, embroiderer, and engraver, and besides these the carriers and suppliers of the materials, such as merchants, sailors, and pilots for the sea-borne traffic, and waggon-makers, trainers of draught animals, and drivers for everything that came by land. There were also rope-makers, weavers, leatherworkers, roadbuilders and miners. Each individual craft, like a general with an army under his separate command, had its own corps of unskilled labourers at its disposal, and these worked in a subordinate capacity, as an instrument obeys the hand, or the body the soul, and so through these various demands the city's prosperity was extended far and wide and shared among every age and condition in Athens.

(13) So the buildings arose, as imposing in their sheer size as they were in-

imitable in the grace of their outlines, since the artists strove to excel themselves in the beauty of their workmanship. And yet the most wonderful thing about them was the speed with which they were completed. Each of them, men supposed, would take many generations to build, but in fact the entire project was carried through in the high summer of one man's administration. On the other hand we are told that when Zeuxis the painter once heard Agatharchus boasting about how swiftly and easily he painted his figures, his retort was, 'Mine take, and last, a long time.' Certainly mere dexterity and speed of execution seldom give a lasting value to a work of art or bestow a delicate beauty upon it. It is the time laid out in laborious creation which repays us later through the enduring strength it confers. It is this, above all, which makes Pericles' works an object of wonder to us – the fact that they were created in so short a span, and yet for all time. Each one possessed a beauty which seemed venerable the moment it was born, and at the same time a youthful vigour which makes them appear to this day as if they were newly built. A bloom of eternal freshness hovers over these works of his and preserves them from the touch of time, as if some unfading spirit of youth, some ageless vitality had been breathed into them.

The director and supervisor of the whole enterprise was Pheidias, although there were various great architects and artists employed on the individual buildings. For example, Callicrates and Ictinus were the architects of the Parthenon with its cella 100 feet long; it was Coroebus who started to build the temple of initiation at Eleusis, but he only lived to see the columns erected on the lower story and the architraves placed on the capitals. After his death, Metagenes of Xypete added the frieze and the upper colonnade, and Xenocles of the deme of Cholargus crowned it with the lantern over the shrine. Callicrates was the contractor for the third Long Wall, which ran between the original two, and for which Socrates says that he himself heard Pericles propose the decree to the people. . . .

At the same time, still in pursuit of distinction, Pericles had a decree passed to establish a musical contest as part of the Panathenaic festival. He himself was elected one of the stewards and laid down rules as to how the competitors should sing or play the flute or the lyre. At that time and from thenceforward the audience came to the Odeon to hear these musical contests.

The Propylaea, or portals of the Acropolis, of which Mnesicles was the architect, were finished in the space of five years. While they were being built, a miraculous incident took place, which suggested that the goddess Athena herself, so far from standing aloof, was taking a hand and helping to complete the work. One of the workmen, the most active and energetic among them, slipped and fell from a great height. He lay for some time severely injured, and the doctors could hold out no hope that he would recover. Pericles was greatly distressed at this, but the goddess appeared to him in a dream and ordered a course of treatment, which he applied, with the result that the man was easily and quickly healed. It was to commemorate this that Pericles set up the bronze statue of Athena the Healer near the altar dedicated to that goddess, which they say was there before.

But it was Pheidias who directed the making of the great golden statue of

Athena, and his name is duly inscribed upon the marble tablet on the Acropolis as its creator. Almost the whole enterprise was in his hands, and because of his friendship with Pericles all the artists and craftsmen, as I have said, came under his orders.

Plutarch *Pericles* 12–13
tr. I. Scott-Kilvert (Penguin 1960)

H6 Financial Decrees of Callias

There is no contemporary account giving details of the way the buildings of the Acropolis fitted into Athenian life. A number of inscriptions provide evidence on various detailed points of religious procedure, finance and construction. These two decrees tell us something about the last two. In addition to their religious function the temples housed the national treasury and the provisions for security and accurate accounting are impressive. The second decree with its reference to restoration reminds us that the whole scheme took well over a generation to complete and that many older sanctuaries were incorporated in the overall design.

The date of these decrees has occasioned a long-standing controversy. H. T. Wade-Gery in Journal of Hellenic Studies *51 (1931) 57–85, showed that both, although inscribed by different hands, were moved at the same session of the assembly by the same spokesman. Probably 434–3 is right, but there are still advocates of a later date, 422–1: see e.g. H. B. Mattingly in* Proceedings of the African Classical Associations *7 (1964) 35–55. The Greek text was authoritatively published by B. D. Meritt and others in* The Athenian Tribute Lists 1, *p. 160.*

A

Decree of the Council and Commons. Committee in session: Cecropis. Secretary: Mnesitheos. President: Eupithes. Proposer: Callias.

The gods to be paid back the moneys owed to them, now that the 3,000 talents duly voted in Athenian currency have been taken up to the Acropolis for Athene. The moneys to be repaid out of those sums voted for repayment to the gods, alike those that are at present in the charge of the Treasurers of the Greeks, and the remainder of those sums, that is the proceeds of the 10 per cent tax when it is taken. The thirty treasury clerks are to make a precise reckoning of what is due to the gods. The Council is responsible for checking the clerks' assessment. The committee in session are to pay the moneys in conjunction with the Council, and to erase the entry on repayment, after checking the ledgers and minutes and other written records. The priests and religious officials and anyone else who knows are to produce the records. The treasurers for these moneys are to be selected by lot at the same time as the other officials on the same principle as those reponsible for Athene's holy places. They are to deposit the moneys belonging to the gods such as it is right and possible so to deposit, on the Acropolis in the inner cell of the temple; they are responsible for opening and closing the doors of the inner cell, and they are jointly responsible with the Treasurers of Athene for securing them. The Treasurers appointed by lot are to take over from the present Treasurers, the overseers and the officials of the holy places, who are now handling the moneys; they are to count them out and separate them off in the presence of the Council on the Acropolis; they are to receive them from the present officials; they are to make a record on a single tablet of all moneys, including the amount due to each individual god and the total sum, recording the silver and gold separately. The Treasurers at any particular moment are to record the balance on a column, preparing an account of the capital and income belonging to the gods, and of any annual expenditure for the auditors, and are to submit their accounts to scrutiny. They are to draw up their accounts from one Panathenaic festival to the next, as do the Treasurers of Athene. The Treasurers are to set up the columns with the holy balance-sheet on the Acropolis. Once the moneys are paid back to the gods any surplus may be used for the dockyard and the walls and . . .

B

Decree of the Council and Commons. Committee in session: Cecropis. Secretary: Mnesitheos. President: Eupithes. Proposer: Callias.

The marble steps, the golden statues of Victory and the Propylaea are to be made. When these are completed there is to be a survey starting from the south in accordance with the decrees. The Acropolis except for excluded areas, is to be formally demarcated. Ten talents per annum are to be spent on restoration, until the buildings are restored and complete. The Treasurers are to be in charge of the work, and are to instruct the architect to prepare drawings, as for the Propylaea. He is responsible, in association with the overseers, for seeing that the Acropolis is well and truly beautified and that necessary repairs are carried out. The other moneys at present on the Acropolis belonging to Athene and any contributed in the future are not to be used for, or drawn upon for any other purpose over the sum of 10,000 drachmas except for this or for necessary repairs; the moneys are not to be used for any other purpose unless the Commons vote an indemnity (e.g. over special levies). If anyone propose or put to the vote a motion to use the moneys belonging to Athene, without an indemnity being voted, then it is possible on the same conditions that pertain if anyone proposes or puts to the vote a motion to hold a special levy. . . . Each year the Treasurers of the Greeks are to deposit on the Acropolis with the Treasurers of Athene any income for that year. When the due amounts out of the 200 talents voted for payment by the Commons have been paid to the other gods, they are to deposit the moneys belonging to Athene on the right-hand side of the inner cell, and the moneys due to the other gods on the left. . . . If there are any moneys uncounted or unweighed, the present Treasurers, together with the four boards responsible for rendering an account from one Panathenaic festival to the next, are to weigh the gold, silver and silver alloy, and count the remainder . . .

H7 Parthenon Building Accounts

The decision to build the Parthenon as a national shrine was taken of course by the Assembly. A board of commissioners was elected to take charge of the building; elections were annual. They were responsible both for the efficiency and the cost of the operation, and their work was subject to annual review. The accounts, beginning in 447–6 and ending in 433–2 were published on a pillar on the Acropolis; those for 434–3 are the best preserved and appear below. They show the previous year's surplus (very small), the receipts and expenditure. Historical sources (Plutarch Pericles *12, 2) suggest that the temple was ultimately paid for out of tribute from the allies.*

Note that the ivory is being sold off very cheap. For a discussion of the accounts see W. B. Dinsmoor 'Attic Building Accounts' American Journal of Archaeology *17 (1913) 53–80; 25 (1920) 233–45; Alison Burford 'Parthenos and Parthenon'* Greece and Rome *10 Supp. 23–35.*

Report of the commissioners (secretary: Anticles) to the fourteenth Council (original secretary: Metagenes). Archon at Athens: Crates.

Receipts for the year as under:

1,470 dr. — Balance from previous year

---

74 st. — Electrum staters from Lampsacus
$27\frac{1}{6}$ st. — Electrum staters from Cyzicus

25,000 dr. — From the treasurers in charge of finances relating to the goddess
Secretary: Crates of Lamptrai

1,372 dr. — Value of sales of gold, weight 98 dr.
1,309 dr. — Value of sales of ivory, weight 3 tal. 60 dr.

Expenditure

...... — Purchases

Wages

1,926 dr. 200 — To workers quarrying on Mt Pentelicus and loading stone onto carts

---

16,392 dr. — To statuaries, a year's salary

...... — Monthly salaries
...... — Balance from this year
74 st. — Electrum staters from Lampsacus
$27\frac{1}{6}$ st. — Electrum staters from Cyzicus

IG I² 352

H8 Phidias

Originally a painter (Pliny, Natural History *35, 54), he was Pericles's choice to supervise the great building-scheme on the Acropolis (Plutarch,* Pericles *13). Of his own sculpture we have only copies and descriptions, though his was the masterhand behind the Parthenon frieze.*

(a)

After thus defining the periods of the most famous artists, I will hastily run through those of outstanding distinction, throwing in the rest of the throng here and there under various heads. The most celebrated have also come into competition with each other, although born at different periods, because they had made statues of Amazons: when these were dedicated in the Temple of Artemis of Ephesus, it was agreed that the best one should be selected by the vote of the artists themselves who were present; and it then became evident that the best was the one which all the artists judged to be the next best after their own: this is the Amazon by Polycleitus, while next to it came that of Pheidias, third Cresilas's, fourth Cydon's and fifth Phradmon's.

Pheidias, besides the Olympian Zeus, which nobody has ever rivalled, executed in ivory and gold the statue of Athene that stands erect in the Parthenon at Athens, and in bronze besides the Amazon mentioned above, an Athene of such exquisite beauty that it has been surnamed the Fair. He also made the Lady with the Keys, and another Athene ... and likewise a work consisting of two statues wearing cloaks ... and another work, a colossal statue undraped; and Pheidias is deservedly deemed to have first revealed the capabilities and indicated the methods of statuary.

Pliny *Natural History* 34, 53–4
tr. H. Rackham (Loeb 1962)

(b)

We should not forget to mention that this art, carving in marble, is much older than that of painting or of bronze statuary, both of which arose with Pheidias in the 83rd Olympiad, that is, about 332 years later. It is reported that Pheidias himself carved in marble and that the exceptionally beautiful Venus in Octavia's Buildings at Rome is his. What is certain is that a pupil of his was the Athenian Alcamenes, a particularly famous sculptor, several of whose works are to be seen at Athens in the temples, while outside the walls there is the celebrated statue of Venus, which in Greek is known as Aphrodite of the Gardens. Pheidias himself is said to have put the finishing touches to this. Another of his pupils was Agoracritus of Paros, who pleased him, moreover, because of his youthful good looks, and consequently Pheidias is said to have allowed him to pass as the author of several of his own works. . . . That Pheidias is the most famous sculptor among all peoples who appreciate the fame of his Olympian Jupiter is beyond doubt, but in order that even those who have not seen his works may be assured that his praises are well earned I shall produce evidence that is insignificant in itself and sufficient only to prove his inventiveness. To do so, I shall not appeal to the beauty of his Olympian Jupiter or to the size of his Minerva at Athens, even though this statue, made of ivory and gold, is 26 cubits in height. But rather, I shall mention her shield, on the convex border of which he engraved a Battle of the Amazons, and on the hollow side Combats of Gods and Giants; and her sandals, on which he depicted Combats of Lapiths and Centaurs. So truly did every detail lend itself to his art. On the pedestal there is carved what is entitled in Greek the Birth of Pandora, with twenty gods assisting at the birth. Although the figure of Victory is especially remarkable, connoisseurs admire also the snake, as well as the bronze sphinx that crouches just beneath her spear. These are things which should be stated in passing with regard to an artist who has never been praised enough. At the same time, they make us realize that the grandeur of his notions was maintained even in small matters.

Pliny *Natural History* 36, 4, 15–19
tr. D. E. Eichholz (Loeb 1962)

(c)

Pheidias the sculptor had been entrusted, as I have mentioned, with the contract for producing the great statue of Athena. His friendship with Pericles, with whom he had great influence, earned him a number of enemies through sheer jealousy, while others made use of him to test the mood of the people and see what their temper would be in a case in which Pericles was involved. They therefore persuaded Menon, one of the artists working under Pheidias, to seat himself in the market-place as a suppliant and ask for the protection of the state in return for laying information against Pheidias. The people granted the man's plea and a motion for Pheidias's prosecution was laid before the Assembly. The charge of embezzlement was not proved, because from the very beginning, on Pericles' own advice, the gold used for the statue had been superimposed and laid around it in such a way that it could all be taken off and weighed, and this was what Pericles now ordered the prosecutors to do.

However, the fame of Pheidias's works still served to arouse jealousy against him, especially because in the relief of the battle of the Amazons, which is represented on the shield of the goddess, he carved a figure representing himself as a bald old man lifting up a stone with both hands, and also because he introduced a particularly fine likeness of Pericles fighting an Amazon. The position of the hand, which holds a spear in front of Pericles' face, seems to have been ingeniously contrived to conceal the resemblance, but it can still be seen quite plainly from either side.

So Pheidias was cast into prison and there he fell sick and died. According to some accounts he was poisoned by his enemies in an attempt to blacken Pericles' name still further. As for the informer, Menon, a proposal was passed, on Glycon's motion, to make him exempt from all taxes and public burdens and the generals were ordered to provide for his safety.

Plutarch *Pericles* 31
tr. I. Scott-Kilvert (Penguin 1960)

H9 Phidias's Works

(a) Athene (Promachos)
A freestanding bronze Athene dating from about 460. One or two late authorities call it Promachos or Defender, but there is no contemporary authority for this. The spear-tip and helmet-crest were visible far out to sea (Pausanias 1, 28, 2). The statue is probably the one taken to Constantinople and there destroyed in riots in AD 1203. This description by a late author is accurate except that the right hand held a spear.

It rose to a vertical height of about thirty feet. It was dressed in a robe of bronze, the same material as the whole statue; this reaches to the feet and was gathered at several points . . . A military belt was firmly clasped round the waist. Over the breasts and full like them she wore a covering in the form of an aegis, coming down from the shoulders and portraying the Gorgon's head, a masterpiece of sculpture. Her neck, bare and of some length could not fail to delight the eyes . . . Her veins were prominent, and her whole body supple, with the appropriate points . . . On the top of her head a plume of horsehair 'nodded awesomely from above'. Her hair was plaited and fastened at the back; from the front her flowing locks were a feast for the eyes, for they were not completely tucked within the helmet, but it was possible to catch a glimpse of her hair. Her left hand held up the train of her robe; her right was stretched towards the south so as to keep the head slightly inclined that way and her gaze directed to the same quarter.

Nicetas 738B

(b) Zeus at Olympia
This statue was one of the seven wonders of the world (Hyginus Fabularum Liber *223); the Greeks thought it a shame to die without seeing it (Arrian* Discourses of Epictetus *1, 6, 23). The temple had a gallery for people to view it better. Cicero says that Phidias used no model except the ideal beauty seen with the inward eye (Cicero* The Orator *2, 8); one poet has the conceit that either the god came down to earth or Phidias ascended to heaven (*Palatine Anthology App. Plan. *81).*

Dio Chrysostomus, philosophical orator of the Roman Empire, speaks of the statue in his twelfth Oration, saying that it established the image of Zeus as gentle and peaceable, and that anyone who had encountered sorrow, and who stood and contemplated it, would find his grief falling away. Quintilian declared that the statue added something to revealed religion (12, 10, 9). One of the most exciting recent discoveries at Olympia has been Phidias's workshop. The care of the statue was hereditary within his family. The statue was eventually destroyed in a fire in the fifth century AD. We have no copies, and know the statue only from coins.

The god is seated on a throne; he is made of gold and ivory. On his head is a garland representing olive sprays. In his right hand he holds a Victory, also of ivory and gold, wearing a ribbon and garland on her head. In the god's left hand is a sceptre inlaid with metals of various kinds; the bird perched on the sceptre is the eagle. The god is wearing gold sandals and a robe of gold. On the robe are worked figures of animals and flowers of lily. The throne is variegated with gold and jewels, ebony and ivory, with figures painted and carved on it. There are four Victories in dance positions on each leg of the throne, with two more at the foot. On each of the front legs are Theban boys in the grip of Sphinxes, and under these Apollo and Artemis are shooting Niobe's children. Between the legs of the throne there are four bars, holding the legs together. On the one facing the entrance there are seven figures; the eighth has inexplicably disappeared. These would be representations of archaic competitions, seeing that competitions for boys had not yet been established in Phidias's day. They say that the boy tying a headband round his hair is a likeness of Pantarces, a lad from Elis with whom Phidias was in love. Pantarces won the prize in the boys' wrestling in the 86th Olympiad [i.e. 436 BC]. On the remaining bars are Heracles and his company warring with the Amazons. There are in all twenty-nine figures, and Theseus is in the ranks of Heracles. The throne is supported not only by the legs, but by an equal number of pillars standing between the legs. But it is not possible to go under the throne . . .; at Olympia there are wall-like screens to stop you. The screen opposite the door is enamelled in blue; the rest show paintings by Panaenus. Among these we can see Atlas sustaining the heaven and earth, with Heracles at his side ready to relieve him of the load; Theseus and Pirithous; Greece and Salamis with a ship's figurehead in her hand; Heracles wrestling with the lion of Nemea; Ajax raping Cassandra; Oenomaus's daughter Hippodamia with her mother; Prometheus in chains still, with Heracles sweeping up towards him (one of the stories about Heracles is that he killed the eagle which was tormenting Prometheus and released him from his chains); and finally, Penthesilea at her last gasp with Achilles supporting her; and two of the Hesperides holding the apples which they were charged to guard. This Panaenus was Phidias's brother, who also painted the battle of Marathon in the Colonnade of Paintings at Athens. On the higher parts of the throne above the statue's head Phidias has set three Graces on one side, and three Seasons on the other . . . The footstool under Zeus's feet . . . shows golden lions and a relief sculpture of Theseus's battle against the Amazons, the first heroic exploit of the Athenians against an alien enemy. On the base which supports the throne and all the glory of the statue are figures of gold, the Sun-god mounted on his chariot, Zeus, Hera, Hephaestus with one of the Graces next to him, next to her Hermes, next to Hermes Hestia, and after Hestia Love welcoming Aphrodite as she rises from the sea, and Persuasion crowning Aphrodite. There are also reliefs of Apollo and Artemis, Athene, Heracles and at the end of the base Amphitrite and Poseidon, and the Moon, in my view riding on a horse. Some people say that the goddess is mounted on a mule rather than a horse, and tell a stupid story about the mule.

The dimensions of the statue of Zeus at Olympia (height and breadth) have of course been recorded, but I cannot commend those who made the measurements, for the published figures fall far short of the impression the statue makes on the spectator.

There is a story that the gods actually give witness to Phidias's skill. When the statue was completed, Phidias asked the god in prayer if the work was to his liking, and immediately, they say, the god directed a thunderbolt to the very spot on the ground where the bronze urn was still standing in my day. The whole of the ground in front of the statue is paved with stone, not white but black. Round the black pavement is a parapet of Parian marble to hold the streams of oil. Oil is best for the statue at Olympia, and keeps the ivory from deteriorating through the swampy condition of the Altis.

Pausanias 5, 11, 1–5

H10 Erechtheum Construction Records

The Periclean building programme on the Acropolis was not only too vast to be quickly completed, but required such quality of workmanship that progress was bound to be slow. The Erechtheum was begun in 421 BC after the Peace of Nicias. However work was stopped in about 415 or 413 BC when the war was going badly for Athens and not resumed until about 409. This inscription records the survey of that date and provides an insight into the details of the building technique and the care with which the work was done.

The commissioners in charge of the temple on the Acropolis housing the ancient statue, Brosynides of Kephisia, Chariades of Agryle, Diodes of Kephisia, the architect Philokles of Acharnai and the secretary Etearchos of Kydathenaion, in accordance with the decree of the assembly moved by Epigenes inscribed (this record of) the work of the temple as they found it, finished and unfinished, in the archonship of Diokles, in the first prytany, held by (the tribe) Kekropis, in the council (year) for which Nikophanes of Marathon was the first to serve as secretary.

We found the following work of the temple unfinished:

At the corner toward the Kekropion: 4 blocks not in place, 4 ft long, 2 ft wide, 1½ ft thick; 1 cornerstone 4 ft long, 3 ft wide, 1½ ft thick; 5 top-course blocks 4 ft long, 3 ft wide, 1½ ft thick; 1 angle stone 7 ft long, 4 ft wide, 1½ ft thick; 1 round stone not in place, corresponding with the top-course blocks, 10 ft long, 1½ ft high; 2 blocks corresponding with the architraves, 4 ft long, 5 palms wide; 1 column capital not in place and the inner face, 2 ft long, 1½ ft wide, 1½ ft thick; 5 architraves not in place, 8 ft long, 2 ft 1 palm wide, 2 ft thick; 3 architraves in place but still to be dressed, 8 ft long, 2 ft 1 palm wide, 2 ft thick . . .

At the porch toward the Kekropion: Needed, to dress the roof stones over the Maidens on top, 13 ft long, 5 ft wide. To dress the rosettes on the architraves needed.

Stone work completely finished but still on the ground: 11 blocks 4 ft long, 2 ft wide, 1½ ft thick; 1 cornerstone 4 ft long, 3 ft wide, 1½ ft thick . . .

Of each of the following the second joint has not been finished, nor the back joints: 12 blocks 6 ft long, 2 ft wide, 1 ft thick – of each of these the second joint has not been finished, nor the back joints; 5 blocks 4 ft long, 2 ft wide, 1 ft thick – of each of these the second joint has not been finished, nor the back joints; 1 block 5 ft long, 2 ft wide, 1 ft thick – of this the second joint is not begun, nor the back joints.

Cornice stones 4 ft long, 3 ft wide, 5 palms thick: 7 finished smooth, without carving; 5 others, same size, 4 ft of volute and moulding of each were uncarved; of 2 others 4 ft of the volute and 8 ft of the moulding were uncarved . . .

On the wall toward the Pandroseion: 1 block 7½ ft long, 3½ ft wide – the smoothing unfinished; 1 block 6 ft long, 3 ft 1 palm wide, 5 palms thick, on the wall toward the Pandroseion – of this 5 ft of moulding uncarved; 6 pediment stones from the stoa, 7 ft long, 3½ ft wide, 1 ft thick – these are unfinished; 2 others 5 ft long, 3½ ft wide, 1 ft thick – unfinished . . .

4 stone doors 8 ft 1 palm long, 2½ ft wide – of these the rest had been finished but the black stones were still to be set into the panels; 1 side ornament for the east lintel – unfinished; Pentelic marble for the altar of the sacrificing priest, 3 blocks 4 ft long, 2 ft 1 palm high, 1 ft thick, another 3 ft long . . .

IG I^2 372
tr. N. Lewis *Greek Historical Documents, The Fifth Century BC*
(Hakkert, Toronto 1971) p. 39

H11 The Erechtheum Accounts

These accounts date from 407 BC. The names are those of a team of craftsmen; there is no indication of the designer. It will be noticed that about half the craftsmen are citizens and about half resident aliens. In all we know the names of some seventy-one workmen on the Erechtheum. The going rate was evidently sixty drachmas a figure. Only five examples of payments are given here.

To . . . . . . for the figure with the spear	60 dr
To Phyromachus of Cephisia for the young man by the breastplate	60 dr
To Praxias, resident of Melite, for the horse and the man visible behind turning it	120 dr
To Antiphanes of Cerameis, for the chariot, young man and pair of horses being yoked . . .	240 dr
To . . . . . . for the young man painting and the man at his side	120 dr

IG I[2] 374

H12 The Temple of Athene Nike

The little temple of Athene Nike was one of the later additions to the Periclean Acropolis. However this inscription of 449–7 shows that it was part of the plan from the start and it is interesting that the architect is to be Callicrates who worked with Ictinus on the Parthenon. Work on the temple was probably delayed by the complications of the Propylea (completed 432) and it was probably not finished until 427 or 424.

Resolved by the council and the assembly . . . . . . Glaucos proposed: that a priestess of Athene Nike, who would hold holy office for life, be appointed from all Athenians; and that the sanctuary be furnished with doors in accordance with a specification to be drawn up by Callicrates; that the commissioners of public contracts (poletai) put the work out to contract in the prytany of the tribe of Leontis. Also that the priestess receive fifty drachmas and the legs and skins from the public sacrifices; that a temple be built according with specifications to be drawn up by Callicrates, and a stone altar. Hestiaeus proposed: that three men be chosen from the council, and that, having drawn up the specifications with Callicrates, they indicate to the council the way in which the work is to be contracted.

IG I[2] 24+
tr. K. Chisholm

H13 The Treasures in the Hekatompedos 418 BC

The following is an example of a large and important class of inscriptions which indicate the extent of the treasures in the care of the boards of Treasurers. Treasures appear to have been stored in three places, all part of the main sanctuary of Athene Parthenos; the Pronaos or eastern cella of the Parthenon, the Hekatompedos, and the Parthenon or western cella of the temple. Lists were prepared annually but only inscribed at the four-yearly Panathenaea and the surviving lists cover a period from 434 through to the close of the fourth century. See W. S. Ferguson The Treasurers of Athena *and H. T. Wade-Gery in* Journal of Hellenic Studies *Vol. 51 p. 76 ff. It is estimated that the total value of the treasures in this list, one of the shorter ones, is about ten talents. The text is conveniently in R. Meiggs and D. Lewis,* Greek Historical Inscriptions *(Oxford 1969) no. 76.*

The four annual boards (of treasurers) which rendered accounts from Panathenaia to Panathenaia transmitted the following objects in the Hekatompedos shrine to the treasurers Pythodoros of Halai and colleagues, for whom Phormion son of Aristion of Kydathenaion was secretary; and the treasurers for whom Phormion son of Aristion of Kydathenaion was secretary transmitted to the treasurers Anaxikrates of Lamptrai and colleagues, for whom Euxenos son of Euphanes of Prospalta was secretary: 3 gold bowls weighing 2,544 dr. A gold statue of a maiden on a stele, no weight record. A silver aspergillum, no weight record. 2 gold crowns weighing 80 dr. A gold crown which the Nike has, weighing 60 dr. 8 silver bowls weighing 400 dr. A silver drinking cup weighing 200 dr. A silver drinking cup of Zeus Polieus weighing 200 dr. A gold crown weighing . . . A gold diadem weighing 63 dr. 4 gold crowns weighing 135 dr, 2 ob. A gold crown weighing 18 dr, 3 ob. 2 gold vessels weighing 293 dr, 3 ob. A gold vessel weighing 138 dr, 2 ob. A gold vessel weighing 119 dr. A gold crown weighing 26 dr, 3 ob. A silver vessel weighing 192 dr. A silver censer weighing 1,000 dr. During the year were added: a gold crown weighing 1,250 dr. A gold crown weighing . . . A gold crown weighing 35 dr.

IG I^{2} 268+
tr. N. Lewis *Greek Historical Documents, the Fifth Century BC* (Hakkert, Toronto 1971) p. 30

H14 Praxiteles

The greatest Athenian sculptor of the fourth century, as Phidias of the fifth. His father seems to have been called Cephisodotus, and a son of that name became a well-known sculptor. Praxiteles was particularly famed for his marble statues, which he liked to have painted by a painter named Nicias. A useful study is G. E. Rizzo Prassitele *(1932). Iris Love has recently found the base of Praxiteles's Aphrodite in a circular shrine at Cnidos. The reference to Cicero is 4* Verrine *2, 4; 60, 135.* Hermes and the Infant Dionysus *at Olympia is an original of Praxiteles.*

(a)

In addition Praxiteles, who had a higher reputation for his work in marble (because of his larger output), produced some outstanding works in bronze as well: *The Rape of Persephone, The Restoration of Persephone, Dionysus drunk,* besides the famous *Satyr* nicknamed 'Celebrated' by the Greeks; the statues which stood in front of the temple of Fortune; the *Aphrodite* destroyed in the flames when the temple caught fire in Claudius's reign (a statue comparable to the world-famous marble one); *The Woman with a Garland, The Woman putting on a Bangle, The Woman with a Basket* . . . He also produced a statue of Apollo as a boy lying with a bow at close quarters in wait for the approach of a lizard (the so-called *Lizard-slayer*). Two statues specially worth seeing represent opposed emotions, *The Weeping Lady* and *The Laughing Whore.* Some people identify the latter with Phryne and discern in it the sculptor's love for her and her own visible pleasure in her professional reward. One statue shows something of his generosity. He put a charioteer of his own on a chariot by Calamis; he did not want a man with such a high reputation for portraying horses to be disgraced by his portrayal of a human being.

Pliny *Natural History* 34, 69

(b)

I have dealt with Praxiteles and his period in writing of sculptors in bronze, but he surpassed himself in the splendour of his work in marble. Works by him are to be found in the Ceramicus at Athens. But supreme among Praxiteles's works, indeed the outstanding statue in the whole world is the *Aphrodite* which many people have voyaged to Cnidos specially to see. He had carved two statues of Aphrodite, and was offering them for sale simultaneously. One was clothed, and preferred for that reason by the people of Cos, who were offered either at the same price, and thought this one decent and respectable. The people of Cnidos bought the one they rejected, and it became far more famous. Later King Nicomedes offered to buy it from the Cnidians, promising to discharge the City's enormous national debt, but they preferred to face the worst, and were right to do so, for the fame of

Cnidos was owing to Praxiteles's statue. The shrine of the statue is completely open so that the goddess's image (made, they believe, with her express approval) can be viewed from every side and is equally marvellous from any . . . Praxiteles also carved the *Eros* which was the subject of one of Cicero's charges against Verres, once the glory of Thespiae, now standing in the gallery of Octavia; also another nude *Eros* in Parium on the Propontis, of equal renown to the *Aphrodite* of Cnidos . . . At Rome Praxiteles's works comprise: *Flora, Triptolemus and Demeter* in the gardens of Servilius, figures of *Good Luck* and *Good Fortune* on the Capitol, as well as *Maenads,* so called *Thyiads, Caryatids* and *Sileni,* and an *Apollo* and a *Neptune* in Asinius Pollio's collection.

Pliny *Natural History* 36, 20–23

H15 Sculpture in Marble

Greece is particulary rich in fine marble especially on Paros, Naxos and from Mount Pentelicon in Attica. Pliny's reference to coloured marbles reflects a Roman predilection. The Greeks polished the skin of marble statues and coloured the drapery.

That completes my account of the sculptors in marble, and of the craftsmen with the highest reputation in that field. While writing on the subject, it occurs to me that at that period marble with markings on it was of no reputation. They worked in marble from the Cycladic Islands, and from Thasos, which was valued as highly as the slightly more bluish marble from Lesbos. For a general account of marbles, including the mottled variety, we have to wait for an occasional mention in the pages of that learned exponent of the life of luxury, Menander. Marble columns were found in temples, not for decorative purposes (there was no appreciation of their value for that purpose), but to provide the strongest possible supports.

Pliny *Natural History* 36, 5, 6

I CULT AND BELIEF

It must never be forgotten that to the majority of Greeks there was no distinction between secular and sacred. All life was sacred, and the rhythms of the year were marked by ritual both in the household and in the religious festivals. The arrangements for the larger state festivals were carefully regulated as part of the religious ritual (see especially nos. I 5–11; I 16), while in the fifth century the participation of the allies added an Imperial dimension and enhanced Athenian prestige. There were also pan-Hellenic religious festivals in which the various states came together in worship and competition.

Traditional beliefs and practices began to be questioned in our period, partly as a result of the spread of the ideas of the Ionian scientists, which was facilitated by the growth of sophistic education. In some of the philosophical sources we can see the emergence of rationalist debate (see nos. I 24 and 28). For Greek religion generally see M. P. Nilsson *A History of Greek Religion* (Oxford University Press ²1949), W. K. C. Guthrie *The Greeks and their Gods* (Methuen 1950); for specific topics see also H. W. Parke *Festivals of the Athenians* (Thames and Hudson 1976), H. W. Parke and D. E. W. Wormell *The Delphic Oracle* (Blackwell 1956).

I1 Athene's Land

City and land generally are sacred to Athene. No matter how the worship of other gods is established in the villages, they hold Athene just as much in honour.

Pausanias 1, 26, 6

I2 A Hymn to Athene

No doubt an adaptation of popular hymn-writing

Pallas, our city's protector,
queen of a land
supreme in piety,
mighty in war,
rich in poets,
come to us bringing
our ally
in battles and war,
Victory, our chorus's friend,
our enemies' enemy.
Come to us now,
our art needs you
to favour our triumph
now if ever.

Aristophanes *Knights* 581–94

I3 The Rivalry of Poseidon and Athene

The story is told in a number of sources: Herodotus 8, 55; Plutarch Themistocles *19; Pausanias 1, 24, 5; 1, 26, 5; Athene was a pre-Greek goddess of the land, associated with the owl. Poseidon was perhaps originally the sky-god of the immigrant Hellenes, Zeus under another name, who, displaced by Zeus, becomes god of the sea. The Pandrosium is a sacred enclosure on the Acropolis; the Thriasian plain is around Eleusis. The flood may be a folk-memory of the tidal waves accompanying the eruption of Santorini.*

In the time of Cecrops the gods determined to claim a city each to do them special honour. Poseidon reached Attica first, struck the centre of the Acropolis with his trident, and opened up the sea-water now called Erechtheis. After him came Athene, called Cecrops as witness of her occupation, and planted an olive which is still shown in the Pandrosium. The two were in fierce rivalry over the territory. Zeus divided them, and appointed arbitrators, not Cecrops and Cranaus, or Erysichthon as some say, but the twelve gods. By their verdict the land was assigned to Athene on the evidence of Cecrops that she was the first to plant the olive. Athene called the city Athens after herself. Poseidon was furious and flooded the Thriasian plain and submerged Attica.

Apollodorus *The Library* 3, 14, 1

14 The Temples of Athens

Synoecism means the unification of Attica which is supposed to have taken place under Theseus.

Before the synoecism the city was identical with the present Acropolis and the area under it towards the south. The evidence for this is that the ancient temples of Athene and of other gods stand either on the Acropolis, or, if outside, in that area of the city – the temples of Olympian Zeus, Pythian Apollo, Earth, and Dionysus in the Marshes, the god still honoured in the older Dionysia in the month of Anthesterion by the Athenians, and their Ionian descendants. There are other ancient temples in the same area.

Thucydides 2, 15

15 The Panathenaic Festivals

(a)

Panathenaea: Two Panathenaic festivals are held at Athens, one annually and one, called the Great Panathenaea, every four years. Isocrates in *Panathenaicus*. Erichthonius the son of Hephaestus was the first to celebrate the festival (so Hellanicus and Androtion, both in *Atthis* book I). Before that it was called the Athenaea (by Istrus in *History of Attica* book III).

Harpocration *Lexicon* s.v. *Panathenaea*

(b)

Panathenaea: The feast and competition of the Panathenaea was originally established by Erichthonius, son of Hephaestus and Athene, and reinstituted by Theseus, who drew the villagers into the city. The competition is held every four years.

Scholiast to Plato *Parmenides* 127a

(c) *This decree dates from about 355–4.*

. . . . . . with a view to the holy and . . . . . . celebration of the annual festival, prepared with all excellence annually for Athene by the people of Athens, and to performance of all necessary arrangements for the splendid organization of the festival by the religious officials in perpetuity, the Commons decreed in addition to endorsing the views of the Council that the religious officials should offer two sacrifices, one to Athene and Health, and one offered in the Old Temple as of old, and give five portions to the committee in office, three to the nine archons, one to the ministers of the goddess, one to the religious officials, three to the military authorities, and the usual shares to the Athenian celebrants and to the basket-bearers. The rest of the meat is to be shared among the Athenians. From the forty-one minas out of the new contributions the religious officials are to purchase cattle, or organize the procession in association with the officers in charge of the cattle, and to sacrifice all these cattle on the great altar of Athene, except for one on the altar of Victory, making a careful selection beforehand from the best cattle, and sacrificing to Athene Polias and Athene Victory, and distributing the meat from all the cattle purchased with the forty-one minas to the common people of Athens in the Ceramicus, just as in other distributions of meat . . .

W. Dittenberger *Sylloge Inscriptionum Graecarum*
1, 271 (Leipzig[3] 1915)

(d)
Branch-bearers . . . By branch-bearers he means the old men, since at the Panathenaic festival the old men processed with branches.

Scholiast to Aristophanes *Wasps* 544

(e)
For whom are we to prepare the sacred robe? A sacred robe richly embroidered was woven for Athene Polias and carried in the Panathenaic procession.

Scholiast to Aristophanes *Birds* 827

(f)
Sauce for the Panathenaea . . . Since all the Athenian colonies sent an ox for sacrifice at the Panathenaic festival there was no shortage of meat, everyone had their fill and ate more than they needed owing to the quantity of meat.

Scholiast to Aristophanes *Clouds* 386

(g)
Dance: The boys performed an armed dance at the Panathenaea.

Scholiast to Aristophanes *Clouds* 988

16 Thesmophoria

A women's festival held in the autumn throughout Greece

(a)

The Thesmophoria, a festival of the Greeks including mysteries (the latter also called Skirrophoria). According to the more mythical account the reason for their celebration is that at the time when the Maiden was carried off by Pluto while gathering flowers, a swineherd named Eubuleus was feeding his pigs at the same spot, and they were swallowed up in the Maiden's abyss. So in honour of Eubuleus the pigs are thrown into the abysses of Demeter and the Maiden. Women named 'Drawers-up' who have purified themselves for three days bring up the rotten portions of the pigs which have been thrown down into the holy halls. They go down into the holy places, bring up the remains and set them on the altars. It is believed that anyone who takes a portion and mixes it with his seed will enjoy a good harvest. They say too that there are snakes down in the abysses which eat the majority of the offerings. For this reason a noise is made while the women draw up the remains and replace them with the great images, to induce the snakes, which they believe to be protectors of the holy places, to go away . . . The pigs, as I have already said, are thrown down, because of their prolificity, as a contribution to the growth of crops and human beings in thanksgiving to Demeter, since she by providing Demeter's own grain made mankind civilized. This is the mythological explanation. I offer a scientific explanation. It is called Thesmophoria because Demeter is called Thesmophoros; she established laws or ordinances (*thesmous*) by which men must work for their sustenance.

Scholiast to Lucian *Dialogues with Prostitutes* 2, 1

(b) *A hymn to Demeter and the Maid*

Come in grace and kindness,
goddesses, to your grove,
where no men may look on
the holy rites, as in torchlight
  you reveal your immortal faces.

Come, o come, we pray you,
our Ladies of the Festival.
If ever you have come in answer
to our prayers, come now, be present
  with us here, we implore you.

Aristophanes *Thesmophoriazusae* 1148–59

I7 Anthesteria

A three-day festival of Dionysus in February – Cask-opening, Day of Cups, Day of Pots – a feast of revocation of the dead and blessing on the year. Buckthorn and pitch were apotropaic. It is possible that the masquerade of the dead was transferred to the later festival of Dionysus and contributed to the growth of tragedy. For the festival see Jane Harrison Prolegomena to the Study of Greek Religion *Cambridge [3]1922, pp. 32–76.*

(a)

On the eleventh day of the month Anthesterion they broach the new wine, calling the day Pithoigia (cask-opening). It was apparently an ancient custom to pour a libation from the wine before drinking any and to pray that the use of the powerful draught might bring them protection rather than harm.

Plutarch *Questions from Banquets* 3, 7, 1

(b)

Day of Pollution: In the Feast of the Cups in the month of Anthesterion, in which they believe that the souls of the dead arise. They used to chew buckthorn and anoint their doors with pitch.

Photius *Lexicon* s.v. *miara hemera*

(c)

Doorwards: Out through the door. 'Doorwards, Spirits of the Dead (*Cares*), Anthesteria is over.' Some say that the words were spoken for the mass of Carian servants; during the Anthesteria they have a holiday and no work. When the festival is over they pack them back to work with the words, 'Doorwards, Carians, Anthesteria is over.' Others explain the proverbial saying, 'Doorwards, Spirits of the Dead, Anthesteria is over', on the grounds that the souls are circulating through the city during the Anthesteria.

The Suda s.v. *thuraze*

18 Thargelia

A harvest festival in the May–June period, sacred to Apollo and more vaguely to Artemis. The Eiresione is named from the wool (eiros) *twined round branches and hung with first fruits.*

(a)
Thargelia: An Athenian festival named from thargelia, i.e. all the fruits of the earth. Celebrated in the month Thargelion. To Artemis and Apollo.

Etymologicum Magnum s.v. *Thargelia*

(b)
Thargelos is a pot full of seeds.

Hesychius *Lexicon* s.v. *Thargelos*

(c)
You've torn up my Eiresione ... At the Pyanepsia and the Thargelia the Athenians hold a festival in honour of the Sun and the Seasons. The boys carry branches twined with wool (hence the name Eiresiones), and hang them up in front of the doors.

Scholiast to Aristophanes *Knights* 729

(d)
'Doubly-flourishing' is used of a boy who is flourished or blessed on both sides, i.e. whose father and mother are both alive ... The men of old, in saying that those who have both parents living are 'doubly-flourishing', add that such boys used to be responsible for the Eiresiones. This depends on the words of Pausanias: 'The Eiresione is an olive branch garlanded with wool, with various fruits of the earth hanging from it. A doubly-flourishing boy carries it out and sets it in front of the doors of Apollo's temple at the festival of Pyanepsia' ... The boys used to sing a song:

> Eiresione brings
> figs and rich cakes
> and a pot of honey
> and oil in addition
> and a cup of pure wine
> for her to drink and sleep.

After the festival they bring them out of the fields and set them by the doors.

Eustathius *Commentary on Homer Iliad* 22, 496, p. 1283

I9 Arrephoria

(a) Arrephoroi *mean carriers of the* arre, erre *or* herse, *which are no doubt sacred objects of some kind.*

One feature astonished me. It is not widely known, so I will describe the events. Two girls live near the temple of Polias; the Athenians call them Arrephoroi. They are boarded for a time with the goddess. When the festival comes round they perform the following ritual by night. They set on their heads objects given them to carry by the priestess of Athene; the nature of these objects is not known to either giver or bearers. Now there is within the city not far away an enclosure dedicated to the goddess called Aphrodite in the Gardens, and there is a natural underground passage leading down through it. The girls make their descent by this. They leave down below the objects they are carrying, and bring back something else which is carefully wrapped up. The girls are then dismissed and others brought on to the Acropolis in their place.

Pausanias 1, 27, 3

(b) *The derivation of Arrephoria from Arretophoria (i.e. carrying of objects which may not be named) is a false one. But it is clear that the ritual was directed in different form to more than one goddess. The parallel with the Thesmophoria may be just. The ritual has been called the Thesmophoria of the unmarried girl.*

The same rites (*sc.* as the Thesmophoria) are also called the Arretophoria and are celebrated with the same intention over the fertility of crops and humans. These two sacred objects which may not be named are formed of cereal paste and carried round; they are images of snakes and of the forms of men. They also use fir-cones owing to the prolificity of that tree. These too are thrown into the holy places called holy halls . . . as a contribution to the growth of crops and human beings in thanksgiving to Demeter, since she by providing Demeter's own grain made mankind civilized.

Scholiast to Lucian *Dialogues with Prostitutes* 2, 1

110 Bouphonia or Dipolia

Bouphonia means the Murder of the Ox, Dipolia the festival of Zeus of the City. The ritual is a curious one. Perhaps the ox, having eaten the sacred meal, has become holy. It must be sacrificed; equally it is sacrosanct. Therefore its slayer must be cast out. The scholiast alone mentions cows: this may perhaps indicate an original offering to a goddess usurped by Zeus.

(a)

There is a statue of Zeus by Leochares, and one called Zeus of the City. I will tell the customary sacrificial practice to this last without giving the traditional explanation. They place on the altar of Zeus of the City barley mixed with wheat, and leave it unprotected. The ox which they are keeping ready for the sacrifice goes to the altar and takes the grain. One of the priests is called the ox-slayer. He kills the ox, throws the axe down on the spot – that is what the ritual prescribed – and runs away. The others, as if in ignorance of the murder, bring the axe to trial.

Pausanias 1, 24, 4

(b)

The Dipolia is a festival at Athens, in which on the fourteenth of Skirrophorion they sacrifice to Zeus of the City. It is a representation of what happened about the cakes and the cows.

Scholiast to Aristophanes *Peace* 419

(c)

They selected girls named water-carriers. They carried water so that the men will sharpen the axe and knife. Of the men who did the sharpening one passed the axe, a second struck the ox, a third slit its throat. After this they skinned it and everyone had a share of the meat. When this was over they sewed up the ox hide, stuffed it with straw and erected it, looking just as it did in life; they yoked it to a plough as if it were at work. They then held a trial for murder and summoned all those who took part in the operation to make their defence. The water-carriers put the blame on those who did the sharpening rather than on themselves. The sharpeners accused the man who handed over the axe, he blamed the man who struck the blow, he blamed the man who slit the throat, and he charged the knife. As this was incapable of speech it was condemned for murder. From that time to the present those I have mentioned perform the sacrifice of the ox at the Dipolia in Athens in the same way. They set cakes of ground barley and mealies on a bronze table, herd the oxen and drive them round, and the one which tastes the offerings is sacrificed.

Porphyry *On Abstinence* 2, 29–30

I11 Callynteria and Plynteria

These were festivals in the month of Thargelion, sweeping and washing. The first is the sweeping out of the temple, the second the ceremonial bathing of the image of Athene in the sea. This last, when the image of the goddess was taken out, was a day of great power, dangerous and 'unlucky'. All the sanctuaries were roped off (Pollux Onomasticon *8, 141) to keep out evil influences. The event referred to is the return of Alcibiades from exile to Athens in 408.*

He had disembarked on the day on which they were celebrating the Plynteria in honour of the goddess. The Praxiergidae perform these rites, which may not be revealed, on the twenty-fifth of Thargelion. They strip the image of its adornments and wrap it up. This is why the Athenians account that day supremely unlucky and forbid any work.

Plutarch *Alcibiades* 34

I12 A Festival of Dionysus

This passage from Aristophanes is of course from the comic stage, and has strong elements of parody: still it gives a glimpse of a spring fertility festival. The last two lines bring in an element of contemporary politics (425 BC).

DICAEOPOLIS: Peace; keep silence.
CHORUS: Quiet all! Didn't you hear the invocation to silence?
Here's the man we want. This way, out of the road,
everyone. It looks as if he's coming out to sacrifice.
DICAEOPOLIS: Peace; keep silence.
Basket-bearer, a little forward.
Xanthus, set the phallus erect.
Daughter, put the basket down and we'll begin.
DAUGHTER: Mother, pass over the ladle.
I must pour the sauce over the cake.

DICAEOPOLIS: Splendid! Lord Dionysus,
let my celebration of this festival,
my sacrifice, my honouring of the Country Dionysia,
with all my household, be acceptable in your sight –
and no military service. And may
the Thirty Years' Peace turn out well for me.

Aristophanes *Acharnians* 237–52

I13 Survival of Ancient Ritual

Chionides was writing comedies in the first half of the fifth century.

The author of *The Beggars*, a play attributed to Chionides, says that when the Athenians offer the Dioscuri breakfast in the City Hall, they set the table with cheese, cake, ripe olives and leeks, in commemoration of their traditional way of life.

Athenaeus 4, 137e

I14 Sacrifice

Pherecrates in his comedy The Deserters, *probably to be dated to 429, shows the gods complaining about sacrificial practice. An old story told how Prometheus had cheated the gods by offering Zeus the choice of a large attractive looking parcel consisting of bones and gristle, and a small unattractive one containing the meat. It is important to remember that as the Greeks, except perhaps for athletes, did not eat much meat, a sacrifice was therefore a treat. The 'wafers' are the sacrificial cakes.*

THE GODS: When you sacrifice do to Our Persons divine
you first from the animal take
And give for your part what's been ours from the start;
and then – here I blush for your sake –
Don't you cut off the meat of the legs from the feet
right up to the edge of the groin,
And strip to the bone and take for your own
the succulent flesh of the loin?

And even the chine don't you file quite fine
    ere We get it, We dogs on the floor,
Each man from his neighbour concealing his shame
    with a dressing of wafers galore?

Pherecrates in Clement *Stromateis* 7, 846
tr. J. M. Edmonds *The Fragments of Attic Comedy* I
(Leiden 1957) p. 217

115 The Gifts of Demeter

The rites of Demeter and Kore were celebrated at Eleusis. The myth is told in the Homeric Hymn to Demeter *or Ovid* Fasti *4, 393–620. The standard book on Eleusis is G. E. Mylonas* Eleusis and the Eleusinian Mysteries (*Princeton University Press 1961*).

In the first place, our city was responsible for the provision of our primary physical necessity. The story is familiar, but can be told again. Demeter in her wanderings after the rape of the Maiden, reached our land. She was well-disposed towards our forebears because of services which none but initiates may hear, and gave them two supreme gifts, grain, which enables us to rise above the level of animal life, and the holy rite, which offers its participants more joyous hopes about death and eternity. Our city knew its duty to gods and to mankind. With these blessings in our care, we did not keep them to ourselves, but shared them freely with all men. Every year we continue with the holy celebration; it was we who taught mankind the uses, cultivation and benefits to be gained from the fruit of the earth.

Isocrates *Panegyricus* 28–9

116 Athenian Decree Regulating the Offering of First-fruits at Eleusis

Eleusis was the centre of one of the most famous mystery-cults. Demeter, the earth-mother or corn-mother, was honoured here together with her daughter, Kore, the Maiden (Persephone), the grain-spirit, who was raped by the king of the Underworld, Dis or Pluto (his very name means 'riches'), but allowed to return to earth for part of the year – clearly a myth of the corn, growing, harvested, buried, coming to life again. The myth became a parable of the life of man, and initiates were offered a better fate after death.

This inscription relating to the offering of the first-fruits at Eleusis is remarkable in its completeness (I have omitted an appendix). Unfortunately the date is uncertain, and suggestions have varied from about 445 to 415.

The terms are for the most part clear. The sacrificial flour was a mixed flour specially ground from the best grain. The house of Eumolpus was an aristocratic family with special rights and responsibilities for the cult. The Sacrifice of Three involved a bull, ram and goat. The goddesses are Demeter and Kore, the God Pluto, the Goddess presumably again Kore. The politicizing of the cult in the final clause is to be noticed.

The text with some useful notes is in R. Meiggs and D. Lewis Greek Historical Inscriptions *(Oxford 1969) no. 73. There is an important discussion in P. Guillon 'Le décret Athénien relatif aux prémices d'Eleusis et la paix de Nicias'* Bulletin de Corr. Hell. *86 (1962) 467–75. For a discussion of the date see M. Guarducci 'Intorno al decreto Ateniese sulle primizie per le dee de Eleusi'* Rivista di Filologia *89 (1961) 283–95.*

Secretary: Timoteles of Acharne.
Decree of Council and Commons.
Tribe in office: Cecropis. Secretary: Timoteles. Chairman: Cycneas.
Draft proposals.

The Athenians shall offer to the two goddesses the first-fruits of their crops in obedience to tradition and to the oracle from Delphi.
From every 150 bushels of barley: not less than $\frac{1}{4}$ bushel.
From every 150 bushels of wheat: not less than $\frac{1}{8}$ bushel.
Anyone whose harvest is greater or less than this is to offer first-fruits proportionately. The collection is to be made by the demarchs, deme by deme, and handed over to Eleusis to the religious officiants at Eleusis. Three granaries are to be constructed at Eleusis in accordance with tradition at whatever place the officiants and architects determine, and paid for from the goddesses' treasure; they shall store there the grain received from the demarchs. The allies are also to offer first-fruits after the same principles. The cities are to appoint collectors of the grain by what method they demand the grain best collected. When it has been

collected it is to be despatched to Athens. Those who accompany it are to hand it over to Eleusis to the religious officiants at Eleusis. If they do not issue a receipt within five days of due notice of delivery from the representatives of the contributing city, the officiants are to be fined 1,000 drachmas each. The same applies to receipts for delivery by the demarchs. The Council are to choose heralds and send them to the cities, to give notice of the Assembly's decrees, in the immediate situation without delay, and at such time in the future as seems suitable.

The hierophant and torchbearer at the mysteries shall instruct the Greeks to offer the first-fruits of their crops in obedience to tradition and to the oracle from Delphi.

The quantity of grain received from the demarchs is to be recorded on tablets deme by deme, and that from the cities, city by city, and the record deposited in the Eleusinion at Eleusis, and in the council-headquarters.

The council shall send notice also to all the other Greek cities, where they deem it practicable, announcing the principles on which the Athenians and their Allies are offering first-fruits, and encouraging them, without laying it on them as an obligation, to do the same in obedience to tradition and to the oracle from Delphi, if they so will; the officiants are to receive any contributions from these cities on the same terms.

Sacrifice is to be offered from the sacrificial flour according to the principles established by the house of Eumolpus. From the proceeds of the barley and wheat there is to be offered a Sacrifice of Three with gilded horns to each of the two goddesses, an unblemished sheep to each of Triptolemus, the God, the Goddess and Eubulus, and an ox with gilded horns to Athene.

The officiants are to sell the surplus barley and wheat and join with the Council in making offerings to the two goddesses, in accordance with decisions of the Commons at Athens, appending an inscription to the offerings declaring that they were derived from the first-fruits of the crops, and the names of the Greeks making the first-fruit offering.

These who take this action shall have many blessings, and rich and fruitful harvests, those who do no harm to the Athenians, the city of Athens or the two goddesses.

IG I^2 76

I17 The Blessings of Initiation

These passages are separated by possibly as much as five centuries. The dates of the Homeric Hymns are uncertain; like the epics they were first transmitted orally, and no one author can be ascribed to them. Cicero (106–43 BC) was Rome's greatest orator, concerned with philosophy as well as politics.

(a)

Blessed among men on earth is he who has seen these things.
But he who is uninitiate in the holy rites, who has no lot in them,
does not enjoy a like fate when he lies in death beneath broad-spreading darkness.

Homeric Hymn to Demeter 479–82

(b)

Your Athene has plainly made outstanding contributions to human life, gifts from heaven, but none better than those Mysteries. They educated us out of a life of barbarous rusticity into civilization. The ceremonies are called initiations, and we recognize in them the first principles of living. We have gained from them the way of living in happiness and dying with a better hope.

Cicero *Laws* 2, 14, 36

I18 Profanation of the Mysteries

In 415 as the Athenian fleet was about to sail for Sicily a charge was brought that one of the commanders, Alcibiades, had joined with some friends in parodying the Eleusinian Mysteries. At much the same time it was discovered that all through the city the phalluses on the Herms had been broken. There was an uproar, denunciations, charges of conspiracy to discredit Alcibiades. Andocides is reconstructing the scene sixteen years later. The close link between religion and politics is important. See also no. K8.

Pythonicus rose to his feet in the Assembly, saying, 'Gentlemen, you are proposing to be involved in all the danger of sending out this mighty expedition. I shall produce evidence that one of your commanding officers, Alcibiades, has joined with others in a celebration of the Mysteries in a private house. If you grant immunity to him on my nomination, a slave of one of those here present, not an initiate himself, will tell you about the Mysteries.' Alcibiades spoke at length to rebut the charge. The committee in office decided to ask non-initiates to leave, and themselves to fetch the lad Pythonicus named. They then went and brought a slave of Polemarchus's son Archebiades, named Andromachus. Once they voted him immunity he declared that the Mysteries had taken place in Pulytion's house, and named Alcibiades, Niciades and Meletus as celebrants, and others as present and observers ... He was the first to lodge information, giving a list of those involved. Polystratus was arrested and executed, the rest escaped and were condemned to death *in absentia.*

Andocides *On the Mysteries* 11–13

I19 Religious Duties

First of all, then, show devotion to the gods, not merely by doing sacrifice, but also by keeping your vows; for the former is but evidence of a material prosperity, whereas the latter is proof of a noble character. Do honour to the divine power at all times, but especially on occasions of public worship; for thus you will have the reputation both of sacrificing to the gods and of abiding by the laws.

Isocrates *To Demonicus* 13
tr. G. B. Norlin (Loeb 1928)

I20 Providence

A view, attributed to Socrates, closely similar to that found in many Victorian textbooks of theology.

Don't you think that the original creator of mankind was acting with beneficial providence in endowing men with their several senses, eyes to see the visible, ears to hear the audible? What use would scents be to us without the gift of nostrils? What capacity would we have to identify sweet and dry and all those delectable flavours if we had no tongue planted in us with a capacity for discrimination? More, don't you see providence in the working of the body? Our capacity for sight is weak, so it is shut in by eyelids which open when we want to use that faculty and close in sleep. Eyelashes grow on the lids to protect our sight from the wind. Eyebrows overlay the eyes so that no drop of sweat from the head can damage them. Our faculty of hearing admits sounds of all kinds without clogging up. Again all animals have incisor-teeth for cutting, molars for grinding the food passed on from them. So too the mouth which receives and passes on the food which animals want is set near the eyes and nostrils; but what passes out from the body is unpleasant, and the passages for that are set as far as possible away from the organs of perception. All these are providently arranged; have you any doubt whether they are the product of chance or design?

Xenophon *Memorabilia* 1, 4, 5–6

I21 Socrates's Prayer

'Dear Pan and all you other gods of this place, grant me to be beautiful within. May all that I own without harmonize with all that I am within. May I place riches in wisdom. May I enjoy no more wealth than a man of moderation can stand.'

Plato *Phaedrus* 279b–c

I22 A Religious Man

Someone next said: 'Hermogenes, it's your job to tell us who are these friends of yours and to demonstrate their great power and their interest in you, to justify your pride in them.'

'All right. Greeks and foreigners alike believe that the gods know everything about the present and future; that's clear enough. At any rate all cities and peoples use seers to ask the gods what they ought or ought not to do. Clearly too we believe they have the power of blessing and cursing; at any rate, everyone prays to the gods to save them from harm and grant them blessings. It is these gods, omniscient and omnipotent as they are, who are my friends. They look after me; they never forget me day or night wherever I go and whatever I'm engaged in doing. They have foreknowledge of the consequences of any action and send me messengers in the form of noises or dreams or birds to tell me what I ought or ought not to do. I have never had cause to regret paying attention to these; it is when I've ignored them that I've suffered for it.'

Socrates said: 'No difficulty in believing that. What I'd like to know is what service you offer to hold their friendships.'

'It doesn't cost much, by Zeus,' said Hermogenes. 'I sing their praises; that doesn't cost anything. I always give them back a share of all they give me. As far as possible I avoid profane language; and I never willingly tell lies where I call them to be witnesses.'

'By Zeus,' said Socrates, 'if you with that character have the gods' friendship, it looks as if the gods approve of decent behaviour.'

Xenophon *Symposium* 4, 46–9

I23 The Superstitious Man

Theophrastus, who died in 287, was Aristotle's successor at the Lyceum. This 'character' portrays an attitude which was probably much the same in earlier times.

Superstition is of course a kind of cowardice in face of the divine. We might characterize the Superstitious Man in the following terms. He washes his hands and asperses himself with water from the Three Springs and puts a laurel-leaf from a temple-precinct in his mouth before going out for the day. If a cat runs across the road he refuses to budge till someone else has passed or he has thrown three pebbles across the road. If he sees a snake in his house, he invokes Sabazios if it is red; if a sacred snake he establishes a shrine on the spot. On passing one of the smooth stones which stand at crossroads, he pours a libation of oil from his flask and drops to his knees in worship before proceeding. If a mouse gnaws through a bag of barley, he goes straight off to the diviner to ask what he should do: if the answer is, 'Take it to the saddler's and have it patched', he ignores the advice, and goes through an apotropaic ritual. He's noted for continually purifying his house on the ground that it's been 'visited' by Hecate. Owls hooting while he's out and about put him out of face: he won't go on without calling out 'Athene is queen'. He avoids treading on a grave or coming into contact with a dead body or a woman in childbirth: 'better not to risk pollution', he says. On the fourth and seventh of each month he has wine mulled for the whole family, goes out and buys myrtle-boughs, frankincense and holy pictures, and on his return spends the whole day offering sacrifices and garlands to the Hermaphrodites. If ever he has a dream he's off to the interpreters, the seers, the augurs, to ask what god or goddess he should propitiate. He applies for initiation into the Mysteries of Orpheus and pays a monthly visit to the hierophants accompanied by his wife, or, if she is not available, by his children and their nurse. He is meticulous about going down to the sea to asperse himself. If he sees a figure of Hecate at a crossroads with a crown of garlic, he goes straight back home, washes his head, and calls in priestesses telling them to purify him by carrying round a squill or young dog. If he sees a lunatic or an epileptic he shudders and spits into his lap.

Theophrastus *Characters* 16

I24 Rationalism

A fragment from a satyr-play by Critias, one-time friend of Socrates, and one of the Thirty Tyrants.

There was a time when human life was disorganized,
like the life of animals. Force ruled.
There was no reward for virtue,
no punishment for crime.
Then, I believe, human beings invented laws
as executioners, so that Justice might be dictator
over all alike, and hold violence in subjection.
Criminals were punished.
Now the laws prevented
open crimes of violence.
Covert crime continued. At this point, I believe,
Some ingeniously clever man first
invented for mortals fear of the gods, to bring
the sanction of fear on criminals, however covertly
they might act or speak or plan.
So he invented divinity,
'There exists an immortal divine being,
hearing and seeing without bodily senses, marking
their acts with perfect wisdom, wearing a divine form,
ready to hear all that human beings say
able to see all that they do.
Though you plot a crime in silence
the gods will know; they are
omniscient.' With sounds like these
he introduced the most welcome of all doctrines,
and veiled the truth in lies.
He proposed as a home for the gods the place where
his proposal would have the most powerful effect,
the region from which, as he knew, terror came
as well as succour for those in distress,
the circumference of the sky, where he saw
the flashing lightning and the fearful crash
of thunder, and the star-strewn face of heaven,
the glorious workmanship of time, the craftsman.
From there the blazing molten mass of the meteor falls,
and showers of rain come down to earth.
He instilled these fears into mankind,

used them to establish this gorgeous myth
of a god in a worthy habitation,
and extinguished lawlessness by law.

Critias fr. 25
H. Diels and W. Krantz *Die Fragmente der Vorsokratiker* (1952)

I25 Free Thought and Persecution

Protagoras of Abdera was a leading sophist charging a fairly heavy fee. His celebrated aphorisms are often quoted out of context. It is not clear whether the first (which is discussed in Plato's Theaetetus*) refers to mankind as a whole or any individual. The second is a wry reference to the poet Simonides, who asked for one day to answer the question, then two, then four, and so on. The Athenians were not usually intolerant; the story, if true, suggests a period of political stress when the favour of the gods was important. Cicero* (de Natura Deorum *1, 23, 63) reiterates the story.*

Protagoras was the first to assert that there are two opposing sides to every question. He would even develop a series of arguments along these lines, being the first to do so. He opened one of his works with the words: 'Man is the measure of all things, of the existence of the existent, and the non-existence of the non-existent.' He mentioned that the soul did not exist apart from the senses (so Plato writes in *Theaetetus*) and that all statements are true. He opened another work with the words: 'As regards the gods: I have no grounds for knowing whether they exist or not. There are many obstacles to knowledge – the obscurity of the subject and the brevity of human life.' Because of this preface he was deported by the Athenians and his writings were collected from their owners by an official and publicly burned.

Diogenes Laertius 9, 51–2

126 Omens before Battle

Sacrifices were regularly made before battle and omens consulted. Even so, some latitude of interpretation was possible, as the following passage shows. See A. D. Nock 'Religious Attitudes of the Ancient Greeks', Proceedings of the American Philosophical Society *85 (1942) 472–82.*

As long as the Boeotians were on the left wing they were in no hurry to join battle. But once the Athenians were established opposite the Spartans and they themselves drawn up on the right opposite the Achaeans, they promptly declared that the sacrifices were favourable, and gave the word to prepare for battle.

Xenophon *Hellenica* 4, 2, 18

127 Omens and Portents

But at the very moment when all the preparations were complete and the enemy, not suspecting any move of this kind, were off their guard, there occurred a nocturnal eclipse of the moon. This terrified Nicias and those of his men who were sufficiently ignorant or superstitious to be disturbed by such a sight. Eclipses of the sun towards the end of the month were by this time understood even by the uneducated to be caused in some way or other by the shadow of the moon. But in the case of the moon, what it could be that crossed her path and caused her while she was at the full to lose her light and give off so many different colours, they found far more difficult to explain. They were convinced that it must be a supernatural portent and a warning from the gods that fearful calamities were at hand.

The first man to attempt to explain in writing the illumination and eclipse of the moon was Anaxagoras, and his account was the boldest and the most lucid of all. But this was a recent theory, nor did it enjoy much repute: in fact, it was still treated as a secret, confined to a small circle and only communicated with great caution rather than with confidence. Public opinion was instinctively hostile towards natural philosophers and visionaries, as they were called, since it was generally believed that they belittled the power of the gods by explaining it away as nothing more than the operation of irrational causes and blind forces acting by necessity. For this reason even Protagoras was driven into exile and Anaxagoras imprisoned, till Pericles managed to rescue him with great difficulty, while Socrates, although he had nothing whatever to do with this kind of speculation, was nevertheless put to death for his connexion with philosophy. It was not until later that the glorious fame of Plato shone forth, and served, not only through the example of his life, but also through his teaching that the forces of nature are subject to a higher principle, to dispel the odium which had attached itself to such theories, thereby enabling them to circulate freely. At any rate, Plato's friend Dion remained unperturbed, although an eclipse of the moon took place at the time when he was to embark at Zacynthus for his conspiracy against Dionysius, and he continued his voyage to Syracuse, landed there, and drove out the tyrant.

It happened that at that moment, however, Nicias did not even have an experienced soothsayer with him. His former intimate associate, Stilbides, who had done much to hold his superstitious fears in check, had recently died. And, indeed, as Philochorus has pointed out, from the point of view of men engaged in an evacuation, the eclipse, so far from being a bad omen, was a positive advantage, since an operation of this kind, carried out under the fear of discovery, needs concealment above all else, while light is fatal to it. In any event the normal practice, as Autoclides mentions in his commentaries, was to delay action for no more than three days following an eclipse of the sun or moon. Nicias, however, persuaded the Athenians to wait for another whole cycle of the moon, as if he could not see that the planet had been purified of the darkness and restored to its normal brilliance, the moment it had passed out of the region which is overshadowed by the earth.

Nicias now became more and more oblivious of his other duties and completely absorbed in sacrifice and divination.

Plutarch *Nicias* 23–4
tr. I. Scott-Kilvert (Penguin 1960)

I28 Science, Religion, or Both?

Anaxagoras of Clazomenae was the most famous philosopher of the mid-fifth century, Lampon a religious leader, Thucydides (not the historian) a leading oligarch, ostracized in 443.

There is a story that Pericles was once sent from his country estate the head of a one-horned ram. Thereupon Lampon, the soothsayer, when he saw how the horn grew strong and solid out of the middle of the creature's forehead, declared that the mastery of the two dominant parties in the city – which at that time were led by Thucydides and Pericles respectively – would be concentrated in the hands of one man, and that he would be the one to whom this sign had been given. Anaxagoras, on the other hand, had the skull dissected and proceeded to demonstrate that the brain had not filled its natural space, but had contracted into a point like an egg at that place in the cavity from which the horn grew. On that occasion, so the story goes, it was Anaxagoras who won the admiration of the onlookers, but not long after Lampon came into his own, for Thucydides was overthrown and the entire control of affairs fell into Pericles' hands.

Plutarch *Pericles* 6
tr. I. Scott-Kilvert (Penguin 1960)

I29 Vortex Dethrones Zeus

A comic view of the effect of the scientific revolution. The voice referred to in the first line is the voice of the Clouds.

STREPSIADES: Name of Earth, what a voice, solemn, spectacular out of this world!
SOCRATES: Of course. These are the only gods. All other religion is just nonsense.
STREPSIADES: But Zeus – name of Earth! – Olympian Zeus – isn't he a god?
SOCRATES: Zeus! What Zeus? Don't talk rubbish. There isn't any Zeus.
STREPSIADES: What d'you mean?
Who makes the rain? Answer me that before you go any farther.
SOCRATES: *They* do of course. And I'll prove it you by irrefutable evidence –
come along now. When did you ever see it raining and no cloud in the sky?
Zeus ought to be able to give the clouds a holiday and rain out of a clear sky.
STREPSIADES: Apollo, that's right. What a splendid piece of graft.
And I always used to think the rain was Zeus pissing into a sieve.
Ah, but who causes the thunder? It makes me go hot and cold to talk about it.
SOCRATES: *They* do. The thunder is the sound of their rolling.
STREPSIADES: You've an answer for everything. How?
SOCRATES: They are hydroelectric spheres. A disequilibrium of forces
operates the law of motion. Hydrostatics in suspension
become hydrodynamics. Result: collision of mass, explosion, resonance.
STREPSIADES: But the disequitable force that operates the laws of motion – that's Zeus.
SOCRATES: Oh, no. It's an atmospheric vortex.
STREPSIADES: Vortex? Well I never did.
Poor old Zeus is non-existent. Vortex is on the throne instead.

Aristophanes *Clouds* 363–81

J COMMUNITY AND SOCIAL LIFE

The Athenian polis did not regulate the life of each individual to the extent that Sparta did. The Athenian citizen could eat where and how he wanted, choose his friends and entertainments. Leisure was the prerogative of freemen and citizens, indeed primarily of the upper classes. Freedom from earning one's living meant time for the more important functions of man, becoming involved in politics, representing one's polis at one of the Panhellenic festivals; for the common man the high points of life would be the city festivals in which he could participate by sacrificing, going to the theatre, joining in processions, games and official sacrifices. Leisure as we understand it was paralleled in the symposia, or dinner parties, which could have political implications as well.

The Excavations of the Athenian Agora Picture Books (The American School of Classical Studies at Athens) are a useful guide to the archaeological evidence. On this topic see especially: no. 1 'Pots and pans of classical Athens'; no. 9 'Lamps from the Athenian Agora'; no. 12 'An ancient shopping center: The Athenian Agora'.

For a fuller treatment of the buildings consult R. E. Wycherley *The Stones of Athens* (Princeton University Press 1978) and on civic planning and amenities the same author's *How the Greeks Built Cities* (2nd edition, Macmillan, 1962).

For evidence from Old Comedy see V. Ehrenberg *The People of Aristophanes* (Methuen 1974) and on specific topics, H. A. Harris *Greek Athletes and Athletics* (Hutchinson 1964) and M. I. Finley and H. W. Pleket *The Olympic Games: The First Thousand Years* (Chatto and Windus 1976).

J1 The Polis as a Community

The word polis cannot be translated, for it denoted something outside our experience today; for the Greeks 'politika' *(politics) embraced moral, cultural and religious matters, as well as what we mean by political affairs; anything, in fact, which was of common concern to the whole community. Hence Aristotle's remark, often mistranslated as 'man is a political animal', means 'man is a creature whose natural instinct is to live in a polis'; i.e. the polis is the only organization within which man can fully realize all his capacities and potential. Some idea of the enormous range of the meaning of polis can be seen from the following examples drawn from H. D. F. Kitto* The Greeks *(Penguin 1951):*

(a) *Ship of State*

CREON: Gentlemen, as for the polis, the gods
have brought it safely through the storm, on even keel again.

Sophocles *Antigone* 162–3

(b) *The Whole People*

CREON: It has been proclaimed to the polis that no one
should give him a funeral with honour, or mourn for him,
but leave him unburied, his body a meal for birds
and dogs, a disgrace for all to see.

Sophocles *Antigone* 203–6

(c) *Constitutional Government*

CREON: Is the polis to tell me how to rule?
HAEMON: You see how you've spoken just like a little boy?
CREON: What? Is anyone but me to rule over this land?
HAEMON: It is no polis that is ruled by one man alone.

Sophocles *Antigone* 734–7

(d) *All my Fellow Citizens*

CHORUS: Did you see, did you see
O whole polis, this wise man, this super-intelligent man . . .

Aristophanes *Acharnians* 971–2

(e) *'Everybody knows that'*

JOCASTA: You may be certain that this is how he told the tale,
it is not possible for him to change it now;
for the polis heard it, not I alone.

Sophocles *Oedipus the King* 848–50

tr. K. Chisholm after H. D. F. Kitto

J2 Passing the Time

The Agora or the city-centre was the great place to meet for a chat. Some shops were better-known resorts than others. The barber's, then as now, was the place to catch up with the latest news. See also Plutarch Nicias *30 for his description of how the news of the disaster in Sicily in 413 reached the Athenians through gossip in a barber's shop.*

Everyone of you frequents the scent-shop, the barber's or the saddler's, or wherever, and the majority of you those closest to the city-centre, and not so many those more distant. So if any of you has any criticism of those who come into my premises, the same criticism is valid against those who frequent the other shops – that means the whole population of Athens, for you all like lounging and gossiping here, there and everywhere.

Lysias 24, 20

J3 The Scene at the Palaestra

When we went in, we found that the boys had finished the sacrifices there, and had pretty well completed the religious business, and were all playing knucklebones in their best dress. Most of them were playing in the open air in the courtyard, but some were in a corner of the dressing-room playing at odd-and-even with a large number of knucklebones which they were taking out of small boxes. Lysis was among these. He stood out among the youngsters and older boys with his garland and his good looks; the sort of person you would call not just a good-looker, but good generally. We went over to the other side and sat down – it was quiet there – and chatted to one another.

Plato *Lysis* 206e–7a

J4 Importance of Horse Racing at the Major Festivals

This passage refers to Alcibiades (see no. L3). Winning a race at one of the major religious festivals could confer great political prestige; these events were of Panhellenic importance, both because of their religious aspect as a common act of worship and celebration of the god or gods, and because of their political importance in bringing together the city-states of Greece. In times of war a truce would be declared so the Games could be held.

About the same time my father, seeing that the festival assembly at Olympia was beloved and admired by the whole world and that in it the Greeks made display of their wealth, strength of body, and training, and that not only the athletes were the objects of envy but that also the cities of the victors became renowned, and believing moreover that while the public services performed in Athens redound to the prestige, in the eyes of his fellow-citizens, of the person who renders them, expenditures in the Olympian Festival, however, enhance the city's reputation throughout all Greece, reflecting upon these things, I say, although in natural gifts and in strength of body he was inferior to none, he disdained the gymnastic contests, for he knew that some of the athletes were of low birth, inhabitants of petty states, and of mean education, but turned to the breeding of race-horses, which is possible only for those most blest by Fortune and not to be pursued by one of low estate, and not only did he surpass his rivals, but also all who had ever before won the victory.

Isocrates *The Team of Horses* 31–4
tr. G. B. Norlin (Loeb 1928)

J5 Hunting

Game and hounds are an invention of the gods Apollo and Artemis . . . My advice to the young is not to despise hunting or any other training. These help people to be good in war and in other activities which cannot fail to lead to nobility in thought, word and act.

Xenophon *On Hunting* 1

J6 An Attack on Athletes

From Autolycus, *a lost play of Euripides*

There are thousands of things wrong with Greece,
but the athletes are the worst of all.
Living properly – they don't know about it
and they don't care. How could any man
be a slave to his jaw and a servant to his belly,
and outstrip his father's glory?
They can't cope with poverty, can't swim
with the tide. They've no idea of good character
and take obstacles hard.
When young they're famous and add to their country's
repute. When old age comes grimly on them,
they're like cloaks with frayed ends.
I blame Greek practice.
We make a fuss of them,
do them honour, give them free meals.
Wrestlers, sprinters,
discus-throwers, boxers –
what good do their crowns do their country?
Will they fight the enemy
with discuses? Drop their shields
and repel the invader by sprinting?
Oh no; they've more sense than to face
cold steel. I say that the garlands
should go to wise statesmen, heroes,
sound advisers, good citizens,
those who prefer good words to deadly action
and bring an end to war and revolution. That's
a blessing to any city, to all Greece.

Euripides fr. 284

J7 A Dinner Party

Ion of Chios was a contemporary of Sophocles and a tragic poet whose lost memoirs are cited for his recollections of various fifth-century Athenians. Themistocles was responsible for the Greek victory over the Persians at Salamis. For Cimon see no. B3. Serious drinking began after dinner.

Ion says that while still a teenager he came from Chios to Athens and dined with Cimon at Laomedon's house. When the wine was served Cimon was invited to sing. He gave quite a pleasant performance and the guests favoured him as a cleverer man than Themistocles, who knew how to make his country prosperous and powerful, but not how to sing or play the lyre. After that, as you would expect with the drink circulating, conversation turned easily to Cimon's achievements. They recalled his outstanding exploits, and he himself recounted one of his own stratagems which he thought particularly shrewd.

Plutarch *Cimon* 9, 1–2

J8 Good and Bad Dinner Parties

In Plato's Symposium *they send the entertainers away and conversation reigns; in Xenophon's they have the best of both worlds. (See no. J9.)*

Conversation about poetry reminds me too much of the wine-parties of second-rate and commonplace people. Such men, being too uneducated to entertain themselves as they drink by using their own voices and conversational resources, put up the price of female musicians, paying well for the hire of an extraneous voice – that of the pipe – and find their entertainment in its warblings. But where the drinkers are men of worth and culture, you will find no girls piping or dancing or harping. They are quite capable of enjoying their own company without such frivolous nonsense, using their own voices in sober discussion and each taking his turn to speak or listen – even if the drinking is really heavy. In the same way gatherings like our own, if they consist of men such as most of us claim to be, call for no extraneous voices – not even of poets. No one can interrogate poets about what they say, and most often when they are introduced into the discussion some say the poet's meaning is one thing and some another, for the topic is one on which nobody can produce a conclusive argument. The best people avoid such discussions, and entertain each other from their own resources, testing one another's mettle in what they have to say themselves.

Plato *Protagoras* 347c–8a
tr. W. K. C. Guthrie (Penguin 1956)

J9 After-dinner Entertainment

The tables were cleared, a libation offered and a hymn sung. A man from Syracuse now came in to entertain the guests. He had with him a flute-girl, a dancing-girl with spectacular abilities, and a boy, a good-looker, to play the lute and dance. The Syracusan made his living by producing this show. The flute-girl and the boy played on their instruments, and there was general satisfaction with their performance. Socrates commented, 'The perfect dinner-party, Callias! An unexceptionable meal, followed by a feast for eyes and ears.' 'How about ordering some perfume,' said Callias, 'to have a feast for the nose as well?'

Xenophon *Symposium* 2, 1–3

J10 Parasites

The word parasite originally means dinner-guest. It comes to be used for the man who gets his meals at another's expense, as a mere sponger. They seem to have appeared first towards the end of the fifth century, but their prominence in Middle Comedy suggests that they became a regular feature of social life in the fourth. We know of one nicknamed Soup, because he was always present at the start of a meal. Athenaeus cites a number of passages. This, from Timocles's Dracontium, *is not unsympathetic.*

Then am I to permit all and sundry
to denigrate the parasite? No fear.
There's no more valuable group for these things.
If you account sociability a virtue,
the parasite practises it comprehensively.
You're in love! he'll help you without hesitation.
You've some business in hand? It'll be his business
to be at your side, making his patron's rights his own.
He's second to none in admiring his friends.

They enjoy free dinners?
Who doesn't? Man, demigod, god –
Who says No to spending time like that?
Not to go on all day about it,
I think I have convincing evidence
of the high honour a parasite's life enjoys.
They receive the same honour for their services
as Olympic victors do — free meals.
Anywhere which doesn't charge
should be regarded as a City-hall.

Timocles in Athenaeus 6, 237d–f

J11 Food

The Athenians, except for athletes, ate meat rarely (see also no. I14).

(a) *Telecleides was a writer of Old Comedy.*

I like hot scones, I don't like wild pears,
I adore roast hare on girdlecake.

Telecleides in Athenaeus 14, 648e

(b)

. . . drinking honeyed wine
from an aromatic cup,
with a cheese-snack . . .

Telecleides in Athenaeus 4, 170

(c) *The following passage possibly refers to a rival poet's provision of refreshments for the audience; in which case the speaker may be Victory.*

After a time he tried to win my love
with ripe olives and cakes; chervils did the trick.

Telecleides in Athenaeus 2, 56d

(d) *Aristomenus was another writer of Old Comedy.*

I'll have a spot of breakfast and be back –
two or three nibbles at a loaf of bread.

Aristomenus in Athenaeus 1, 11c

(e) *From* The Slave Trainer *by Pherecrates, also a writer of Old Comedy.*

A: Tell me how dinner's getting on.
B: You're going to have a slice
of eel, a squid, roast
lamb, a sausage,
boiled foot, liver, rib,
plenty of birds, cheese
in a honey-sauce, a slice of beef.

Pherecrates in Athenaeus 3, 96c

(f) *Magnes was a writer of Old Comedy.*

Have you ever seen pancakes smoke and
sizzle, when you pour honey on them?

Magnes in Athenaeus 14, 646f

(g) *Ecphantides was a writer of Old Comedy.*

When he had to buy boiled pig's trotters for his meal.

Ecphantides in Athenaeus 3, 96c

J12 Riddles

Riddling was a favourite party-game. Those who failed to guess the answer had to drink a cup of wine mixed with sea-water without stopping to take breath. Middle Comedy makes use of riddles for comic purposes. One frequent form was to give a complex definition with a simple answer as in Antiphanes's Sacred to Love.

A: When I want to say 'pot' to you am I to say 'pot'
or 'a hollow-bodied vessel formed on a whirling wheel,
moulded of earth, cooked in another of the Mother's halls,
pregnant with tender-fleshed forms, milk-fed and stewing,
from the new-born flock'?

B: God, you'll be the death of me,
I'm sure, if you can't say in ordinary language 'pot of meat'.

A: All right. Now shall I say 'mingling with rivers from the golden bee
the creamy flood from bleating goats, resting
in a flat cover of the virgin daughter of chaste Deo,
playing the millionaire in a myriad delicate integuments'
or shall I say in plain language 'a cake'?

B: I'd rather 'a cake'.

A: How about 'sweat from Bromius's spring'?

B: Cut it out. Say 'wine'.

A: 'The dewy fount of the nymphs'?

B: Leave it out. Say 'water'.

A: 'The breath of cassia streaming through the upper air'?

B: Too long. Say 'myrrh'.

A: Nothing like that?

B: No – and no more questions.
It seems to one a waste of time to follow those
who never call a thing by its own name, but twist a mass of words round it.

Antiphanes in Athenaeus 10, 449b–d

J13 Games

(a) Phaininda *was a ball-game, later called* harpastum, *and very popular. There is a late account of the game in Sidonius Apollinaris 5, 17; see also the anonymous* Laus Pisonis *185 ff. The rules are quite unclear; even H. A. Harris* Sport in Greece and Rome, *p. 87 ff, is not over-illuminating.*

He caught the ball,
triumphantly passed it to one player, sold another a dummy,
knocked it out of another's hands, helped another up after a tackle,
with ringing shouts ...
'Out of court ... too far ... pass him ... over his head ... at your feet ...
in the air ... too short ... pass it back in the scrimmage.'

Antiphanes in Athenaeus 1, 15a

(b) Cottabus *was a game of jerking wine from a bowl at a mark; like squash it required a supple wrist. Plato, the comic dramatist, not the philosopher, in* The Troubles of Zeus, *showed a game among the gods with forfeits. Heracles is perhaps playing with Aphrodite.*

A: Have a game of cottabus, while I go
inside and get some supper.
HERACLES: Fine.
But is there a bowl?
A: The mortar will do.
HERACLES: Fetch one, and some water. Bring
the wine-cups. We'll play for kisses.
A: Kisses? I can't have that. It's not
genteel. I'll lay the stakes –
the shoes she's wearing,
and your cups.
HERACLES: Whew! This
is better than the Isthmian games.

Plato in Athenaeus 15, 666d

(c) *This game sounds like kiss-in-the-ring. Pollux was a grammarian who wrote on the meanings of Greek words in the second century AD.*

The Kissing Game is named from kissing or canoodling, as Crates suggests in *Games* ... a play in which the poet says something about pretty well all the games there are. Thus:

She stands in the middle
of the men as they dance, and plays
the Kissing Game, of course kissing
the good-lookers.

Pollux *Onomasticon* 9, 114

(d) 'Cities' *is also mentioned in Hesychius (s.v.) Photius (s.v.) and in Zenobius 5, 67. Photius describes it as a game with seven pebbles (each?). Cratinus was a fifth-century dramatist.*

The game involves a number of pebbles and a board marked off by lines into squares. The board is called the 'city' and each of the pebbles is a 'dog'. The pebbles are divided into two by colour, and the skill of the game consists in taking a pebble of the opposite colour with two of the same colour. Cratinus has a joke on the subject:

CHORUS: Pandion's son, king of a prosperous city, do you know the one we're speaking of?

THESEUS: Oh yes – the city they play with the dog.

Pollux *Onomasticon* 9, 99

J14 Drink

The Greeks normally mixed wine with water, a ratio of three parts water to one of wine (Hesiod) was a temperate one; one to one was considered inebriating. Alcaeus, the late seventh-century poet, gives a proportion, of one of water to two of wine: a strong mixture.

(a)

Let us drink. Why are we waiting for the lamps? Day is a finger.
Lift down the large ornamental cups . . .
The son of Semele and Zeus gave men wine
to drown. Mix one to two, and pour it out
brimful, so that one cup presses hard on
the next.

Alcaeus fr. 41 (Bergk) Z 22 (Lobel-Page)

(b) *In this scene from an old comedy play* Corianno *even the strong 2:1 mixture is considered too watery.*

OLD WOMAN: Glyce, it's undrinkable.
GLYCE: Too much water?
OLD WOMAN: Nothing but water!
GLYCE: What did you do? Damn it all, how did you mix it?
CHILD: Two of water, mummy.
GLYCE: And wine?
CHILD: Four.
OLD WOMAN: Go to hell. Do you think you're mixing wine for frogs?

Pherecrates in Athenaeus 10, 430e

K SOME GLIMPSES OF LIFE

Life in the great age of Athens was dominated by the Peloponnesian war and the subsequent political upheavals, yet there is a continuity of pattern on the smaller scale, the day-to-day life of the citizen working in the fields or in a workshop, attending the assembly to deal with the running of the bureaucratic machinery, perhaps involved in a law suit, as juror, plaintiff or defendant.

For pictures to illustrate the artefacts of everyday life see *The Excavations of the Athenian Agora Picture Books* (The American School of Classical Studies at Athens) especially nos. 1, 6, 8, 9, 11 and 14.

For more detail see V. Ehrenburg *The People of Aristophanes* (Methuen 1974); J. E. Jones, A. J. Graham and L. H. Sackett *An Attic Country House* (British School of Archaeology 1973); E. S. Stavely *Greek and Roman Voting and Elections* (Thames and Hudson 1972).

Two important books on the sea are J. S. Morrison and R. J. Williams *Greek Oared Ships 900–322 BC* (Cambridge University Press 1968) and M. Amit *Athens and the Sea, a Study in Athenian Sea Power* (Brussels 1965).

K1 Athenians in Attica

In 431 war broke out and those who lived in the countryside were brought within the city walls. Thucydides speaks of the old way of life.

The Athenians lived for the most part in independent communities in the countryside. Even after the synoecism old habits stuck, and the majority from early times down to the present war were to be found living among the fields with all their families. They were not easily persuaded to move, especially as it was not long since they had taken up their establishments again after the Persian War. They were deeply discontented at abandoning their homes and their traditional ancestral shrines, and having to change their life-style and give up what each had come to regard as his own city.

Thucydides 2, 16

K2 The Ephebic Oath

The ephebe was a young man of military age; there are many references to the oath they took on beginning service. For a recent discussion see P. Siewert 'The Ephebic Oath in Fifth-century Athens' Journal of Hellenic Studies *97 (1977), pp. 102–12.*

Traditional oath of the Epheboi which they must swear:

1 'I will not disgrace these sacred arms,
2 and I will not desert the comrade beside me wherever I shall be stationed in a battle line.
3 I will defend our sacred and public institutions,
4 and I will not hand over (to the descendants) the fatherland smaller, but greater and better, so far as I am able, by myself or with the help of all.
5 I will obey those who for the time being exercise sway reasonably and the established laws and those which they will establish reasonably in the future,
6 if anyone seek to destroy them, I will not admit it so far as I am able, by myself or with the help of all.
7 I will honour the traditional sacred institutions.
8 Witnesses are the gods Aglauros, Hestia, Enyo, Enyalios, Ares and Athena Areia, Zeus, Thallo, Auxo, Hegemone, Herakles, and the boundaries of the fatherland, wheat, barley, vines, olive-trees, fig-trees.'

tr. P. Siewert
'The Ephebic Oath in Fifth-century Athens'
Journal of Hellenic Studies 97 (1977) (after J. Plescia)

K3 A Council of War

Xenophon the Athenian served with Cyrus when he rebelled against his brother the Great King of Persia. The use of Greek mercenary soldiers had increased greatly in the fourth-century BC. The Persians particularly liked to have them because their discipline and fighting skills were considered superior to native troops. See H. W. Parke Greek Mercenary Soldiers from the Earliest Times to the Battle of Ipsus *(Oxford 1955).*

The following extracts are taken from the Anabasis *Xenophon's account of the expedition against the Great King (see also no. K4).*

With their generals arrested and the captains and soldiers who had gone with them put to death, the Greeks were in an extremely awkward position. It occurred to them that they were near the King's capital and that around them on all sides were numbers of people and cities who were their enemies: no one was likely in the future to provide them with a chance of buying food. They were at least a thousand miles away from Greece: they had no guide to show them the way: they were shut in by impassable rivers which traversed their homeward journey: even the natives who had marched on the capital with Cyrus had turned against them, and they were left by themselves without a single cavalryman in their army, so that it was evident that, if they won a victory, they could not kill any of their enemies, and if they were defeated themselves none of them would be left alive. With all this to reflect upon they were in a state of deep despondency. Only a few tasted food that evening, and a few lit fires. Many of them did not parade by the arms that night, but took their rest just where each man happened to be, and could not sleep because of their misery and their longing for their home lands and parents and wives and children, which they thought that they would never see again. . . .

Xenophon was no different from the rest, and now in their difficult position he was as miserable as anyone else and could not get to sleep. However, he got a little sleep in the end and had a dream. He dreamed that there was a thunderstorm and that a thunderbolt fell on his father's house and then the whole house was on fire. He woke up immediately, feeling very frightened, and considered that in some respects the dream was a good one, because in the midst of his difficulties and dangers he had dreamed of a great light from Zeus; but in other respects he was alarmed by it, because the dream seemed to him to have come from Zeus in his character of the King and the fire had seemed to blaze all round him and this might mean that he would not be able to leave the King's country but would be shut in on all sides by one difficulty or another. But what is really meant by having a dream like this can be seen from what happened after the dream. . . .

Dawn was just breaking when the new officers were chosen, and they came to the centre of the camp and decided to post sentries and call the soldiers to a meeting. When the rest of the army were assembled, Chirisophus stood up first and spoke. . . . After him Xenophon stood up. He had put on the best-looking uniform that he could, thinking that, if the gods granted victory, victory deserved the best-looking armour, or if he was to die, then it was right for him to put on his best clothes and be wearing them when he met his death. He began his speech as follows: 'Cleanor has spoken of the natives' perjury and treachery, and I feel sure that you agree with what he has said. If, then, we want to make friends with them again, we shall have to be very downhearted indeed, when we consider what happened to our generals, who, because they trusted in their good faith, put themselves into their hands. But if our purpose is to take our arms in our hands and to make them pay for what they have done and for the future to fight total war against them, then, with the help of heaven, we have many glorious hopes of safety.'

Just as he was saying this, someone sneezed, and, when the soldiers heard it, they all with one accord fell on their knees and worshipped the god who had given this sign. Xenophon went on: 'I think, soldiers, that, since an omen from Zeus the Saviour appeared just when we were speaking about safety, we ought to make a vow that we will give thank-offerings to the god for our safety in the place where we first reach friendly soil, and we should also vow to offer sacrifices to the other gods to the best of our ability. Whoever agrees with this, put up his hand.'

Then they all raised their hands, and afterwards they made their vows and sang the paean.

Xenophon *Anabasis* 3, 1, 2–3; 3, 1, 11–13; 3, 2, 1–4; 3, 2, 7–9
tr. R. Warner (Penguin 1950)

K4 The Sea

The Greeks, and the Athenians in particular, were never at home far from the sea, as this famous episode in the march through the mountains of Asia Minor tells.

They came to the mountain on the fifth day, the name of the mountain being Thekes. When the men in front reached the summit and caught sight of the sea there was great shouting. Xenophon and the rearguard heard it and thought that there were some more enemies attacking in the front, since there were natives of the country they had ravaged following them up behind, and the rearguard had killed some of them and made prisoners of others in an ambush, and captured about twenty raw ox-hide shields, with the hair on. However, when the shouting got louder and drew nearer, and those who were constantly going forward started running towards the men in front who kept on shouting, and the more there were of them the more shouting there was, it looked then as though this was something of considerable importance. So Xenophon mounted his horse and, taking Lycus and the cavalry with him, rode forward to give support, and, quite soon, they heard the soldiers shouting out 'The sea! The sea!' and passing the word down the column. Then certainly they all began to run, the rearguard and all, and drove on the baggage animals and the horses at full speed; and when they had all got to the top, the soldiers, with tears in their eyes, embraced each other and their generals and captains.

Xenophon *Anabasis* 4, 7, 21–5
tr. R. Warner (Penguin 1950)

K5 A Prosperous Athenian Metic

For evidence about the property of Cephisodorus, another Athenian metic, see no. D2(b).

Lysias was the son of Kephalos, grandson of Lysanias, and great-grandson of Kephalos. His father was by birth a Syracusan but moved to Athens because he wished to live in that city and also because Perikles, son of Xanthippos, persuaded him to do so, as he was a personal friend of Perikles and they were connected by ties of hospitality, and he was a man of great wealth. But some say that he moved because he was banished from Syracuse when Gelon was tyrant. Lysias was born at Athens in the archonship of the Philokles who succeeded Phrasikles, in the second year of the eightieth Olympiad, and at first he was a schoolmate of the most prominent Athenians; but when the city sent the colony to Sybaris, which was afterwards renamed Thourioi, he went out with his eldest brother Polemarchos (for he had two others, Euthydemos and Brachyllos), their father being already dead, to share in the allotment of land. This was in the archonship of Praxiteles, and he was then fifteen years old. He remained there, was instructed by the Syracusans Teisias and Nikias, acquired a house, had a share of the allotment, and was a citizen for thirty-three years, until Kleokritos was archon at Athens. But in the next year, when Kallias was archon, in the ninety-second Olympiad, when the misfortunes in Sicily had happened to the Athenians and unrest had arisen among the allies in general and especially those who dwelt in Italy, he was accused of favouring Athens and, with three hundred others, was banished. Arriving at Athens in the archonship of the Kallias who succeeded Kleokritos, when the Four Hundred already had possession of the city, he remained there. But when the battle of Aigospotamoi had taken place and the Thirty had taken possession of the city, he was banished after having been there seven years. He was deprived of his property and lost his brother Polemarchos, but he himself escaped from the house in which he was kept to be executed (for it had two doors) and lived at Megara. But when the men at Phyle set about their return to Athens, he was seen to be more helpful than anyone else, since he supplied two thousand drachmas and two hundred shields and, when sent with Hermes, hired three hundred mercenaries and persuaded Thrasydaios of Elis, who had become his guest-friend, to give two talents. For these services Thrasyboulos, after the restoration of the exiles to the city and in the period of anarchy before Eukleides, proposed a grant of citizenship for him, and the popular assembly ratified the grant, but when Archinos had him up for illegality because it had not been previously voted by the council, the enactment was declared void. And after losing his citizenship in this way, he lived the rest of his life at Athens with all the rights of citizenship except the vote and eligibility to office, and died there at the age of eighty-three years or, as some say, seventy-six or, as others say, over eighty; and he lived to see Demosthenes as a youth. They say he was born in the archonship of Philokles.

Four hundred and twenty-five orations attributed to him are current. Of these Dionysios and Caecilius and their school say that two hundred and thirty-three are genuine, and he is said to have lost his case with only two of them. There is also his speech in support of the enactment against which Archinos brought suit and deprived him of citizenship, and another against the Thirty. He was very persuasive and concise and produced most of his speeches for private clients. There are also Textbooks of Rhetoric prepared by him, and Public Addresses, Letters and Eulogies, Funeral Speeches, Love Speeches, and a Defence of Socrates addressed to the judges. In the matter of his diction he appears to be easy, although in fact he is hard to imitate. Demosthenes in his speech against Neaira says that he was in love with Metaneira, a fellow-slave with Neaira; but later he married the daughter of his brother Brachyllos. Plato also mentions him in the *Phaedrus* as an able speaker and older than Isocrates.

[Plutarch] *Moralia* 835C–836A
tr. N. Lewis *Greek Historical Documents* (Hakkert, Toronto 1971)

K6 A Dispute between Hill-farmers

One Callicles is prosecuting an unknown defendant for damage done to his farm by flooding because the latter built a wall damming up a public watercourse. The defendant denies the allegations, and gives a vivid picture of a mountain farm.

The intervening space between our properties is a public right of way. Around our properties the country is hilly, with the unfortunate result that water runs down partly on to the bridle path and partly on to our properties. Further, the water which comes down on to the path is carried downwards along the path so long as it has free passage, but if it encounters any obstacle there is nowhere for it to overflow except on to our farms. Whenever there was a heavy storm, gentlemen, my property used to be inundated. Before my father took it over it was owned by a man who did not like the countryside at all, a city type, and who neglected it. Two or three times the water flowed in and damaged the property, and was making a regular channel. Furthermore, as I have learned from eye-witnesses, the neighbours used to take shortcuts trespassing on our property. My father saw these facts, and built this perimeter wall . . . Callicles claims that I am causing him material damage by walling off the watercourse. I shall demonstrate that this is not a watercourse but our private property. If it were not admitted to be our private property, then a legal claim might lie against us for building on public land. But no one challenges our assertion. There are fruit trees growing on the land, vines and figs. No one could dream of planting fruit trees in the bed of a river! No one would bury his ancestors there! But both these are facts, gentlemen.

And the trees were planted before my father built the wall; the tombs are old and go back to before we acquired the property! Gentlemen, there could be no stronger argument; the facts speak for themselves.

Demosthenes *Against Callicles* 10–14

K7 An Action for Assault

A pompous plaintiff named Ariston, whose tone the speech-writer catches beautifully, describes how he was assaulted. Panactum was a frontier fort used for training.

Two years ago I was put on garrison-duty and sent to Panactum. The sons of the defendant Conon were camped next to us – unfortunately. This was the start of our violent hostility, as I shall tell you. These men every day spent all their time from breakfast on drinking. They never let up during our whole period on garrison-duty. We of course behaved away from Athens exactly as usual. By dinner-time they were already drunk and disorderly, towards our batmen and later towards ourselves. They alleged that the boys smoked them out while cooking dinner or were insolent or something; they beat them up, emptied their jerries over them, and actually pissed on them. They used any form of insult and violence. This upset us. We remonstrated with them. They laughed at us and carried on as before. So our whole mess unanimously – not just myself – reported the matter to the commanding officer. He gave them a sharp rebuke, not only for their abominable behaviour to us, but for their general demeanour in camp. Did they change? Were they ashamed? That very evening as soon as it was dark they jumped on us using filthy language and going on to offer me violence. They made such a noise with their shouting round the tent that the commander and his lieutenants arrived with some of the other soldiers, and saved us from suffering immediate damage – or perhaps inflicting it after our sottish treatment. After all this it was not surprising if there was some mutual hostility on our return . . .

It happened that we were turning back from Persephone's temple, and walking past the Leocorion when we met them. As we passed, one of them whose name I do not know, set about Phanostratus and held him prisoner. The defendant Conon with his son and Andramenes's boy fell on me. They pulled off my cloak, tripped me up, and knocked me into the mud, kicked me and pummelled me so that they split my lips and closed up my eyes. They left me in such a state that I could not get up or utter a sound. I lay there and listened to them. It was terrible; I would not dare to repeat some of it in your presence. But I will tell you one clear piece of evidence of his violent character and his prime responsibility for the whole episode. He began to crow like a victorious gamecock and his associates encouraged him to flap his elbows against his ribs like wings.

Demosthenes *Against Conon* 3–6, 8–9

K8 Sequel to the Mutilation of the Herms

The sale of property (in 414–3) of those condemned for mutilating the Herms *in 415–4 was recorded on stone. Fragments of ten columns are extant of which three samples are given below. (Part of the first column, a list of slaves, is given in no. D2(b). The left-hand figure is a sales tax. The text is in R. Meiggs and D. Lewis* Greek Historical Inscriptions *(Oxford 1969) no. 79.*

3 ob   18 dr standing crop at Thria
3 ob   20 dr standing crop at Athmonon
Total, including sales taxes, 4,723 dr 5 ob.

(Property of) Polystratos son of Diodoros, of Ankyle:
2 dr 1 ob   202 dr Faithful

. . . .

(Property of) Panaitios:
[lost]   70(?) dr 104 amphoras 7 choes of pure Attic wine
3 dr   260 dr beehives in the field at Is - - - - - - -
1 dr 1 ob   100 dr two female work oxen at Ar - - - - - - -
[lost]   [lost] 4 cows and - - calves
[lost]   [lost] 84 sheep and their young
7 dr 3 ob   710 dr 67 goats and their young

(Property of) Polystratos son of Diodoros, of Ankyle:
[lost]   [lost] house in Kydathenaion with a double-folding front door, adjoining the temple of Artemis Amarysia at Athmonon
[lost]   [lost] property at Ankyle south of the hillock where the temple . . .

(Property of) Alkibiades son of Kleinias, of Skambonidai:
[lost]   two-door chest
[lost]   four-door chest

90 dr	10 Milesian-work beds
16 dr	4 tables
17 dr	low couch, one-armed
11 dr	plain screen
[lost]	double-ended Milesian-work bed
[lost]	6 perfume jars
[lost]	5 stools
1 dr 1 ob	bench
[lost]	2 wicker baskets
[lost]	reed mat

tr. N. Lewis
Greek Historical Documents (Hakkert, Toronto 1971)

K9 A Book Collector

Euripides was perhaps the first serious book collector at Athens. We first hear of the book-trade during the Peloponnesian War (Aristophanes Birds *1288). For an interesting discussion see J. A. Davison* From Archilochus to Pindar *(Macmillan 1968) pp. 86–128.*

'Tell me, Euthydemus, is what I hear true, that you have accumulated a large collection of books written by the so-called learned?'

'Yes, indeed, Socrates,' he said. 'I'm still collecting too. I want my library to be as complete as possible.'

Xenophon *Memorabilia* 4, 2, 8

K10 Construction of a Footbridge

An inscription datable to 421–0, bringing before us a piece of public works. The name Rheitus was given to two salt-water creeks at Eleusis (Pausanias 1, 38, 1; Hesychius s.v.). The temple referred to dated from the sixth century and was destroyed by the invading Persians in 480.

Secretary: Prepis, son of Eupherus.
Decree of the Council and Commons.
Tribe in office: Aigeis. Secretary: Prepis. Chairman: Patrocles. Motion moved by Theaeus.

Decided: to bridge the Rheitus on the town side, using stones from the ruins of the old temple at Eleusis, left behind from the building of the wall, for the complete security of the priestesses carrying the holy images. The width is to be five feet to prevent the passage of wheeled traffic but permit the movement of pedestrians to the ceremonies. They are to use stones to cover the channel of the Rheitus following the proposals of the architect Demomeles. If they are not ...

W. Dittenberger *Sylloge Inscriptionum Graecarum* 86 (Leipzig[3] 1915)

L SOME PEN-PORTRAITS

The most rounded portraits we have from contemporary or even later sources are of the great and the famous. An indirect view of the 'Man in the Agora' can be gleaned from the literature, especially comedy (Aristophanes) and oratory (Demosthenes, Lysias, Isocrates). From inscriptions we have the names of more Athenian citizens than of any other city, yet we know nothing of their characters as individuals, only their characteristic behaviour as an assembly.

For further reading on the famous see H. D. Westlake *Individuals in Thucydides* (Cambridge University Press 1968) which contains chapters on Pericles, Cleon, Nicias, Alcibiades and Demosthenes as well as Spartan leaders.

L1 Pericles

Born about 495 of an aristocratic family, he was the dominant figure in Athenian politics from about 463 to his death in 429. He directed Athenian imperial policy, and led Athens into the war with Sparta. His claim that he never caused any Athenian to wear mourning (see (d) below) is decidedly dubious, but he rightly gave his name to an age of remarkable achievement.

(a)

Pericles belonged to the tribe Acamantis and the deme Cholargus. His family was of the highest nobility on both sides. His father Xanthippus, victor over the Persian King's generals at Mycale, married Agariste, granddaughter of the great Cleisthenes who so gallantly expelled the family of Pisistratus and brought the dictatorship to an end, instituted legislation, and introduced a constitution carefully devised to promote security and a common mind. She in her sleep dreamed that she had given birth to a lion; a few days later Pericles was born. His general appearance was impeccable, apart from a disproportionately long head. This is why almost all his statues are helmeted: it seems that the sculptors were unwilling to expose his deformity to ridicule. The Athenian dramatists used to nickname him schinocephalus (*schinus* is another word for 'squill') . . .

The poet Ion says that Pericles had an autocratic and arrogant attitude, and that his overbearing contained a contemptuous sense of superiority over others . . . When Zeno heard people calling Pericles's aloofness an arrogant concern for his own reputation, he used to suggest that they might show a similar concern for their reputations, on the view that a pretence to honour unconsciously produces a habit of dedication to it . . .

In his younger days Pericles was very shy of facing the commoners. His similarity in feature to the tyrant Pisistratus had been remarked, and those of an older generation noted his attractive voice and swift fluency of speech, and were astonished at the likeness. His wealth, ancestry and powerful friends led him to fear ostracism. At first he refused to touch politics, but showed outstanding skill and courage in military service. However, after Aristides's death, and Themistocles's exile, and during Cimon's continual absence from Greece on campaigns, Pericles finally decided to throw in his lot with the popular party, taking up the cause of the underprivileged masses instead of the rich élite. This was contrary to his character which was anything but democratic.

Plutarch *Pericles* 3–7

(b) *Eupolis was one of the great writers of Old Comedy. The passage refers to Pericles; it comes from a play called* The Demes. (See also B 16.)

A: He was the greatest orator of all.
When he rose to his feet, like a champion runner,
he could give the others three yards start.

B: You call him speedy, but it wasn't just speed.
A kind of Persuasion lived in his lips.
He cast a spell on us. He was the only orator
who left his sting behind in his audience.

Eupolis fr. 94K

(c)

Pericles, by his position, intellectual ability and manifest incorruptibility, exercised a free control of the commoners: he led them instead of being led by them. He did not attain power by improper means. He did not speak to please them; such was the esteem in which he was held, that he could risk their anger by standing in their way. If ever he thought them over-confident and dangerously above themselves, he would reduce them to panic by his words; if they were in a state of irrational alarm he would restore their confidence. Theoretically Athens was a democracy; in practice power was in the hands of the first citizen.

Thucydides 2, 65

(d)

No Athenian ever wore mourning because of any action of mine.

Pericles in Plutarch *Pericles* 38

L2 Socrates

Athenian thinker (469–399) executed by the restored democracy.

(a) *Phaedo on Socrates*

Echecrates, that was the end of our friend, a man we would say to be the best of his time in our experience, supreme in wisdom and moral integrity.

Plato *Phaedo* 118a

(b) *Xenophon on Socrates*

He was as I have described him, so pious that he never acted without guidance from the gods, so upright that he never did the smallest injury to any man, but was most helpful to all who came in contact with him, so self-disciplined that he chose virtue before pleasure, so intelligent that he was faultless in judging good from bad, self-reliant with no need of advice, masterly in defining and expounding this sort of area and challenging others, convincing them of wrong and turning them to decency and morality. To me he seemed the embodiment of goodness and happiness.

Xenophon *Memorabilia* 4, 8, 11

(c) *The Indictment*

'Socrates is guilty of refusing to honour the gods honoured by the state and of introducing other new divinities. He is also guilty of corrupting the youth.'

Xenophon *Memorabilia* 1, 1, 1

(d) *The underlying charge*

Gentlemen of Athens, you executed Socrates the Sophist because he was clearly responsible for the education of Critias, one of the Thirty anti-democratic leaders.

Aeschines 1, 173

(e) *A comic view of Socrates. The Clouds address him.*

Hail, high-priest of subtle bilge, tell us what you're now requesting.
Of all the present-day professors you're the only one we've time for –

apart from Prodicus. We value his wisdom and his judgment. You,
swaggering along the streets as your eye darts shifty glances,
barefoot, putting up with trouble, looking disdainfully, all for us.

Aristophanes *Clouds* 359–63

(f) *Alcibiades on Socrates*

'I propose to praise Socrates, gentlemen, by using similes. He will perhaps think that I mean to make fun of him, but my object in employing them is truth, not ridicule. I declare that he bears a strong resemblance to those figures of Silenus in b statuaries' shops, represented holding pipes or flutes; they are hollow inside, and when they are taken apart you see that they contain little figures of gods. I declare also that he is like Marsyas the satyr. You can't deny yourself, Socrates, that you have a striking physical likeness to both of these, and you shall hear in a moment how you resemble them in other respects. For one thing you're a bully, aren't you? I can bring evidence of this if you don't admit it. But you don't play the flute, you will say. No, indeed; the performance you give is far more remarkable. Marsyas c needed an instrument in order to charm men by the power which proceeded out of his mouth, a power which is still exercised by those who perform his melodies (I reckon the tunes ascribed to Olympus to belong to Marsyas, who taught him); his productions alone, whether executed by a skilled male performer or by a wretched flute-girl, are capable, by reason of their divine origin, of throwing men into a trance and thus distinguishing those who yearn to enter by initiation into union with the gods. But you, Socrates, are so far superior to Marsyas that you produce d the same effect by mere words without any instrument. At any rate, whereas we most of us pay little or no attention to the words of any other speaker, however accomplished, a speech by you or even a very indifferent report of what you have said stirs us to the depths and casts a spell over us, men and women and young lads alike. I myself, gentlemen, were it not that you would think me absolutely drunk, would have stated on oath the effect which his words have had on me, an e effect which persists to the present time. Whenever I listen to him my heart beats faster than if I were in a religious frenzy, and tears run down my face, and I observe that numbers of other people have the same experience. Nothing of this kind ever used to happen to me when I listened to Pericles and other good speakers; I recognized that they spoke well, but my soul was not thrown into confusion and dismay by the thought that my life was no better than a slave's. That is the condition to which I have often been reduced by our modern Marsyas, with 216 the result that it seems impossible to go on living in my present state. You can't say that this isn't true, Socrates. And even at this moment, I know quite well that, if I were prepared to give ear to him, I should not be able to hold out, but the same thing would happen again. He compels me to realize that I am still a mass of imperfections and yet persistently neglect my own true interests by engaging in public life. So against my real inclination I stop up my ears and take refuge in flight, as Odysseus did from the Sirens; otherwise I should sit here beside him till I was an old man. He is the only person in whose presence I experience a sensation of which I might be thought incapable, a sensation of shame; he, and he alone, positively makes me ashamed of myself. The reason is that I am conscious that there is no arguing against the conclusion that one should do as he bids, and yet that, whenever I am away from him, I succumb to the temptations of popularity. So I behave like a runaway slave and take to my heels, and when I see him the conclusions which he has forced upon me make me ashamed. Many a time I should be glad for him to vanish from the face of the earth, but I know that, if that were to happen, my sorrow would far outweigh my relief. In fact, I simply do not know what to do about him. b c

'That is the effect which the "piping" of this satyr has had on me and on many other people. But listen and you shall hear how in other respects too he resembles the creatures to which I compared him; and how marvellous is the power which he possesses. You may be sure that none of you knows his true nature, but I will reveal him to you, now that I have begun. The Socrates whom you see has a tendency to fall in love with good-looking young men, and is always in their society and in an ecstasy about them. (Besides, he is, to all appearances, universally ignorant and knows nothing.) But this is exactly the point in which he resembles Silenus; he wears these characteristics superficially, like the carved figure, but once you see beneath the surface you will discover a degree of self-control of which you can hardly form a notion, gentlemen. Believe me, it makes no difference to him whether a person is good-looking – he despises good looks to an almost inconceivable extent – nor whether he is rich nor whether he possesses any of the other advantages that rank high in popular esteem; to him all these things are worthless, and we ourselves of no account, be sure of that. He spends his whole life pretending and playing with people, and I doubt whether anyone has ever seen the treasures which are revealed when he grows serious and exposes what he keeps inside. However, I once saw them, and found them so divine and precious and beautiful and marvellous that, to put the matter briefly, I had no choice but to do whatever Socrates bade me. d e 217

'Believing that he was serious in his admiration of my charms, I supposed that a wonderful piece of good luck had befallen me; I should now be able, in return for my favours, to find out all that Socrates knew; for you must know that there was no limit to the pride that I felt in my good looks. With this end in view I sent away my attendant, whom hitherto I had always kept with me in my encounters with Socrates, and left myself alone with him. I must tell you the whole truth; attend carefully, and do you, Socrates, pull me up if anything I say is false. I allowed myself to be alone with him, I say, gentlemen, and I naturally supposed that he would embark on conversation of the type that a lover usually addresses to his darling when they are *tête-à-tête*, and I was glad. Nothing of the kind; he spent the day with me in the sort of talk which is habitual with him, and then left me and went away. Next I invited him to train with me in the gymnasium, and I accompanied him there, believing that I should succeed with him now. He took exer- b c cise and wrestled with me frequently, with no one else present, but I need hardly say that I was no nearer my goal. Finding that this was no good either, I resolved to make a direct assault on him, and not to give up what I had once undertaken; I felt that I must get to the bottom of the matter. So I invited him to dine with me, behaving just like a lover who has designs upon his favourite. He was in no hurry d to accept this invitation, but at last he agreed to come. The first time he came he rose to go away immediately after dinner, and on that occasion I was ashamed and let him go. But I returned to the attack, and this time I kept him in conversation after dinner far into the night, and then, when he wanted to be going, I compelled him to stay, on the plea that it was too late for him to go.

'So he betook himself to rest, using as a bed the couch on which he had reclined at dinner, next to mine, and there was nobody sleeping in the room but ourselves. e Up to this point my story is such as might be told to anybody, but you would not have heard the sequel from me but for two reasons. In the first place there is, as the proverb says, truth in wine – whether one adds "and in children" or not is of no significance – and in the second it would be wrong, when one is setting out to compose a panegyric, to allow so proud an exploit on the part of Socrates to remain unknown. Besides, I am in much the same state as a man suffering from snake-bite. They say that such a man cannot endure to reveal his sufferings except 218 to those who have experienced the like; they are the only people who will understand and make allowances if his agony drives him to outrageous speech and behaviour. Now I have suffered a bite more painful than that in the most sensitive part in which one can be bitten; I have been wounded and stung in my heart or soul or whatever you like to call it by philosophical talk which clings more fiercely than a snake when it gets a hold on the soul of a not ill-endowed young man. Seeing too that your company consists of people like Phaedrus, Agathon, b Eryximachus, Pausanias, Aristodemus, as well as Aristophanes, not to mention Socrates himself, people who have all had your share in the madness and frenzy of philosophy – well, you shall all hear what happened. You will make allowances both for my actions then and for my words now. As for the servants and any other vulgar and uninitiated persons who may be present, they must shut their ears tight against what I am going to say.

c 'Well, gentlemen, when the light was out and the servants had withdrawn, I decided not to beat about the bush with him, but to tell him my sentiments boldly. I nudged him and said: "Are you asleep, Socrates?" "Far from it," he answered. "Do you know what I think?" "No, what?" "I think that you are the only lover that I have ever had who is worthy of me, but that you are afraid to mention your passion to me. Now, what I feel about the matter is this, that it would be very foolish of me not to comply with your desires in this respect as well as in any other d claim that you might make either on my property or on that of my friends. The cardinal object of my ambition is to come as near perfection as possible, and I believe that no one can give me such powerful assistance towards this end as you. So the disapproval of wise men, which I should incur if I refused to comply with your wishes, would cause me far more shame than the condemnation of the ignorant multitude if I yielded to you."

'He listened to what I had to say, and then made a thoroughly characteristic reply in his usual ironical style: "You must be a very sharp fellow, my dear Alcibiades, if what you say about me is true, and I really have a power which might help you to improve yourself. You must see in me a beauty which is incomparable and far superior to your own physical good looks, and if, having made this discovery, you are trying to get a share of it by exchanging your beauty for mine, you obviously mean to get much the better of the bargain; you are trying to get true beauty in return for sham; in fact, what you are proposing is to exchange dross for gold. But look more closely, my good friend, and make quite sure that you are not mistaken in your estimate of my worth. A man's mental vision does not begin to be keen until his physical vision is past its prime, and you are far from having reached that point."

'"Well," I said, "I have done my part; what I have said represents my real sentiments and it is now for you to decide what you think best for me and for yourself."

'"Quite right," he answered, "we will consider hereafter, and do whatever seems to be best in this as in other matters."

'I had now discharged my artillery, and from the answer which he made I judged that I had wounded him; so, without allowing him to say anything further, I got up and covered him with my own clothes – for it was winter – and then laid myself down under his worn cloak, and threw my arms round this truly superhuman and wonderful man, and remained thus the whole night long. Here again, Socrates, you cannot deny that I am telling the truth. But in spite of all my efforts he proved completely superior to my charms and triumphed over them and put them to scorn, insulting me in the very point on which I piqued myself, gentlemen of the jury – I may well call you that, since you have the case of Socrates' disdainful behaviour before you. I swear by all the gods in heaven that for anything that had happened between us when I got up after sleeping with Socrates, I might have been sleeping with my father or elder brother.

'What do you suppose to have been my state of mind after that? On the one hand I realized that I had been slighted, but on the other I felt a reverence for Socrates' character, his self-control and courage; I had met a man whose like for wisdom and fortitude I could never have expected to encounter. The result was that I could neither bring myself to be angry with him and tear myself away from his society, nor find a way of subduing him to my will. It was clear to me that he was more completely proof against bribes than Ajax against sword-wounds, and in the one point in which I had expected him to be vulnerable he had eluded me. I was utterly disconcerted, and wandered about in a state of enslavement to the man the like of which has never been known.

'It was after these events that we served in the campaign against Potidaea together, and were mess-mates there. Of this I may say first that in supporting hardship he showed himself not merely my superior but the whole army's. Whenever we were cut off, as tends to happen on service, and compelled to go

e

219

b

c

d

e

220 without food, the rest of us were nowhere in the matter of endurance. And again, when supplies were abundant, no one enjoyed them more; at drinking especially, though he drank only when he was forced to do so, he was invincible, and yet, what is more remarkable of all, no human being has ever seen Socrates drunk. You will see the proof of this very shortly if I am not mistaken. As for the hardships of winter – and the winters there are very severe – he performed prodigies; on one b occasion in particular, when there was a tremendous frost, and everybody either remained indoors or, if they did go out, muffled themselves up in a quite unheard-of way, and tied and swathed their feet in felt and sheepskin, Socrates went out with nothing on but his ordinary clothes and without anything on his feet, and walked over the ice barefoot more easily than other people in their boots. The soldiers viewed him with suspicion, believing that he meant to humiliate them.

c 'So much for this subject, but "another exploit that the hero dared" in the course of his military service is worth relating. A problem occurred to him early one day, and he stood still on the spot to consider it. When he couldn't solve it he didn't give up, but stood there ruminating. By the time it was midday people noticed him, and remarked to one another with wonder that Socrates had been standing wrapped in thought since early morning. Finally in the evening after d dinner, some Ionians brought their bedding outside – it was summer-time — where they could take their rest in the cool and at the same time keep an eye on Socrates to see if he would stand there all night as well. He remained standing until it was dawn and the sun rose. Then he made a prayer to the sun and went away.

'Now, if you please, we will consider his behaviour in battle; we ought to do him justice on this score as well. When the action took place in which I won my e decoration for valour, it was entirely to Socrates that I owed my preservation; he would not leave me when I was wounded, but succeeded in rescuing both me and my arms. That was the time too when I recommended the generals to confer the decoration on you, Socrates; here at any rate you cannot find any handle for criticism or contradiction. But the generals were influenced in my favour by the fact that I was well-connected, and their desire to confer the distinction on me was surpassed by your own eagerness that I should receive it rather than yourself. In addition, gentlemen, let me tell you that Socrates was a sight well worth seeing 221 when the army made its disorderly retreat from Delium. I was then serving in the cavalry, whereas he was an infantryman, and after the rout had begun I came upon him marching along in company with Laches, and called out to them not to be down-hearted, and assured them that I would not desert them. And here I had an even better chance of observing Socrates than at Potidaea, because being mounted I had less occasion to be frightened myself. In the first place I noticed b that he was far cooler than Laches, and next, if I may borrow an expression from you, Aristophanes, that he was using just the same gait as he does in Athens, "strutting along with his head in the air and casting side-long glances," quietly observing the movements of friend and foe, and making it perfectly plain even at a distance that he was prepared to put up a strong resistance to any attack. That is how both he and his companion got off safe; those who show a bold front in war are hardly ever molested; the attention of the pursuers is concentrated on those who are in headlong rout. c

'One might find many other remarkable qualities to praise in Socrates, but a description of his general way of life would perhaps be equally applicable to some other people; the really wonderful thing about him is that he is like no other human being, living or dead. If you are looking for a parallel for Achilles, you can find it in Brasidas and others; if Pericles is your subject you can compare him to Nestor and Antenor (and they do not exhaust the possibilities); and you can make d similar comparisons in other cases. But our friend here is so extraordinary, both in his person and in his conversation, that you will never be able to find anyone remotely resembling him either in antiquity or in the present generation, unless you go beyond humanity altogether, and have recourse to the images of Silenus and satyr which I am using myself in this speech. They are as applicable to his talk as to his person; I forgot to say at the beginning that his talk too is extremely like the Silenus-figures which take apart. Anyone who sets out to listen to Socrates e talking will probably find his conversation utterly ridiculous at first, it is clothed in such curious words and phrases, the hide, so to speak, of a hectoring satyr. He will talk of pack-asses and blacksmiths, cobblers and tanners, and appear to express the same ideas in the same language over and over again, so that any inexperienced or foolish person is bound to laugh at his way of speaking. But if a 222 man penetrates within and sees the content of Socrates' talk exposed, he will find that there is nothing but sound sense inside, and that this talk is almost the talk of a god, and enshrines countless representations of ideal excellence, and is of the widest possible application; in fact that it extends over all the subjects with which a man who means to turn out a gentleman needs to concern himself.

'That is what I have to say, gentlemen, in praise of Socrates.'

Plato *Symposium* 215a–222a
tr. W. Hamilton (Penguin 1951)

L3 Alcibiades

The brilliant, unpredictable political leader, ward of Pericles and friend of Socrates, whose love-hate relationship with Athenian democracy led to disaster. The best study is J. Hatzfeld Alcibiade (1940).

(a)

Once he was hard pressed when wrestling. To avoid being thrown he applied his teeth to his opponent's grip and nearly bit through his fingers. The other let go with the words, 'Alcibiades, you bite like a girl.' 'No,' he said, 'like a lion!'

Plutarch *Alcibiades* 2, 2

(b)

(11) The horses he bred were famous in every country, and so was the number of his racing chariots. Nobody but Alcibiades, neither king nor private citizen, ever entered seven of these at the Olympic games. And to have won with them the first, second, and fourth prizes, as Thucydides says, and the third, too, according to Euripides, is an achievement so magnificent that it scarcely leaves further room for ambition in this field. Euripides celebrates his success in this ode:

Son of Cleinias, yours is the name I sing.
Victory shines like a star, but yours eclipses all victories:
What man or hero in all the lands of Greece
Ever triumphed first, second, and third in the chariot race,
Stepped from the course unwearied and crowned with the olive of Zeus,
And heard his name three times acclaimed in the herald's cry?

(12) His success at Olympia was made all the more brilliant by the way in which the various cities vied with each other to do him honour. The people of Ephesus erected a magnificently decorated tent for him, Chios supplied fodder for his horses and a large number of animals for sacrifice, while Lesbos presented him with wine and other provisions which allowed him to entertain lavishly. And in the midst of all this rivalry another episode occurred: we do not know whether Alcibiades was falsely accused of what happened or was genuinely guilty of sharp practice, but in any case the affair served to bring him even more conspicuously into the public eye.

The story is that there was at Athens a certain Diomedes, a respectable man and a friend of Alcibiades, who was keenly ambitious to win a victory at Olympia. He discovered that there was a racing chariot at Argos which was the property of the city and as he knew that Alcibiades had many friends and was extremely influential there, he persuaded him to buy it. Alcibiades made the purchase for his friend, but then entered the chariot for the race as his own and told Diomedes he could do what he liked about it. Diomedes was furious and called upon gods and men to witness how he had been cheated. It seems that this affair also gave rise to a lawsuit and that Isocrates wrote a speech *On the team of horses* for Alcibiades' son. In his speech, however, the plaintiff referred to is not Diomedes but Tisias.

Plutarch *Alcibiades* 11–12
tr. I. Scott-Kilvert (Penguin 1960)

(c) *The Sicilian Expedition*

Alcibiades, Cleinias's son, was the most enthusiastic advocate of the expedition. He was politically opposed to Nicias, who had also criticized him, and was glad to take a different view. But he was above all ambitious for the military command; he hoped to capture Sicily and Carthage, and hoped too that victory would increase his wealth and reputation.

Thucydides 6, 15

(d) *Alcibiades seeks recall from exile*

Phrynichus, who was still in office, disagreed. He thought – quite rightly – that Alcibiades was not interested in oligarchy or democracy; all he wanted was to be recalled by his supporters through a change of constitution.

Thucydides 8, 48

(e)

Alcibiades, Clinias's son, from Athens. Nature seems to have experimented with him to see what he could achieve. All the records of him agree that he was unique alike in virtue and vice. He was born of a leading family in a powerful state, the handsomest man of his generation, qualified for anything, a natural leader (an outstanding commander by sea and land), eloquent, with such exceptional ability as an orator that his presence and words swept opposition aside, wealthy, energetic when occasion demanded, tough, generous, magnificent in his possessions and character, clubbable, amiable, skilled to sense the needs of the moment; yet, as soon as he relaxed and lacked any stimulus to activity, he showed himself luxurious, dissolute, sex-mad and intemperate. Everyone was astonished at the variety of opposed qualities in a single individual.

Cornelius Nepos *Alcibiades* 1

(f) *Among the speeches attributed to Andocides is a fragment of an attack on Alcibiades. It does not seem in Andocides's style; it may possibly be by one Phaeax, though some regard it as altogether unauthentic. The date seems to be 417 and the occasion an ostracism. The orator is expansive: this version is somewhat contracted. The commission on the tribute was in 425.*

So much for myself. But I want to remind you of Alcibiades's past life – though it is hard to know where to begin in such a catalogue of crimes, every one relevant. If I were forced to describe in detail his adulteries, his affairs with other men's wives, his general career of lawless violence, time would run out on me, and I would not be popular with my fellow-citizens in publicizing their private misfortunes. Instead I will enlarge upon his political career and his relations with those nearest to him, and casual encounters with citizens and foreigners.

In the first place it was he who persuaded you to revise the tribute-assessment which Aristides had established with justice to all ... In fact, if you account Aristides a good citizen and a man of justice, you must rank Alcibiades with the lowest of the low, since his policies to the allied states were exactly the opposite ... I regard him as a poor statesman, who looks to the present and ignores the future, favouring popular policies against those which are right.

I am amused that people believe Alcibiades to be concerned about democracy, of all forms of government the one which most favours equality. They are failing to apply deductions from his private life. They should look at his arrogant acquisitiveness. He received a dowry of ten talents on his marriage to Callias's sister. When Hipponicus lost his life as a commanding officer at Delium he claimed another ten, on the grounds that Hipponicus had contracted to add ten more on the birth of a child to his daughter. Despite this dowry, uniquely large in Greek history, he behaved abominably, bringing mistresses, slave and free alike, into the house, so that his wife was compelled for decency to present herself to the magistrate and claim a legal divorce. He now demonstrated his power. He called in his friends, and kidnapped his wife from the city-centre in demonstrative contempt of the magistrates, the laws, and his fellow-citizens. ... Another example of his scandalous behaviour. He induced the painter Agatharchus to accompany him home and then insisted on him painting. Agatharchus demurred with the truthful excuse that he could not do it since he was under contracted obligation to others. Alcibiades said that he would hold him by force if he did not begin painting straight away – and did so too. ... Democracy, freedom counting nothing ... You are responsible. You refrain from punishing violence. You bring secret crimes to book but show admiration for open villainy. That is why our young men spend all their time in the law-courts instead of on the athletics track. That is why our old men do all the fighting, while the young make speeches. Our young men take Alcibiades as their standard.

[Andocides] *Against Alcibiades* 10–22

L4 Theramenes

*The leading Athenian statesman during the latter part of the war with Sparta. Like the Vicar of Bray he turned up no matter which party was in power. He was much vilified for his veering and shifting, but received Aristotle's approbation (*Constitution of Athens *28.5, no. A2). For an interesting treatment see A. Harding 'The Theramenes Myth'* Phoenix *28 (1974) 101–11.*

(a) *Theramenes takes the lead in establishing the oligarchy of Four Hundred in 411.*

Theramenes, Hagnon's son, was one of the leaders in the dissolution of democratic government; he was a man of some skill in oratory and politics.

Thucydides 8, 68

(b) *Thucydides on the compromise constitution of the Five Thousand, in which Theramenes also had a share. (See also Aristotle's approval* Constitution of Athens *33 no. A2.)*

In particular for the first time in my life the Athenians obviously enjoyed a good constitution. It was a moderate compromise between oligarchy and democracy, and began to help Athens to recover from disaster.

Thucydides 8, 97

(c) *A view from comedy in 405. Theramenes came from Cos, and was an adopted Athenian: Chios had at this time broken away from Athens.*

(i) An act worthy of a man
with his wits about him
sailing round the world
always ready to shift
to the sunny side of the boat,
not like some statue,
keeping one position,
always on the move,
to where favour lies –
the act of a clever man,
a man like Theramenes.

Aristophanes *Frogs* 533–41

(ii) Theramenes? A clever fellow, never at a loss.
He'll watch the storm-clouds break and toss
and keep dry. Not Chios – Cos.

Aristophanes *Frogs* 968–70

(d) *Critias attacks Theramenes.*

'I would have you know that his present actions are nothing new. He is a traitor by nature. I will remind you of his record. Originally he had been honoured by the democracy because of his father Hagnon. Yet he was the leader in subverting the democracy for the rule of Four Hundred, and took a prominent place among them. He realized that opposition to the oligarchy was gathering, and was the first to champion the democracy against them. That's why he is nicknamed Buskin. A buskin is designed to fit both feet; Theramenes faces both ways.'

Xenophon *Hellenica* 2, 3, 30–31

(e) *Theramenes's death. See also Xenophon* Hellenica *2, 3, 56.*

What pleasure I take in Theramenes! What a noble spirit! We may weep when we read the story, but a great man does not need tears over his death. He was thrown into prison by order of the Thirty Tyrants. He drank down the poison like a thirsty man. Then he threw the dregs out of the cup so that they rang, laughed at the sound, and said, 'For my dear Critias!'

Cicero *Tabletalks at Tusculum* 1, 40, 96

L5 Demosthenes

Demosthenes, the greatest of fourth-century orators, lived from 384–322. In later life he boasted the consistency of his warnings against the imperial ambitions of Philip of Macedon, but the record does not so show him, and he seems rather to have been jockeying for his personal power against his rivals. The high patriotism he voiced was an inspiration at the time and subsequently; see e.g. K. Freeman It has All Happened Before *(F. Muller 1941) where his words are applied to the Nazis. He was eventually condemned for venality and banished. Whatever his character and policies, by any standards he was an exceptional orator. See A. W. Pickard-Cambridge* Demosthenes and the Last Days of Greek Freedom *(Putnam 1914); W. Jaeger* Demosthenes: The Origin and Growth of his Policy *(Cambridge University Press 1938).*

(a) *Demosthenes's early lack of success*

And yet when he first came before the people he was interrupted by heckling and laughed at for his inexperience: this was because his manner of speaking appeared confused and overloaded with long periods, and his expression contorted by a formality which his audience found harsh and wearisome. It appears too that his voice was weak and his utterance indistinct and that he suffered from a shortness of breath, which had the effect of breaking up his sentences and making his meaning difficult to follow. At last, when he had left the assembly, and was wandering about the Piraeus in despair, he met another orator named Eunomus of Thriasia, who was by then a very old man. Eunomus reproved him and said: 'You have a style of speaking which is very like Pericles', and yet out of sheer timidity and cowardice you are throwing away your talents. You will neither stand up to the rough and tumble of the assembly, nor train your body to develop the stamina that you need for the law-courts. It is through your own sheer feebleness that you are letting your gifts wither away.'

Plutarch *Demosthenes* 6
tr. I. Scott-Kilvert (Penguin 1973)

(b) *Demosthenes as an orator*

Demosthenes's style, without frills or jokes, was concise, forceful and serious; it did not 'smell of burnt midnight oil' as Pytheas scoffed, but of sobriety and care and the embittered, dour manner attributed to him.

Plutarch *Comparison of Demosthenes and Cicero* 1
tr. K. Chisholm

(c) *Demosthenes cuts a sorry figure on an embassy to Philip.*

Demosthenes promised us torrents of words. He said he would make a speech about our just claims to Amphipolis and the origin of the war, which would sew up Philip's mouth with a dry reed, persuade the Athenians to allow Leosthenes to return, and Philip to restore Amphipolis to Athens . . .

Demosthenes's turn to speak arrived. Everyone was attentive, ready to hear oratory of exceptional power. (We learned later that his boastful promises had been reported to Philip and his court.) Everyone settled down to listen. The creature mouthed an introduction of sorts; it was obscure and dead with terror. He advanced a short way into his theme, then suddenly stopped speaking and didn't know what to say, and finally broke off his address altogether. Philip saw what a state he was in, and encouraged him, telling him not to imagine that he was an actor who had irreparably ruined a play, but to keep calm and try gradually to recollect his speech, and to deliver it as prepared. But once he had been thrown off balance, and lost the thread of his script, Demosthenes was incapable of picking it up again. He tried, but the same thing happened. Silence fell, and the herald asked us to leave.

Aeschines *On the Embassy* 21, 34–5

(d) *Demosthenes defends his political career.*

Philip's depredations and appropriations before the outset of my political career I will omit. I do not think any of them concern me. The restrictions he underwent from the first day of my entry into public life are what I shall recall and render account of, after making this preliminary point. There was one advantage, gentlemen, which lay in Philip's hands. Among the Greek states, not in isolated instances but everywhere, there came into existence a crop of corrupt, abominable traitors beyond all previous memory. With them as accomplices and collaborators he worked on the deteriorating condition of the Greeks and their internal dissensions, and made these worse. He used deception or offers of money or wholesale corruption, and divided them into numerous parties, when their interests were one and the same – to curb his rising power. Now at a time when the Greek states were in this condition, gentlemen, and still failed to understand the gathering disease that was growing among them, what conduct, what course of action was it proper for Athens to adopt? This is the question before you of which you should demand an account from me, because the man who took his political stand at this point was myself. Should she have abandoned her spirit and pride, Aeschines, and ranked herself with Thessaly and Dolopia in helping Philip to acquire the command of Greece at the expense of all that was good and great in past generations? Or should she have shunned this appalling prospect, but have looked on at what she could long foretell would happen, if no one stood in the way, and let it go on? I should like to ask critics of our policy which party they would have preferred Athens to join, the party of collaboration in the ruin and dishonour of Greece, in which one would include Thessaly and her associates, or the party which turned a blind eye to all that for the sake of private advantage, like Arcadia, Messenia and Argos. Yet many or all of these came out of it worse than we did. If after his success Philip had at once left Greece and made no mischief thereafter, if he had done nothing to damage any of his own allies or the other Greeks, there would have been some reason to criticize and censure the opponents of his measures. But if he was concerned to circumscribe the repute, the pre-eminence, the liberty of every state, indeed I might add their constitution, where he could, how can it have been anything but our most honourable course that we pursued at my instance?

But, to return, what should have been the policy of Athens, Aeschines, in view of Philip's continued machinations to secure a tyrant's control of the Greek world? What should the statesman have advocated or proposed at Athens – this is the important question – who knew in his heart, as I did right up to the moment of my appearance on the platform, that our country has always striven to be first in the world's honour and distinction, has spent more in men and money for glory and the common welfare of Greece than all the Greek states individually for their own, who could see Philip, our antagonist, sustain in search of power and supremacy the loss of an eye, a broken collar-bone, an injured arm or leg, the sacrifice of any part of his body chance might seize from him, in the hope that with the rest of it intact he might live in glory and renown? And yet no one would dare to breathe the idea that it was fitting that a man born and bred in a small and mean city like Pella, as it then was, should have in him such greatness of spirit as to set in his heart the desire and ambition of power over Greece, while we Athenians, who every day in every word we speak, in every spectacle we look on, keep in our minds the memory of noble ancestors, should have in us a spirit so demeaned as by our own offer, our own will, to cede to Philip the place of liberty. It is unthinkable. The only remaining course, therefore, and the course of necessity, was righteous opposition to every unjustifiable action of his against us. That is what Athens did from the beginning, naturally and with justice, and that was the policy I proposed and advised throughout my public career. . . .

Demosthenes *On the Crown* 59–69
tr. A. N. W. Saunders (Penguin 1974)

(e) *In 323 Demosthenes was charged with and found guilty of involvement in a corruption scandal. We happen to have some papyrus fragments of the speech for the prosecution by Hyperides. What follows comprises a few extracts from these fragments.*

Gentlemen of the jury, I was just remarking to those next to me, what a curious thing it would be if Demosthenes were the only man in Athens to be exempt from the laws which enforce an agreement made by a person against his own interests, or from the decrees of the Commons, which you are sworn to observe in your voting, decrees proposed not by one of his enemies but by none other than Demosthenes himself. It must have been a kind of death-wish . . . . . . Demosthenes, you were charged by the People of Athens with having accepted twenty talents illegally . . . . . . From his usual place by the rock cutting he told Mnesitheus the dancer to ask Harpalus how much money there would be to deposit in the Acropolis. He replied, 'Seven hundred talents.' . . . . . . He told you in the Assembly that that was the actual sum. But when the amount deposited was three hundred and fifty talents instead of seven hundred, he kept his mouth shut. He had already had his twenty talents . . . . . . You, Demosthenes, were responsible for the decree proposing that a watch be kept on Harpalus. You did not criticize the failure of the guards; you did not prosecute them when they disbanded. It was neatly timed. Did your service go unpaid? Harpalus paid good money to the backbench politicians who had nothing to offer but noisy heckling. Is it likely that he neglected you, the architect of our policy? It is beyond belief.

Hyperides *Against Demosthenes*

Index of Passages